C000234136

Sidekick

Bulldog to Lapdog: British Global
Strategy from Churchill to Blair

Stephen Haseler

Also by Stephen Haseler

The Gaitskellites
The Death of British Democracy
Euro-Communism (Joint Author)
The Tragedy of Labour
Anti-Americanism
The Politics of Giving
The Battle for Britain: Thatcher and the New Liberals
The End of the House of Windsor
The English Tribe
The Super-Rich: The Unjust World of Global Capitalism
Super-State: The New Europe and its Challenge to America

First published in 2007 by Forumpress

Forumpress
c/o The Global Policy Institute
London Metropolitan University
31 Jewry Street
London EC3N 2EY, UK

ISBN-10: 0-9554975-1-5
ISBN-13: 978-0-9554975-1-3

A catalogue record for this book is available from the British Library.

The publisher has used its best endeavours to ensure that the URLs for websites referred to in the book are correct and active at the time of going to press.

For further information on Forumpress, visit our website: www.forumpress.co.uk

Cover Design and Layout: Ben Eldridge ben@eldridge.com

Sub-editor: Katerina Hadjimatheou

Printed by Lightning Source www.lightningsource.com

Sidekick

Bulldog to Lapdog: British Global
Strategy from Churchill to Blair

Stephen Haseler

Contents

Preface

This book is about Britain's role in a rapidly changing world. But, as my life on both sides of the Atlantic has taught me, any book about Britain must also be a book about America – and about what the British, though not the Americans, believe is a 'special relationship'. Many within Britain's foreign policy elite still see America as Britain's saviour and protector – and thus see the country's future as resting within the American empire, if not exactly as a colony then as a junior partner (or 'sidekick'). This was particularly true for the premiership of Tony Blair and it helps in large part to explain his seemingly inexplicable decision to send British troops to invade the heartland of Arabia in the spring of 2003. Others, of which I am one, see this British fixation with America not just as inherently undignified, but also as deeply damaging. For not only does it act as an obstacle to Britain's more natural future in Europe, but also, by dividing Europe, it hinders the emergence of a healthy transatlantic relationship of equals.

This deep attachment to 'the special relationship' with Washington is the product of the turbulent history of the last century and the long alliance between Britain and the USA stretching over two world wars – the Second World War and the Cold War. This book is an attempt to tell the story of this 'relationship' from its inception in the Roosevelt-

Churchill era in the early 1940s through to the Cold War years and then beyond to Tony Blair's support for Washington's invasion and occupation of Iraq.

I argue – in a theme that runs throughout the whole book – that Britain's dogged belief in this 'special relationship' has its roots in the British political establishment's post-1945 inability to adapt to the loss of its empire. It was a loss that by historical standards was abrupt and profoundly felt. And it led to an insistent search amongst Britain's political class for a continuing world role, even, if need be, for the semblance of one.

Yet, in the new post-1945 world it soon became clear that such a global role – no matter how limited – could only be secured by attaching the country to the new American superpower. And if the price for such reflected glory was that the country should accept the role of junior partner to the USA and become its subordinate geo-political 'sidekick', then so be it. This arrangement suited both sides. Cold War America got a loyal ally and Britain's elites settled for the pretence and pomp of an independent world role.

I also hope to show in this book how this lop-sided 'special relationship' has over the years extracted a high, and growing, price – not least in the human, financial and geo-political costs to Britain of the war in Iraq. More broadly, I argue that it has resulted in a geo-strategic over-dependence upon the United States – a dependence that may well have been a necessity during the Cold War, but in today's new multi-polar era is no longer needed. Dependency is not only undignified and unhealthy, it also tends to breed in the dependent one an underlying resentment – which in turn, as in the case of Britain, has fostered an underlying petty anti-Americanism.

Even more importantly, this fervent attachment of the country's elites to the 'special relationship' remains the major obstacle to building a realistic future for Britain – the kind of future which Tony Blair advocated in his early years in Downing Street. In my view we British have a choice to make – between, on the one hand, a future life in the American empire (of which, as I argue in this book, there are worse fates!) and, on the other, the far better alternative of becoming a leading player in the construction of Europe.

During the latter part of his premiership Tony Blair regularly denounced the idea that such a choice needed to be made. Indeed a consensus began to form that the country could maintain a foot in both the American and European camps (and could act as 'a bridge' between them). Yet as this book goes to press, and Blair's legacy as Prime Minister is being reviewed, it is becoming increasingly clear that he, like John Major and a host of other Prime Ministers before him, simply put off making the choice. He found it simply too difficult to commit fully to Europe – particularly so after 9/11 and the 'special relationship' with George W. Bush. So, as Blair leaves office he leaves a country which is still supporting an American-led war and occupation in the Middle East, is still outside the Euro-zone, and still an awkward partner in the wider EU.

He also leaves a political class which is now flirting with the fanciful idea of Britain's future as lying outside of both the USA and Europe – as some kind of free-floating off-shore 'Tiger economy' (like the low cost Asian 'Tigers'). My American friend, the US State Department Official and student of Britain, Kendall Myers, has recently argued that we British might well, following the bitter lessons of the war in Iraq, finally turn against the 'special relationship'. But he went on to argue that 'what I think and fear is that Britain will draw back from the US without moving closer to Europe. In that sense London Bridge is falling down'. He may be right. I hope he is wrong.

*

Whilst writing this book I have been fortunate enough to be able to look at the 'special relationship' from both the British and the American sides. My own connections with the United States are strong ones. Married to an American for forty years, and with friends and family in the United States, I have gained real insights. And my time as an Englishman in Washington D.C. – in the capital's think tanks and universities – during the Reagan, Bush and Clinton Presidencies in the 1980s and 1990s provided a unique vantage point from which to view the workings of the transatlantic relationship.

During many visits to Washington I have been able to hone my thinking and analysis on transatlantic relations and 'the special relationship' in the company of some real experts – many of whom, of course, will not necessarily share my views and conclusions in this book. My friends Kendall Myers (from the US State Department who achieved his five minutes of fame recently with the quotation I cite at the beginning of the Introduction), Michael Lind (at the New

America Foundation), Mark Falcoff (an AEI scholar) and Stanley Kober (a Cato Institute scholar) have been particularly generous with their time and thoughts. As have other American friends made during the Thatcher-Reagan years such as Elliot Abrams (now a White House special advisor), Sven Kraemer (former National Security Council official), Edwin J. Feulner Jnr. (President of the Heritage Foundation), Peter Rodman (now Deputy Assistant Secretary of State), Bill Schneider (Member of the Pentagon's Defence Policy Board), Bruce Weinrod, Charles Horner, Ben Wattenberg, Richard Perle and numerous others. I have also benefited greatly from my time as a visiting professor at Georgetown University (and a fellow at GCSIS), at Johns Hopkins University, and particularly from my ten-year visiting association with the University of Maryland, Baltimore County.

On the British side, where the 'special relationship' is often taken more seriously than in Washington, I have been able to draw on the views and ideas of a host of political and academic friends and acquaintances throughout British political life, many of the more prominent of whom I refer to in the text. In particular I owe much to my colleagues and friends: the historian, David Carlton (Anthony Eden's unofficial biographer), the political journalists John O'Sullivan and the late Frank Johnson, the former MEP John Stevens (with his indefatigable pro-European convictions), and two 'continentals' – Jacques Reland (fellow member of the Global Policy Institute) and Detlev Albers (Professor at the University of Bremen and my Co-Editor of the academic journal 'Social Europe'). Also, whilst Vice Chair of the Federal Union and a Senior Research Fellow at the Federal Trust I have been privileged to work alongside Ernest Wistricht, John Pinder, and the Director of the Federal Trust, the former MEP Brendan Donnelly.

I am also indebted, so to speak, to a 'special relationship' all of my own. My American wife Bay shares with me a political science background (in her case from Bryn Mawr College), Labour Party experience (in her case the Transport House research department) and a transatlantic life. To say that her own invaluable insights on this subject have helped inform my thinking would be a serious understatement.

Above all I wish to thank those colleagues at London Metropolitan University (and its constituent forerunner, London Guildhall

University) and at its Global Policy Institute for their support in both time and research. Following my doctorate at LSE in 1967 I began my career with this City of London-based higher education institution and, following stints, some of them longish, on the GLC and at numerous American universities and think tanks, have always returned to it.

I also wish to thank Henning Meyer, a PhD candidate and now research fellow at the Global Policy Institute, for all his help in advising on and in preparing the text for publication. The text has also been read in its entirety by Bay Haseler, James Hannah and Katerina Hadjimatheou and their comments have led to real improvements. Needless to say, the responsibility for the work remains entirely mine.

Finally, a note about method. Whilst writing this book I realised that during my many years in the political and academic world in London and in Washington, I had actually met, and had dealings with, many of the public – and not so public – figures whom I was quoting and referring to in the middle and latter part of this text. For this reason parts of this book will read like a memoir – and I hope these personal recollections both enliven the text as well as adding to an understanding of the subject. As these are first-hand accounts they are, in effect, primary sources.

Stephen Haseler
Kensington, London, 2007

Introduction

'We [the Americans] typically ignore them [the British] and take no notice – it's a sad business. [The 'special relationship'] was a done deal from the beginning, it was a one-sided relationship that was entered into with open eyes...There was nothing. There was no payback, no sense of reciprocity.'
Kendall Myers, US State Department (and Specialist on British Politics) December 2006

'The Special Relationship'

It was a coarse, but clear, instruction. 'We want you to get up the arse of the White House and stay there.' This was the mission handed out, in October 1997, by Tony Blair's Chief of Staff Jonathan Powell to Her Majesty's newly-appointed Ambassador to the United States, Christopher Meyer. And it revealed more decisively than any memo or position paper the British Prime Minister's true view of Britain's proper role in the world.[1] This role – the so-called 'special relationship' between Washington and London – had been the centrepiece of British diplomacy ever since the end of World War Two. But it was to become highly controversial during the high-profile events that led up to the Iraq invasion of 2003.

1

This 'special relationship' was on full public display, caught on television camera, in the summer of 2006. At a G8 conference in Russia, held in July during the early days of the Israeli-Hezbollah conflict, the political and personal dynamic between US President George Bush and Tony Blair was revealed in a rare viewing of a 'private' conversation caught on videotape whilst a microphone was accidentally switched on. In it, the US President is seen and heard rejecting the British Prime Minister's suggestion that he, Blair, should go to the Middle East as a kind of advance party for the US Secretary of State. Just as revealing, though, was the personal chemistry of the exchange. The President, noticing Tony Blair sidling up to him, remained in a seated position and offered the off-hand greeting 'Yo Blair'. Blair remained standing and formal. Bush – in the manner he might adopt with an aide – grandly declared his strategy and tactics for dealing with the crisis (to do with 'getting Kofi to talk to Bashar al-Assad of Syria'); and Blair, lurking at the President's elbow, would interject tentative, supplicatory and insinuating comments best suited to a courtier trying to secure an advantage. The British press had a field day with the tape, one newspaper portraying the exchange in the manner of an English public school as the 'frat-boy' President and the 'fag' Prime Minister.[2]

This publicly viewed private exchange between President and Prime Minister simply reinforced what had become a well-entrenched worldwide image of the Bush-Blair (American-British) relationship. And it attracted an unusual amount of scorn and derision from around the world. During the height of the crisis, as Tony Blair was jetting around the world gathering support for Bush's Iraq policy, even the mild-mannered Nelson Mandela was moved to describe him as 'America's Secretary of State'. Blair's 'poodle image' sometimes led to embarrassing public encounters. During a press conference in Berlin in the immediate aftermath of the Iraq invasion Blair was asked pointedly whether in his discussions with the German Chancellor he 'represented Britain or the Bush administration' at which point Chancellor Schröder quickly intervened apparently to save his guest from further ridicule – 'the British Prime Minister represented Britain' he asserted with a straight face.[3] Another devastating assessment of Blair's role came later from former US President Jimmy Carter – a natural ideological ally of New Labour if there ever was one – who reflected in his 2006 book *Faith and*

Freedom that Tony Blair had 'surprised and disappointed' him by being 'compliant and subservient' to the Bush Administration, a posture that, in his view, was decisive in Bush's decision to invade Iraq.[4]

Blair's visceral support for the 'special relationship' and the place it gave him at court in Washington had, though, never been hidden from the British public. Indeed, it had been publicly proclaimed, adopted, defended, even celebrated, particularly so during the run up to the Iraq war of 2003. By the time of the invasion of Iraq, with Britain's troops alongside those of the United States, in London at any rate, the 'special relationship' had become a given – assuming almost the proportions of a force of nature, as though there was no possible alternative for the country. It was also being openly sold as a clever tactic by wise men in London. Through the good offices afforded by the 'special relationship', British would have a say in American policy – a say that would be denied to us should the country line up with the sceptical Europeans. Britain – the argument ran – would be able to soften American militancy and persuade the US administration to secure UN support for the projected invasion. Britain would become 'Greece to the US's Rome', a characterisation that could be heard in the smooth tones of Britain's Ambassador to the UN, Jeremy Greenstock, who, in the aftermath of the Iraq crisis gave the somewhat patronising opinion that the 'combination of US power and British tactical subtlety is a good one'.[5]

Such a view was in no way the exclusive preserve of Prime Minister Blair and his immediate circle. For genuine support for and commitment to the 'special relationship' was to be found widely throughout the British political establishment. It had become a fixed point of reference for what might be called the 'official view' or the 'official mind'. This 'official mind' attempts to describe the governing strategic thinking held in the upper reaches of Whitehall and Westminster, of the political parties, of the intelligence services and of the armed forces. This 'official mind', or mind-set, is the accumulated product of decades of foreign policy experience – most of which was formed in the aftermath of the Second World War – and, since then, has hardly changed. Neither the Suez conflict in 1956, nor the end of the four decades of the long Cold War in 1989 – with all its implications for a new world order and a new role for Britain – nor even the defeat in Iraq, has altered 'official' thinking. In early 2007, as these words are written, Britain still stands poised to sign on to yet another round in

3

the 'special relationship' by replacing the Trident nuclear deterrent with another American-made and controlled system.

Britain's foreign policy establishment – and its 'official mind' – is, however, becoming more than just isolated. It is becoming unrealistic. For it remains impervious to the growing 'Atlantic divide'. Long before the 2003 Iraq crisis British and American values were increasingly diverging on such questions as religion, guns and minorities (the so-called 'Guns, God and Gays' syndrome). The two countries were also differing on the death penalty, as many American states continued with executions and Britain, together with all EU nations, had abolished it. Intriguingly, as early as 2001 US Secretary of State Condoleezza Rice, recognising this growing gap, saw the need for a transatlantic 'values debate' whereas the British government did not. The 'official mind' tends to proceed as though British and American global interests are at one – even though they are also clearly diverging in some key areas of the world – not least in the Israeli/Palestinian conflict, over relations with energy-rich Russia and on environmental questions.

The 'official view' is not shared by the British people. In fact, in the period before the Iraq invasion the British public underwent an historic shift in their view of foreign policy as they turned increasingly against Britain aligning herself with the USA. Under the headline 'Britons reject Blair's closeness to the US' *The Independent* reported that an NOP poll which it had commissioned revealed that 64% of those polled thought it was more important for Britain to have good relations with its EU partners than with the US whilst 25% believed the relationship with the US should take priority.[6] Two years later views had hardened. A YouGov survey carried out for *The Spectator* in August 2006 showed that only 14% believed Britain should continue to align itself with the USA.[7] And in an ICM/Guardian survey, also in August 2006, 63% of respondents thought Blair 'had tied Britain too closely to the US'.[8]

'A World Role': The Imperial Legacy

What, then, was the ultimate motive for such national abasement? And what possible reasoning could lurk behind the abandonment by Britain's national leadership of even the appearance of British dignity and independence? Paradoxically, the answer may well lie in the British political elite's continued fixation – some half a century following the demise of empire – with the need for a global role for the country (and for themselves). Yet, the cold reality of 1945 was that this desperate need for a global role could no longer, realistically, be met through British power alone: instead a global role could be re-created by association, by the acceptance of a junior partnership with the USA. For the British Prime Minister, power, no longer inherent, could nonetheless, because of the 'special relationship', rub off on Downing Street.

The two architects of post-war British foreign policy, Ernest Bevin and Winston Churchill were determined to continue the world role. Bevin spoke famously of needing 'a bomb with the union jack on top of it'; Churchill remained an unalloyed imperialist to the end of his days. And a world role of some sort has been sought by every British Prime Minister of the Cold War era bar one. Only Edward Heath showed no real interest – directing his strategic thinking towards a regional, European, role for the country.

This lingering imperial impulse was not a belief in a colonial future. Rather, it was a somewhat inchoate, but seriously held, view that Britain was some kind of special country – a reduced but still exceptional, even superior, power which can help guide less fortunate nations. Following 9/11, as George W. Bush talked of 're-ordering the world' and pursued a forward strategy including invasion, Tony Blair echoed these sentiments as he talked approvingly of a world re-ordered by 'liberal interventionism'.

All the Prime Ministers of the post-war era were the sons and daughter of the imperial British – the people who had inhabited the greatest power on earth at the centre of an empire upon which the 'sun never set'. Attlee, Churchill, Eden and Macmillan grew up in the hey-day of empire, Heath, Wilson and Callaghan in the 1920s and 30s when the empire was still intact. During Thatcher's and Major's formative years, in the period after the 'victory' of the Second World War, 'Empire Day' was still being celebrated in Britain's schools.

1945 Plus: A Sidekick is Born
Yet the empire had effectively come to an end during the 1939-45 war; and Britain had to come to terms with both reduced power and status as well as the arrival of a new superpower. Britain's future role was not certain. The fact was that the British were not only reduced, they were also alone. And the tough negotiations with Washington over the post-war loan had begun to put to rest any illusions of 'Anglo-

American cousinhood' created by the war-time alliance. It taught
Britain's politicians that the US was a separate nation, one which like
all others keenly pursued its own interests without much sentiment.
The Washington elite who assumed world leadership after 1945 were
mainly 'Anglos' by background but at the same time they were first
and foremost tough realistic American patriots – as the decision to
drop the nuclear bomb on Japan revealed. The idea that during the
war the Roosevelt administration had acted in British interests was a
figment of Britain's war propaganda. Indeed, all the evidence shows
that Franklin Roosevelt's geo-strategy was to support Britain against
the Germans but then, in the peace with the Soviet Union, replace the
British empire as the leading force in the west. President Woodrow
Wilson had set the tone when, meeting some earlier British diplomatic fawning during his post-war visit to Europe in 1918, he stated
bluntly to the British delegation that 'you must not speak of us who
come over here as cousins, still less brothers – we are neither'.[9]

Indeed, amongst some in post-war Britain a bitter resentment of
America took hold. They took the view that Britain had fought the
war alone, that the Americans were late in, and that when they came
they were insensitive – creating the popular jibe about the 'yanks'
being 'over here, over-paid and over sexed'. It amounted to a somewhat repressed but quite real anti-Americanism. On the Tory right it
was part of a nationalist and imperialist objection to America's supplanting Britain as a global power; and on the left it was ideological,
deriving from opposition to American capitalism. In the very early
post-war years the debate about Britain's future went unresolved
with influential voices calling for everything from 'third force' neu-
trality to continuing the wartime alliance with the Soviet Union.

But, as the Cold War heated up and threatened to boil over in the
Berlin and Korean crises a new correlation of global forces emerged
which made the British decision easy. With the overarching threat
posed to Western Europe by Soviet military power many west
European governments, seeing the urgent need to defend themselves,
were prepared to accept US leadership of an alliance and even put up
with a well-defined junior partner role. For the British it became crys-
tal clear that, short of an unthinkable alliance with Russia, the country had no alternative.

It was at this point that Britain's sidekick strategy began to take
serious form. The USA was the leader of a system and Britain was

America's top friend (or at least was vying for the privilege with West Germany). As top friend, Britain would, crucially, be allowed to play a minor global role. Britain became the new superpower's bridge to Europe; and as the Cold War developed a cash-strapped Britain would be urged by Washington to keep its 'world role' east of Suez as part of the US alliance system ringing the Soviet Union. In 1956 during the Suez crisis Prime Minister Anthony Eden misjudged both British power and American resolve but the schism was quickly papered-over, and junior partner status resumed. Later the American diplomat Dean Acheson would famously remark that post-war Britain had 'lost an empire but not yet found a role'. Yet, Acheson was wrong: the country had indeed found a role – as America's staunchest ally. As the superpower's junior partner. A sidekick was born.

*

Although Cold War geo-political exigencies and fears may have created the 'special relationship' there were deep underlying forces at work within Britain that, once the 'relationship' was forged, helped cement the alliance. Britain and the United States had, after all, been brothers-in-arms in both world wars – particularly so in the Second World War. And in the aftermath of the Second War the British, or at least a large section of them, began ingesting a powerful 'Anglo-American cousinhood' mythology. The historian Correlli Barnett has chronicled what he calls British 'myth-making about America' and the 'myth of cousinhood and common interest'. He points to romantic ideas about the destiny of the English-speaking peoples and to the 'pan Anglo-Saxonism' of the early twentieth century upper class English (a sentiment boosted by the large number of marriages of financially strapped aristocrats to American heiresses). Former Prime Minister Arthur Balfour gave full vent to these sentiments at the influential Anglo-American Pilgrim's Society in 1917 when he opined that 'we both spring from the same root...are we not bound together forever?' Even as late as 1954 Winston Churchill could argue at a State Department dinner that 'only the English-speaking peoples count: that together they can rule the world'.[10]

The Winston Churchill narrative was crucial here, a true story of drama and courage that would run and run. The great war leader had saved Britain by cementing a strong relationship with the United States and in a 'hands across the ocean' gesture American forces had joined British at D-Day to liberate a benighted continent. The war had been Britain's 'finest hour' but was also a joint venture with the American cousins. And the Churchill story was all the more compelling as he himself was half-American – his mother hailing from the Jeromes of New York – and thus a walking, talking example of the cousinhood. A later Prime Minister of the Churchill generation, Harold Macmillan, was another half-American, and continued the cousinhood myth in his 'father-son special relationship' with President John F. Kennedy. The post-Churchill leadership generation was less biological and more ideological in their pro-Americanism. Margaret Thatcher had certainly imbibed the 'cousinhood' of the war, but she was also an ideological 'free-market' pro-American. And her contemporaries amongst Labour's social democrats were, in essence, attracted by the American dream – wanting the egalitarianism and upward mobility of the New World for Britain.

Churchill, as well as embodying the Anglo-American 'special relationship', also remains the symbol of British power and independence – the personification of John Bull and the country's ambivalent attitude towards the continent. The great man died in January 1965 four years after Britain, under a Tory government, had first applied to join the Common Market. It was to apply again in 1968, and finally joined in 1973. The arrival of a strong and successful European trading bloc – ever evolving into a more political community – posed real problems for Britain's leaders and their continuing need for a world role. The Americans were supportive of European integration and wanted Britain to join. But should the country fully launch itself into a European future then an independent world role would become impossible. And the 1970s saw a bitter clash between pro and anti Common Market forces in which the opponents of British entry argued that the country's links with the Commonwealth – a surrogate term for a 'world role' – were at stake.

Britain's great Common Market debate ultimately served, however, to reinforce the 'special relationship' with America. A European future, a 'European destiny', was always an alternative future – to that of the American future – for Britain and the British. But the Common Market debate unleashed some basic British prejudices about the continent that have lasted – and remain extremely powerful, perhaps even decisive, in the current controversy over the Euro and the European constitutional arrangements. These prejudices go deep. And a long way back. They may well have formed during the French Revolution and the Napoleonic wars when the gripping fear of revolution among the English upper classes bred ideas that died hard: comparisons between Protestant 'liberty' and Catholic 'authoritarianism', between British 'liberty' and continental tyranny, and, above all, between British stability and continental turmoil. Britain was an island of freedom and stability, an exceptional place, and this 'exceptionalism' demanded we keep our distance from Europe.

This powerful bias would have been swept aside if twentieth century history had taken a different course. Instead, the British struggle against the axis powers in Europe and the 'victory' in the Second World War reinforced this notion of exceptionalism. As I outline in Chapter Three the empire and the war gave the post-1945 British a huge sense of superiority, made more obdurate by the experience of evident national decline. A superior people fallen on hard times would have little truck with continental neighbours. After all, as the story had it we British had saved, indeed rescued, the continent for democracy. Thus the popular imagery unleashed by the British tabloid press: the Germans were totalitarian; the French were weak and untrustworthy; the Italians were a joke and unstable. All in all, the continent was bad news. It was a mindset which could allow a British Prime Minister on the eve of the twenty-first century to deliver the extraordinary statement that 'all our problems have come from mainland Europe and all the solutions have come from the English-speaking nations of the world'.[11] All in all, the post-war British had a real attitude problem with their neighbours. It was an awkwardness that helped cement the other relationship – the American relationship.

1989 and 9/11
When the Berlin Wall came down in 1989 the verities of the Cold War structures fell with it. The lack of a common enemy meant that the rationale for NATO – and for US leadership of Europe – came to an end. And for the British, the 'special relationship' – which had been grounded by the Cold War – was also brought into question. The early 1990s saw a new burst of European integration with plans for the birth of a single currency. It was yet another opportunity for Britain to be 'at the heart of Europe'. But old habits die hard. The Euro-zone was born

in 1999, but Britain was to stay out. Britain's establishment looked long and hard at a European future but ultimately decided against it. They would stick with what they knew – 'the special relationship'.

This decision represented a huge missed opportunity. The clear fact is that Britain has always had a choice. There *was* an alternative role available to that of superpower sidekick. Indeed, Tony Blair's government had, before 9/11, toyed with this alternative. Since coming to power in 1997 the New Labour Prime Minister had been preparing Britain to join the Euro-zone, had taken the lead at St. Malo in 1998 in creating a European defence force, and regularly talked of Britain having a 'European destiny'. Yet, this European future dissolved, virtually overnight, following the 2001 '9/11' attacks upon Manhattan and Washington. In the frenetic days that followed the American President was declaring that everyone was either 'with us or against us'. And, when push came to shove, for Blair and much of this generation of British political leaders their very DNA told them that in a world crisis the umbrella of the super-power was the place to shelter. Building a new superpower in Europe took second place to accepting the protection and power of an old one.

By contrast, France took a different route. And French statecraft during the post 9/11 era became, for the British, both intriguing and frustrating – largely because in many respects it was a mirror image of that of the UK. France, like Britain, is a medium-sized country; it has a similar population and economy, and it is a for-mer colonial power still seeking some kind of a global role whilst a member of the EU. Yet France showed that for European nations a junior partner role to the US was not pre-ordained, and that an alternative approach – of independence – could be constructed. Although the Iraq war temporarily divided Europe (with essential-ly neo-conservative governments in Spain and Italy as well as Britain supporting Washington) France was able to show how a new geo-political grouping of France and Germany ('core Europe'), together with a strategic alliance with Russia, could potentially equal the power of the United States – particularly should Britain ultimately join in.

Of course, Blair's decision to throw his and his country's lot in with the United States was based upon much more than geo-political assessment. Domestic politics was also involved. A key here was the crucial political role of one man and his media empire – Rupert Murdoch. Murdoch had come to prominence in Britain as a key supporter of the Thatcher revolution – and his News Corporation had taken an active part in the revolution by winning a stand-up fight with the print trade unions and revolutionising Fleet Street.

Murdoch became a critic of staid, traditional Britain – royal family as well as trade unions – and, initially at any rate, his supposed refreshing antipodean radicalism forged an alliance with New Labour. Murdoch's empire supported Blair in the 1997 general election and Blair's public relations team (particularly Alastair Campbell) always believed that the support of the mass circulation *Sun* newspaper was central to their electoral success. Indeed, following 1997 the Murdoch media empire (which included *The Sun, The Times, The News of the World* and Sky Television) became, if not a member, then certainly an outrider, of the power coalition that sustained New Labour. And slowly but surely Murdoch's view of the world became New Labour's view of the world. Once Murdoch became an American citizen (in order to be able legally to own television stations as well as newspapers) he added a fervent pro-Americanism to his existing pro-business ideology. His media empire – particularly evident in the Fox News Channel – propagated the full Bush patriotic agenda, most notably the 'war on terror'. Karl Rove, George Bush's electoral strategist, openly proclaimed that it was the Democratic Party's perceived weakness in the 'war on terror' that lost it the 2004 Presidential election. Thus, 'terror' became a very useful mechanism for keeping the western public behind parties whose economic policies they might not otherwise support.

Bush's 'war on terror' – and the interventionist policies, principally the invasion of Iraq that it fostered – suited the personal temperament and personality of the British Prime Minister. The almost compulsive need for a global role that was felt widely throughout the British political-military-intelligence establishment meshed well with Tony Blair's obvious personal need for celebrity. For through 'a global role', and only through a 'global role', could he secure a place on the world stage and in the centre of events where politics meets mass television and becomes celebrity (a location well mined by his good friend and mentor Bill Clinton). Blair's people consciously, and unconsciously, copied the great Washington celebrity Presidency. In Downing Street the televised 'Presidential' setting with the little carpeted walk up to the podium in front of the assembled press was a direct copy.

Tony Blair: Celebrity and Empire

Despite appearances the 'special relationship' began to fray somewhat once the Cold War was over. To accept American dominance under the exigencies of a Cold War was one thing; but to continue with it after the Warsaw Pact posed no threat was another. John Major entered Downing Street as the Cold War was ending and much of his premiership took place as the world was coming to terms with its unravelling. Major was a transitionary figure. Tony Blair who followed him in 1997 took office after half a decade had passed in which no Soviet threat existed. And, in these circumstances, to renew the 'special relationship' with such passion was somewhat unthematic and odd. The answer lay, though, in the momentous events of 9/11 and more specifically in the American reaction to them.

The strong and quasi-messianic American reaction to 9/11 changed Blair's world – as completely as 9/11 itself had changed Bush's. American power was to be projected into Afghanistan and then deep into the Middle East and a 'war on terror' was declared that would force nations to choose to be 'with us or against us'. Bush's new aggressive role found few friends but this gave Blair and the British a belated, and unexpected, chance to get back into the 'world role' business, and through the sidekick mechanism, create a global role for Britain and for Blair himself.

As Blair seized this role two aspects of his personality coincided. The 'global war on terror' would provide a world platform for Blair. The office of the British Prime Minister was a good second-rank position. But as an emissary of George Bush – in places where Bush was not particularly welcome – Blair could reach to a new level. The role of globe-trotting sidekick to the superpower would give him a certain political credibility around the world and open doors in every continent. It would not give him power but it would certainly give him fame. It was a golden opportunity for launching himself as a global celebrity. The young Prime Minister was a natural communicator in the mass media-driven age. He gloried in political television and had learned from Bill Clinton the arts of camera-dominated statesmanship. He had subtly copied the trappings of the American

Presidency's media apparatus – including introducing into British politics the previously frowned-upon televised Prime Ministerial Press Conference.

But alongside the relish for celebrity there was also another powerful element at work in the make-up of Tony Blair. It amounted to a surprising residual imperialist streak. For those closely following the evolution of British foreign policy a speech given by Tony Blair in Chicago in April 1999 had seemed odd and somewhat disturbing. It was delivered during the height of the Kosovo crisis and the air war over Serbia and had a decidedly triumphalist tone about it. Downing Street allowed it to be described in grandiose terms as the 'The Blair Doctrine'. Before Bush – and before 9/11 – it revealed a Prime Minister keen to break with the past international system. It was a bold declaration of intent to abandon the sacred UN rules of 'non-interference' in the affairs of sovereign nations. It went beyond peace-keeping and peace-making into support for outright interventionism against regimes the west did not like. For this purpose Serbian leader Milosevic and Iraqi leader Saddam Hussein were lumped together as regimes worth overthrowing.[12]

This was the neo-conservative agenda of interventionism based upon democratisation – albeit delivered in liberal language. It amounted to an unabashed proposition of an imperial vocation for the west. And it was exactly the same argument that was being developed in the Washington neo-conservative think tanks that were plotting the overthrow of Saddam in the latter days of the Clinton administration. It was liberal imperialism, but imperialism nonetheless.

This echo in Tony Blair of nineteenth century imperial rulership was surprising – because in domestic electoral politics he had sold himself as a modern, egalitarian, democratic, man. Perhaps, though, this imperial impulse should have surprised no one. After all, Blair was a product of an elite educational system that during Blair's teenage years in the early 1970s had still, and incredibly, not broken with an earlier public school mission and ethos so brilliantly dissected by the historian Correlli Barnett in his book *The Collapse of British Power*.[13] The traditional English public school ideal of a ruler of empire involved creating in the young men the self-confidence of a 'born to rule' variety – born to rule that is primarily over non-white masses – combined with a Christian, and essentially evangelical, moral sense. And, importantly, the morality often induced a crusading, rather than compromising, character. Superficial mannerisms and differences apart, the similarities between Blair and Bush are striking. George Bush, the privileged fraternity boy and born-again Christian, and Tony Blair, the privileged public school boy and Christian true believer, fit Correlli Barnett's nineteenth century imperialist rulership profile almost perfectly. The only difference between them was that Bush led an empire. But, then, by 'sidekicking', Blair could pretend to lead one as well.

The sad – or pathetic – truth, however, was that the major decision of Blair's premiership may well have been based upon a huge misjudgement. For it tied Britain not to the ruler of the world, but rather to an empire that was powerful but waning. Even as the American superpower flexed its considerable muscles in the Middle East during the Iraq invasion it was becoming clear that for the twenty-first century the United States was destined to become a great power only – one amongst equals in a new multi-polar world. It was not, as Tony Blair gambled it would be, the lone superpower that could impose its will on the world.

In short, Blair read the significance of 9/11 all wrong. For Washington's reaction to 9/11 – the neo-conservative attempt to impose America's will on the globe – was a false dawn. But in the early light of this false dawn Tony Blair – desperately seeking a 'world role' – threw his and his country's lot in with Washington. In the process he divided the EU and set back for some years Britain's relationship with the continent which he had argued was its destiny.

1. Blair, 9/11, and Iraq

'History will judge Blair as a defender of Bush's agenda over Britain's'
Former Cabinet Minister Chris Patten, September 2005

On the morning of 11th September 2001, just as the planes were en route to explode into the twin towers of the World Trade Centre, Britain's Prime Minister, Tony Blair, was in the southern English seaside town of Brighton preparing to address the Trades Union Congress. He was about to deliver a watershed speech which would open the campaign for Britain to join the Euro-zone. It was to be a campaign that would finally resolve the country's long, awkward relationship with Europe, and help Britain to fulfil what Blair had called her 'destiny' in Europe.

But just before Blair was due to set off for his trip from his hotel to the conference centre, the chairman of the conference, Bill Morris of the TUC, announced from the platform that a plane had struck the World Trade Centre in New York and that Blair might be held up. In the event, Blair cancelled his speech, returned to London, appeared on television to announce that Britain would stand 'shoulder to

15

shoulder' with the Americans and, fatefully, also put Britain's European campaign on hold.

It was a campaign that was not to be revived – for the atrocity in New York was to profoundly alter New Labour's whole approach to Britain's future role in the world. In Washington the reaction to 9/11 allowed a stalled Bush administration to develop a new, aggressive foreign policy as the influential, but contained, neo-conservatives clustered around the American Enterprise Institute and the Pentagon were to seize their moment. The 'Statement of Principles' of the Project For a New American Century (signed by Dick Cheney, Donald Rumsfeld, Paul Wolfowitz, Elliot Abrams, Norman Podhoretz and others in 1997) was dusted off, and for a time became the handbook of President George W. Bush himself. It was highly critical of Clinton's foreign policy, sought a new defence buildup, and called for a new global vision based upon 'military strength and moral clarity'.[1] This political takeover of the US government led to aggressive uni-lateralism – including an extraordinary bid for global supremacy which included the invasion of Iraq, a Middle Eastern nation that did not threaten the United States.

The raw assertion of US power had real implications for Britain, for it gave the Prime Minister, should he want it, a special, though subordinate, role in which Downing Street was assigned the task of junior partner and global advocate of US policy. It was a role per-fectly suited to Tony Blair and to many in the British intelligence services and military. After a half-century of global decline – with America now off-balance and seeking a sidekick – here was a rare and real chance to place Britain at something near the centre of world events. And Blair took it.

For some time before 9/11 the British Prime Minister had begun to see himself as a global, rather than European, player – a posture made more credible when Britain stood alongside the Americans than when it was lost amongst the Europeans. The Kosovo crisis had been a turning-point for Blair. Here was America and NATO, without a UN mandate, laying down the rules for the post Cold War world. And he had gone further, seeing himself, in tandem with Washington's power, as a re-maker of the world. In a strange, somewhat discordant speech in Chicago in April 1999, delivered during the air war over Kosovo, he went as far as outlining a new international doctrine. He declared that 'Bismarck had been wrong' to say that 'the Balkans was not worth the bones of a single Pomeranian Grenadier'; he singled out Slobodan Milosevic and Saddam Hussein as 'dangerous men'; and, more importantly, he attempted to overthrow the basic UN doctrine of 'non-interference' in other countries' affairs in favour of a new idea of 'regime change'. It amounted to a call for a new world order in which western intervention and 'regime change', on western terms and for western reasons, was now acceptable.[2] In Blair's mind, America (with Britain at her side) would lead the charge – in what was nothing less than a rationale for a new updated phase of liberal – or neo-liberal – imperialism. With 9/11 as its galvanising force, this new western assertiveness ended up with the invasion of Iraq.

Only days after 9/11, with the wind in his sails, Tony Blair could return to this theme at the Labour Party Conference of 2001 when he displayed a relish for the coming business of, in his own words, 're-ordering the world'.[3] The formula – which was being worked on in Washington as Blair spoke – was clear: the mission would be couched in liberal tones – 'bringing democracy' – but Washington (with London in tow) was going to 're-order' the world on western terms. And it was going to do so by a combination of western military power (to be put on show in the invasion of Iraq) and the on-going westernising process of globalisation.

On the ground in Britain though, the public remained hostile to the prospect of an Iraqi invasion. At the time, and for years afterwards, the British public could simply not understand why Blair had sided with Bush and joined in the fateful 2003 invasion. It was, after all, a bizarre, slightly unreal decision for a Labour Prime Minister to take. All the opinion polls showed decisive majorities against the invasion, an opposition made manifest by a massive march and rally in central London; the main European partners were against it, the intelligence was not clear-cut; and the UN could not be squared. Yet, in the face of all this, Britain's left-of-centre progressive-minded premier went ahead and committed British troops to the American-led war.

Blair thus nailed his colours, and with them his legacy, to the mast of a conservative Christian Evangelical Republican President. Former Cabinet Minister Chris Patten could write that 'history will judge Blair as a defender of Bush's agenda above Britain's'.[4] It was a coruscating verdict. Blair had taken the 'special relationship' to a new level.

Invasion: The 'Special Relationship' in Action
By March of 2003 the whole British political class – Tony Blair and his cabinet, the majority of New Labour MPs, and the vast majority of Conservative MPs – took the fateful decision to sign up with George W. Bush and invade Iraq. And the British did more than just support the Americans in the UN, they also sent troops – the largest contingent after the US. And following the invasion the British, for the first time since imperial days, took over the military occupation of Arab lands (in the south of the country around Basra). Indeed, to the late twentieth century British mind the very idea of British troops occupying a heartland Arab nation after having toppled its government would have seemed an act of blatant imperialism, a return to inter-war mentalities, and wildly far-fetched.

The Iraq war was a 'defining moment' for Britain's relationship with the Arab world, but also for Britain's 'special relationship' with the United States of America. It was a rare and decisive either/or moment in the Anglo-American relationship. The Americans badly wanted British support, but were mainly interested in full-hearted diplomatic support in the run up to war. At no time did they insist upon Britain sending large numbers of troops. The American Defence Secretary, Donald Rumsfeld, had always had misgivings about the need for British – or any other – troops to support 'Operation Iraqi Freedom', and on the eve of war went as far as publicly stating that they were not needed.[5] Again on the eve of war, with Blair's continued premiership in some doubt, the President himself made a last minute friendly offer to let him off the hook. Bush suggested that Britain need not send troops should it lead to the Blair government falling. Yet even given these opportunities, Blair, in an act of breathtaking eagerness to please, sent the troops anyway.

Britain had some clear choice before it in the run-up to war. It could have sided with France and Germany and stood aside – a course which would have put at risk the country's relations with Washington. But Washington would have tolerated – some in the Pentagon would have preferred – Britain simply supporting the US politically and diplomatically without sending troops (as Harold Wilson did during the Vietnam War even whilst being pressured by President Lyndon Johnson to go further). The Americans would also have accepted a British decision to send only a very small, token, non war-fighting force. That Blair decided to go the 'Full Monty' of an invasion and occupying force showed Blair's utter determination both to please Washington and to play a global role. From Downing Street's perspective, once the decision to support the US politically had been taken, the damage with public opinion had been done. There was nothing to lose from sending significant numbers of troops, and much to gain in the scramble for reconstruction contracts in the occupation phase.

The spring invasion of Iraq in 2003 was the culmination of an extraordinary phase of Downing Street directed British foreign policy in which the British PM and some of the higher echelons of the intelligence and military establishment not only took momentous decisions but also took real risks with Britain's geo-political position in Europe. By siding with invasion and occupation Blair took Britain into the potentially momentous 'clash of civilizations' as he alienated Britain from Arab and broader Islamic opinion, perhaps for generations. He also took the lead in dividing Europe by breaking with its two senior members, France and Germany. Whilst Germany and France led the opposition to the war, New Labour PM Tony Blair was joined by conservative Prime Minister Jose Maria Aznar of Spain, ultra-conservative Prime Minister Silvio Berlusconi of Italy, and the leaders of a host of eastern European candidate countries, in supporting the Bush White House.

Why?

In the months following Blair's fateful decision, large numbers of British people – both within and without the Westminster village – were asking themselves one question about their Prime Minister. Why did he do it? Why did Tony Blair take his country to war in Iraq when no apparent immediate British national interest was involved? Why did he put at risk his relationships with his fellow EU leaders? And why – a question asked after the revelations that Saddam possessed no useable weapons of mass destruction – was he prepared to deploy exaggerations and half truths in order to do it?

Yet, as the dust settled following the war, the answers to these questions, although never stated, became progressively clear. It became obvious that, from Downing Street's perspective, once Washington had made up its mind to go to war, the British Prime Minister – any British Prime Minister – had no alternative but to support the President of the USA. In sum, Britain's 'special relationship' demanded it; and when an American President goes to war, and asks for Britain's support, such support is normally given.

This time too it was automatically given. Although this time there were new factors. There was a split in the western camp. In all previous great global crises – during the Korean War, the Cuban missile crisis, the Vietnam War (when western differences were kept low profile), the first Gulf War and air war over Serbia – the west had been politically united. But over Iraq the major continental powers not only opposed Washington, they campaigned against it in the UN. Blair was forced to choose between America and Europe. But for Blair it was not a difficult or agonising choice. From Downing Street, the western geo-political power correlation looked clear. Washington was still the stronger of the two western contestants. Bush was adamant and committed, and would go to war anyway. And the Franco-German security core, although an intriguing new development (particularly so with Russia as an ally) was in its infancy.

Martin Kettle, a commentator with good connections to Downing Street, suggested that Blair supported the invasion and the post-war US policy in Iraq, for quite straightforward reasons – he argued bluntly that Blair believes that 'what happens in the US defines the limits of the possible for Britain'.[6] In other words, according to this Blairite thesis, it was simply 'impossible' not to support the USA.

It was difficult though to sell such a raw idea of subordination to the British public – so a more palatable posture was struck. It had been outlined decades before by Sir Pierson Dixon, Britain's UN Ambassador at the time of the Suez Affair. He had argued ruefully that 'if we cannot entirely change American policy, then we must, it seems to me, resign ourselves to a role as counselor and moderator'. And he added that: 'It is difficult for us, after centuries of leading others, to resign ourselves to the position of allowing another and greater power to lead us.'[7] Half a century later, Tony Blair might not have put it exactly that way; but Britain as America's 'counselor' and 'moderator' was a role he had openly advocated as Prime Minister.

So, as the tension rose in the run up to invasion, the official British line became what the well-informed columnist and author Peter Riddell came to describe as a 'hug them close' strategy – the idea being that by 'hugging them close' Britain would secure greater influence with the Americans than by breaking with them.[8] Blair put out the word that his closeness to Washington was calculated: that in return for his support Bush was agreeing to support a revival of the stalled Middle East 'peace plan' which would secure a long-term Israeli-Palestinian agreement. Four years later, as Blair again lent his support to the US in the Israeli-Lebanon-Hezbollah war, he was still allowing it to be known that he was imminently set to get Washington's 'green light' for such a new 'peace initiative'.

Tony Blair: American Conservative

Tony Blair's support for the United States in the war in Iraq was simply the tip of an iceberg, a symptom of a much deeper commitment. For, by the time of his second term as premier he had basically adopted the whole Bush-American world-view. So much so that, like Margaret Thatcher before him, he came to identify with the US more than he did with Britain. On the 18th September 2005 the British media was abuzz with details of an intriguing and revealing comment by Blair about the New Orleans hurricane tragedy – seen at the time as a turning-point in the popularity of President George W. Bush. The BBC reported that Blair had told Rupert Murdoch that BBC reporting of the New Orleans hurricane tragedy had been 'full of hate at America and gloating about our [sic] troubles'.[9] The use of 'our' was highly revealing. It revealed not just where the British Prime Minister's true affection, if not loyalty, may have lain, but also that he saw the Bush presidency and his premiership as conjoined, as one political unit with common friends and common enemies.

Blair's identification with the USA had, though, a considerable prime ministerial pedigree. Winston Churchill identified with America – after all he had an American mother. So too did Margaret Thatcher who had a close personal and ideological relationship with President Ronald Reagan. Yet, the Americanisation of Tony Blair was less easy to understand. Blair had no similar blood or ideological ties. His ties were with the presidency: he was very close to *both* liberal-moderate Bill Clinton and conservative-cum-neo-conservative George W. Bush. It was his relationship with the Texan that was somewhat odd, and may reveal that Blair's love affair was, at root, all about power – the power and celebrity of the American presidency.

Yet, over time, the love affair with the presidency turned ideological. Having begun his premiership in 1997 ostensibly as a European social democrat – with an 'ideology' roughly similar to Gerhard Schröder's SPD and slightly to the left of Clinton's 'third way'

Democrats – he later morphed into a full, red-blooded American radical conservative. Blair, breathtakingly, signed on to each of the three components of Bush's radical conservatism – global neo-liberal 'free-market' economics, global political rule from Washington, and Christian-based 'family values'. It was an ideological package that took him into an unlikely political stable – one populated by Wall Street, the Pentagon and the Christian right and, in Europe, by ultra-conservative Prime Minister Silvio Berlusconi of Italy and Prime Minister Jose Maria Aznar of Spain. Blair was the lone supposed European social democrat in such company.

Blair became the chief European advocate of the need to accept 'globalisation'. When used by politicians, 'accepting globalisation' was code for the need to accept a business-driven, cost-cutting agenda. To survive in the global economy – so ran the business argument – nation states need to ensure that their costs, that is wages and taxes, are competitive. Labour markets should also be competitive – that is, flexible enough to make it easy to 'hire and fire'. In the age of globalisation, if governments don't so oblige, then global capital will go elsewhere – principally to lower-cost China and India. In an article in Newsweek in 2006 Tony Blair pulled no punches: 'complaining about globalisation' he said 'is as pointless as trying to turn back the tide. Asian competition can't be shut out; it can only be beaten'.[10]

Since the end of the Cold War there had been a quantum leap in the power of mobile capital over state and labour, and neo-liberals argued that governments need to yield to these 'realities'. Blair was in the forefront of such yielding – constantly arguing that the British people should welcome 'globalisation', not resist it nor even attempt to shape it. All any government could do was to help their population to adapt to the inevitable by helping them to compete – primarily by providing suitable skills and education, the origin of Blair's catch-phrase policy priority: 'Education, Education, Education'. Of course, in this future low tax regime governments would not be able to fund the future welfare state and thus the welfare systems needed 'reform' (with a bigger private sector).

Blair – just like the Wall Street economists who propounded this doctrine – was sustained in it by a sense of almost righteous inevitability. There was, they and he argued, 'no alternative' to this global capitalist dynamic. Those who went with the flow, like neo-liberal New Labour Britain – would be 'winners' – whereas the 'sclerotic' Euro-zone economies would be 'losers'. It was an American message, but increasingly, during the first few years of the twenty-first century, an American conservative message (as some US liberals in the Democratic Party, worrying about outsourcing jobs, began to flirt, more and more, with protectionism). The message was clear: the west would need to 'accept' losing jobs in its manufacturing sector, but would see its service sector grow to make up for the loss, and it assumed that China and India would continue to demand western services. And the message had a warning – that any attempt at trying to use trade or other policies to staunch the loss of jobs in the west was 'protectionist' and self-defeating. It was a message that New Labour, no matter its moral and intellectual roots, could sign up to.

The fact was that Tony Blair's government came to believe – with some justification – that Britain depended on the City of London with its worldwide links. Hywel Williams, one of Britain's most perceptive writers, put it starkly. 'The power of capital over New Labour, with its superstitious veneration of money created Britain's most consistently business-friendly party' he argued; and this business-friendly party, as it promoted 'globalisation', found that, for Britain 'all that is left is the power of the City – the true governor of Britain, with a world-view of global markets that has ended British independence'.[11]

Blair's New Labour also adopted the key underpinning idea of the American economic conservative movement – the notion that western societies need to live with growing *gross* inequality – as a price worth paying for private capital formation. A tolerance for inequality – and for a growing class of super-rich and mega-rich people – had been a feature of several eras of American history, and particularly so in what economist Paul Krugman has called the 'new gilded era' of the post-1980s world.[12] Such tolerance of *gross* inequality had not been present in Britain, certainly since 1945, and not really even during the premiership of Margaret Thatcher – when the stress was on creating a vibrant middle class.[13] But Blair broke with the British post-war consensus, and adopted a much more American approach. In a remark, unthinkable for any social democrat, Blair declared to interviewer Jeremy Paxman just before the 2001 general election, that he simply did not worry about growing inequality, or about the growing class of the super and mega-rich. 'It is not a burning ambition for me that David Beckham earns less money' he revealed.

This key American conservative idea – that inequality does not matter, that social problems are not caused by social divides or even poverty, but rather by issues arising from 'family breakdown' – helped further the idea that the tax bill for welfare could safely be reduced. In the 1980s, the American sociologist Charles Murray was hugely influential in this attempted divorce of economic inequalities from social problems, locating them instead in lack of family stability and personal inadequacies. And reportedly, Rupert Murdoch's aide, Irwin Steltzer, played a role in introducing Charles Murray to Rupert Murdoch and thus to British opinion-formers and public through the *Sunday Times*.[14]

American conservatism won yet another battle in its takeover of New Labour when ideas about Christian 'faith-based solutions' began to appear in New Labour thinking. Throughout his premiership Blair was not overly bashful in proclaiming his Christian views, although he balked at journalists who suggested that his relationship with Bush was based upon a shared Christian faith (and at questions about holding hands in prayer meetings in the White House). But he was less open about his growing Roman Catholicism (or the influence on him of the Roman Catholic beliefs held by his wife); and the word from Downing Street was that he would make public any conversion to Catholicism only when he left office. In any event, although Blair's 'faith schools' programme chimed well with Bush's 'faith-based initiatives', they stood out awkwardly in secular Britain – particularly in secular New Labour (or, for that matter, in old or middle-aged Labour as well). Yet, the New Labour Prime Minister continued to introduce them, and even appointed to the sensitive post of Education Secretary an associate of the Catholic religious cult Opus Dei.[15] Again, more intriguing perhaps than Blair's own American conservative belief system – from the Iraq war to economic and social policy – was the fact that it was tolerated by the bulk of Britain's Labour MPs. Not one MP ever raised in public the issue of Blair's *systematic* support for the American conservative agenda.

Murdoch over Britain

This embracing of American-style radical conservatism by Tony Blair was more than an act of true belief. It was also about hard-nosed domestic politics. For, as it happens, Blair's conservative agenda squared nicely with the world-view and global interests of the media mogul, the Australian-American Rupert Murdoch, the owner of News International and *The Sun* newspaper. Blair decided very early on in his career as opposition leader that he needed, at the very least, to neutralise *The Sun* newspaper, which he believed had decisively hurt Labour in previous elections.

The power of *The Sun* was based upon its mass circulation. It outsold every other daily. It developed a clear and concise political message that, particularly following the Falklands conflict in 1982, associated Thatcherism with patriotism and national success and the left with the failed politics of national weakness, trade union militancy and liberal 'softness' on crime. And its political journalism had a knack of articulating basic populist views and appealing to the often-hidden resentments of its relatively low-income and under-educated mass readership (and widely-held resentments of 'liberal elite', 'politically correct' attitudes).

News International became a major player in British politics (in its foreign and well as domestic policy) during the crises of the 1980s as Margaret Thatcher won her battle with Britain's powerful trade unions. Initially, Murdoch's empire was part of the broad anti-trade union coalition; it also developed a radical, and seemingly progressive, meritocratic edge which, under the influence of *Sunday Times* Editor Andrew Neil took as its targets traditionalist Britain: old money aristocracy, the monarchy and royal family as well as the trade unions.

By the late 1980s it turned into a support system for The Conservative party's campaign for a business-led economic and political culture under the banner of the 'free market'. It also began its systematic, high-volume opposition to the European Community and Union, and Britain's place in it. Murdoch's opposition to a European destiny for Britain had little in common with the chauvinism and nationalism exhibited in his papers, particularly *The Sun* (Murdoch, in fact, was an egalitarian Australian, and a cosmopolitan globe-trotter who was to marry, as his second wife, a Chinese woman). Rather, the key Murdoch concern was what he perceived as the anti-business culture of the EU and its highly regulated, high-tax welfare societies – a culture that he saw as hostile to his own media interests as well. His pro-business, anti-Europe values were bound sooner or later to draw Murdoch to the USA. Murdoch and conservative America were a love affair waiting to be consummated. During the 1990s Murdoch built up considerable media interests in North America and, centring his business there, he became an American citizen on 24th August 2003. The successful political journalism of *The Sun* (and of Thatcherism) translated well to Bush's America. As Murdoch invested in newspapers and television (particularly the Fox News Channel) the key themes of Thatcherism – pro-business patriotism laced with a strong law and order position – played very well indeed. Murdoch's Fox News Channel added to this 'Thatcherite core' appeal the values and concerns of the American Christian right – the so-called three G's, 'God, Guns, and Gays' – that had been missing from Murdoch's British operation.

Tony Blair first met Rupert Murdoch in 1994 – privately, over dinner in the Belgravia restaurant Mosimann's. During this get-together Blair suggested that media ownership rules under Labour would not place Murdoch in a worse position than he was under Thatcher and Major, and Murdoch indicated that his newspapers were not 'wedded to the Tories'.[16] In July 1995, Tony Blair, then the new leader of Her Majesty's Opposition (as official Britain still quaintly called the Leader of the Opposition), decided to board an aircraft and travel 24 hours to a remote island off Australia where he would attend a News Corporation Management conference at Murdoch's Hamilton Island resort on Australia's Great Barrier Reef.[17] From this time on, Blair would continue to seek, and to get, Murdoch's support for his premiership. On 18th March 1997 Murdoch's *Sun*, which had supported the Conservatives ever since Murdoch took it over, announced that 'The Sun Backs Labour' – incidentally also on the very day that the Murdoch-funded neo-conservative magazine *The Weekly Standard* declared that US radical rightist Newt Gingrich was not right-wing enough![18] Blair went on to win not only in 1997, but, with Murdoch's support, in 2001 and 2005 as well.

Murdoch's support for Blair may help explain Blair's own transformation from European social democrat into American radical conservative. Irwin Steltzer was a key aide to Rupert Murdoch, an intellectual guru and 'transatlantic advisor', and a major player in transatlantic Murdoch politics. He epitomised American radical conservatism, and, like many Bush neo-conservatives he possesses an articulate and knowledgeable universalist bravura that gives him the gift of proclaiming – with great confidence – the right course for countries other than his own.[19] Steltzer met Blair on many occasions both before and after he became Prime Minister, and became Blair's advocate in the US. He saw early on that Blair shared many ideas with the American conservative right. 'I know Tony Blair...' he once said, 'Blair is one of Thatcher's children. I think he knows it'. And he saw Blair's Christian beliefs as potentially linking him – beyond Clinton and the American secular liberals – to the conservative right. Steltzer could assert perceptively that 'one thing is clear...the leader of Britain's left-wing party finds it acceptable, politically, to profess his Christianity and to look to the new and old testaments for a central core around which to develop his political program. Of necessity, that requires a cultural stance not very different from that of America's Christian Coalition'.[20]

Whereas Murdoch may have only facilitated Tony Blair's growing American conservatism, he and his newspapers and television stations were decisive when it came to Blair's European policy. Blair had come into office in 1997 with very positive views about Britain joining the Euro-zone, but was never, throughout the whole period of his premiership, able to act on them. Before the 1997 general election Blair was forced into pledging a referendum of the issue for fear of Murdoch supporting Major in the campaign. After entering Downing Street Euro-entry remained an objective of the government, but because of fear about Murdoch's media influence in any referendum campaign, the government was never confident of winning a vote. Thus, a vote was never held, and Britain stayed outside. *The Mail on Sunday* even claimed that in the original, uncensored *Diary of a Spin Doctor*, Downing Street official Lance Price had written that 'apparently we [Downing Street] promised News International [Murdoch's corporation] that we won't make any changes to our European policy without talking to them'.[21]

Another clear, and stark, example of Murdoch's power over New Labour – particularly on the European issue – came in July 2006. Blair's premiership was clearly reaching its final phase, and Gordon Brown's team was preparing for the future transfer of power. Speculation about Brown's political options was rife. Into this vacuum Murdoch issued what amounted to a public 'ultimatum' or 'warning' to Brown. He was told flatly not to try for a quick general election but rather to stay around for eighteen months during which the electorate could judge his merits alongside those of the new Tory leader David Cameron. It became clear that Murdoch, ever the vigilant

Eurosceptic, was worried that Brown might hold a quick election, get a new mandate, and then be free to develop his own European policy. At the time it was becoming clear that a new joint German-Italian-French constitutional initiative was possible and might well be launched after the French Presidential election in the late spring of 2007. Murdoch feared that Gordon Brown, just installed as the new Prime Minister might well sign up to it. Murdoch let it be known that *The Sun* newspaper – the only paper New Labour's leaders cared about – would not support Brown in any quickly-called election campaign. Should he try such a manoeuvre it would support Cameron.[22]

An intriguing aspect of this intervention in British politics from a media organisation run from the USA was not its blatant nature. Rather, it was the nonchalant way it was received by New Labour, the British political class, press and commentariat. There was hardly a peep of protest or a riposte of any note. After a decade of New Labour, and three decades of Thatcherism, Rupert Murdoch, an American citizen, domiciled outside the UK, had become accepted as an arbiter of Britain's future. He had become as powerful as the whole British cabinet combined.

Murdoch's press empire was, though, by no means the sole pressure behind New Labour's growing extreme pro-Americanism. There was also a general pro-US bias amongst other powerful sections of the media world – not least the output of *Daily Telegraph* and *Spectator* owner Conrad Black. The nexus of media and politics which Murdoch and Black bestrode was, in fact, the world inhabited by New Labour – and, later, by David Cameron's Tories too. Blair's team and Cameron's too, were not strictly 'political' in the classic sense. Mixing the political with modern communications techniques they took the world of the media very seriously indeed and they treated media barons as legitimate policy-makers. British politics had come a long way since the early 1970s when it was the trade union leaders who were the 'over-mighty subjects' and held similar power over an earlier Labour administration.

In this process New Labour had ceased to act like a traditional left-of-centre British political party. Rather, with cabinet and party weakened, Blair's team resembled a highly sophisticated public relations company that, media-friendly and brand and image-sensitive, cut out the party (its factions, its MPs, its trade unions, and its activists) and made direct contact with the voter. As New Labour embraced this party-less, American-style politics it automatically became more and more dependent upon media support and approval, and upon business and private money for its campaigning. And the media-cum-business community demanded of New Labour business-friendly policies in return.

It was an embrace that as one commentator put it 'created Britain's most consistently business-friendly party'.[23] And a 'business-friendly party' was an America-friendly party. For New Labour increasingly acted as an amen chorus for the US economic model and as a pressure against British integration in 'social' Europe. And a key part of the business-friendly US economic model was the opening to a global marketised world with its pressures for 'competitive', low cost, low wage, low tax economies with flexible labour markets. As New Labour entered this world it began – often with relish – to join in the Wall Street barrage of criticism against the European Social Model with its 'inflexible', regulated – indeed 'sclerotic' – economies and hugely 'debilitating' welfare states. So powerful was the hold of this business-led consensus in Britain that even the downturn of Wall Street and the puncturing of the hi-tech bubble in 2000 and 2001, the huge and dangerous financial imbalances of the US economy, and the corruption scandals of Enron and others, did not shake New Labour's conviction that neo-liberal economics was the way forward for Britain.

Mandarins, Spies and Submariners

New Labour's love affair with America, though, was not simply about business-friendly and media-mogul-friendly politics. For, as well as the Americanised business and media class, Whitehall's traditionalist 'establishment' was also very much on board for the US connection. 'Atlanticism' ran deep in the corridors of Whitehall. When this Atlanticist faction joined up with the Eurosceptic business class in promoting the 'special relationship' it became a formidable pressure group.

An archetypal Foreign Office Atlanticist was Jonathan Powell, an Oxford contemporary of Tony Blair, who became Blair's Chief of Staff in 1997 and saw him every day sometimes at least a dozen times. Picked out by Blair whilst at the British Embassy in Washington, Powell (an affectation has it pronounced 'Po-ell') is a 'devout Atlanticist who is not much bothered about Europe'.[24] Indeed, pro-American Atlanticism runs in the family, for Powell is the brother of an even stauncher pro-American Atlanticist, Lord Charles Powell (again pronounced Po-ell) who was Margaret Thatcher's chief foreign policy advisor.

The Powells are in one sense very representative figures – representative, that is, of the governing official mindset of top political Britain. Like Tony Blair himself they are the product of public schools and, again like Blair, have just a touch of the old imperial manner, and of its attraction to power – in this case to the power of superpower America. Like the foreign policy establishment they represent, their Atlanticism is ingrained, made so by the historic success of NATO during the Cold War years.

Below this top political level – where the Atlanticist 'special relationship' was held as an act of faith – there were the more pragmatic pro-American Whitehall interest groups: the spies and submariners. Britain's intelligence community had a real 'special relationship' with Washington – based on intelligence sharing not offered to other European nations, which had continued beyond the Cold War years; and Whitehall needed to continue to please Washington for fear it would be cut off. This may help explain the seemingly determined behaviour of John Scarlett, the Chair of the Joint Intelligence Committee, who, throughout the great post-invasion controversy about Britain's intelligence, and the Hutton enquiry into the strange death of a weapons inspector, stood 100% by Blair and his policy even though at least one other intelligence chief was reported as possessing severe misgivings about the war.[25]

The role of the intelligence services is shrouded in mystery, but they have two clear and obvious advantages in Whitehall's power struggles. They are the sole possessor of 'knowledge' and 'information'; and they have total and regular access to the Prime Minister's office, more so than top cabinet ministers.

The other Whitehall pressure group highly supportive of Washington is the British Navy, which ever since the late 1960s has played host to Britain's nuclear weapons which, together with the missiles, are carried in the navy's submarines. To many in Whitehall this 'British bomb' remains the central nervous system of British power and thus the key to the British establishment's 'world role'. Yet, as befits this British nuclear 'world role', Washington is indispensable. For the United States – first through the Polaris and then through the

Poseidon agreements – provided and provides indispensable servicing requirements for the submarine force and crucial satellite targeting systems. The British bomb is independent but only if the British government wants to launch a 'spasm' response. A proper, targeted response needs American input and allows for an American veto over its use whereas, by contrast, the French nuclear weapons system is genuinely independent. These umbilical intelligence and nuclear ties to Washington may explain, perhaps much more clearly than any of the more geo-political and theoretical attachments to 'Atlanticism' (and 'NATO-think'), why exactly it is that Britain's top leadership needs the Americans and needs to 'hug them close'.

'NATO-Think'
Atlanticist 'NATO-Think' – and its key idea that the US is indispensable for European security – remained dominant in London long after the rationale for NATO had arguably dissolved with the fall of the Berlin Wall and the winding down of the Warsaw Pact. And in the post-Cold War years US leadership of the west was given a new lease on life following the decisive US role in the first Gulf War in 1991 and then in the Balkans conflict. Thus 'NATO-Think' continued way beyond its proper sell-by date.

Many in London saw the invasion of Iraq in 2003 as heralding yet another lesson in American leadership of the west. Yet, as the post-invasion occupation failed to meet the minimum objectives of the mission – and the invasion came to be seen as an historic strategic blunder – British advocates of the 'special relationship' found it more and more difficult to make the Atlanticist case. They continued, though, to rest on the 'place at court' argument: that Britain, by staying close to Washington, could influence US policy; that the most suitable role for Britain's government – and the democracy it represents – was, in effect, to be a foreign policy lobbyist in Washington. As Christopher Meyer, in an authentic rendition of the argument, asserted: 'Whether you like it or not there is almost nothing that the United States, as the sole superpower, does that will not affect Britain for better or worse.'[26] Such views were so strongly held that even should the British Prime Minister not be listened to he should continue to 'press and press and continue to press his views [in Washington]'.[27]

Essential to the Atlanticist case for the 'special relationship' was the argument that a 'place at court' gave Britain real influence over

Washington. Some time before the Iraq invasion, the author John Dickie had derided the idea in an influential book called *Special No More*[28]. And, when the dust settled after the Iraq invasion it was clear that Dickie's analysis had been sustained: no real deal between Bush and Blair had been struck, and Britain was getting next to nothing in return for its support.

Advocates of the 'special relationship' pointed to Bush's decision to go to the United Nations before invading Iraq as an example of Blair's influence in Washington. But this was a detour, not a change of course, and was also demanded by Bush's Secretary of State, Colin Powell. One British policy that Blair had been lobbying Washington to implement was his vision of a 'two state solution' to the Israel/Palestine conflict, and in 2004 he had even hosted an international conference on the question (which Condoleezza Rice, Bush's National Security Advisor, had attended). But Blair's initiative got nowhere for it was dependent upon Bush agreeing to put his weight behind it by leaning heavily on Israel (as his father had done). Bush signed on to the theory of a 'two state' formula but refused to put American muscle behind any serious plan to achieve it (such as pressuring Israel to withdraw to the 1967 borders).

Apart from the detour to the UN and the rhetoric on Israel-Palestine, Bush gave nothing else to Blair. By the end of Blair's premiership Blair had adopted Bush's position on the Middle East, rather than the other way round; and during a rather forlorn trip to the region in September 2006 Blair had become so identified with Washington that he was welcomed in Israel but was boycotted by Hamas in the occupied Palestinian territories.

Blair's 'special' influence on the US administration had produced no US movement on Washington's opposition to the Kyoto climate change treaty and no movement on US non-recognition of the International Criminal Court. There was no discernible 'special' treatment for the 'special' ally on a whole range of other questions; indeed there were occasions when Britain was treated by the Bush White House with near-contempt. Britain's Prime Minister, and even its Attorney General, Lord Goldsmith, were prepared to go along with the humiliation of accepting a massive double-standard in American-British relations. At Guantanamo Bay, British citizens were held in an outlaw fashion with no due process and no extradition possible whereas American citizens in a similar situation in Britain may well have been turned over to the US – even if they would have been in danger of receiving the death penalty.[29]

Also, the British government tolerated a one-sided extradition agreement in which – as in the 2006 Enron extradition case – British citizens being sought by America were extradited without a proper pre-trial, and thus were treated completely differently from American citizens whom the British wanted. The Irish lobby in the US Senate was holding up the ratification of an extradition treaty, but the British government, instead of abrogating the British signature on the treaty until the Senate had ratified it, let the extraditions stand.

Ditching 'Our Destiny' in Europe

Blair's support for the American war in Iraq was a mammoth assertion of the importance to Britain of the 'special relationship' – more so because Chancellor Schröder and President Chirac both opposed it. In reality, Blair had to make a choice between America and Europe. However, it was a choice he did not believe existed. For, ever since assuming the premiership in 1997 he had pursued a strategy in which Britain had a foot in both camps. On the one hand Blair could proclaim that 'our destiny lies in Europe' but at the very same time proclaim the utter centrality of the 'special relationship' with the USA. He believed fervently that he could square the circle between Britain as an Atlantic and Britain as a continental power; that Britain could both have its cake and eat it.

Blair had taken this message directly to the heart of core Europe when he addressed the French National Assembly in Paris on 24th March 1998. 'I know that some feel being close with the USA is an inhibition on closer European cooperation' he argued, but 'on the contrary, I believe it is essential that the isolationist voices in the USA are kept at bay and we encourage our American allies to be partners in issues of world peace and security. Strong in Europe. Strong with the United States. That should be our goal'. He resented those who suggested there was indeed a choice. In speech after speech he denounced the idea that the country needed to choose, and he placed himself as the necessary 'bridge' between Europe and the USA. A bridge was necessary. 'The world works better when the US and EU stand together' he argued at the George Bush Senior Presidential Library in Texas on the 7th April 2002. And Britain need not make a choice.

The idea of 'a choice' was also anathema to Blair's powerful Chancellor of the Exchequer Gordon Brown. The sheer pull of the 'special relationship' can be seen in the extent to which Blair's assumed successor was also loath to make a choice. Brown was virtually a candidate for modern European man: meritocrat, Celt, with none of the English problems with France and the continent, and seemingly no hankering after past imperial glory. But since entering office in Whitehall Brown had increasingly come under the sway of Washington. He took holidays in Cape Cod, and became friends with senior American politicians (Democrats mainly), and seemingly completed an intellectual journey from faintly moralistic left-winger to market globaliser.[30] As Britain's Chancellor of the Exchequer he, for a while, became a cheerleader for the US economic model and an advocate for 'reforming' Europe – a favourite theme of market fundamentalists.

Yet, in Labour's early years in government the pro-European impulses still surfaced. Tony Blair was still toying with British entry into the Euro following the general election in the summer of 2001. It was a move which worried Whitehall's Atlanticists. They were already anxious about the change of administration in Washington, for George W. Bush was by no means Bill Clinton, and there was much speculation that Blair and Bush would not hit it off. But following their first meeting at Camp David in February 2001 these fears lessened and by the time of George Bush's visit to Chequers in July 2001 the US-UK relationship appeared as solid as it had been during Clinton's presidency. Tony Blair, with George W. Bush by his side at a joint press conference at RAF Halton, could welcome the US President in the traditional manner. 'It's a very strong relationship' said Blair, 'a very special relationship'.

The new President did, however, place some strains on the relationship. And Blair's great high wire act, of balancing Downing Street between Washington and Brussels, became more and more precarious as George W. Bush developed a global strategy that was far less sensitive to European concerns. American 'unilateralism' had been a theme of the new President well before the 9/11 tragedy, and became a banner under which marched the growing number of nationalists in Washington. Bush had campaigned on a populist 'unilateralist' and 'nationalist' platform in the 2000 Presidential election: and he had made clear his proclivity to put American interests first, even if it meant ignoring the UN and the Europeans. It should have come as no surprise when the new administration failed to ratify the Kyoto treaty, rejected the International Criminal Court, and erected tariffs on steel. Washington's new mood of unilateralism was reinforced, and made official, by the new global security doctrine ushered in following the events of 9/11. In the newly-proclaimed 'war on terror' every nation on earth was put on notice that the US would not tolerate any threat to its primacy, and that every nation had to decide whether they were 'with us or against us'. During the height and heat of the Iraq crisis US-European relationships soured to the point where Washington was talking of 'punishing' France and also of 'de-aggregating' its European policy (code for downgrading the EU connection and dividing and ruling Europe by playing off the European powers against one another).

Following 9/11 Blair's interest in joining the Euro evaporated and when Gordon Brown in November 2001 made public his insistence that five tests be passed before Britain could join, the Prime Minister no longer had the stomach for a fight. The whole push for Europe was placed on hold and the British government only had time, and eyes, for Washington.

Across the channel it was a very different story. American leadership was no longer automatically accepted by continental Europe's two major powers and the Franco-German rejection of Washington was overwhelmingly supported by the European publics (in Britain as well). Blair's government remained loyal, but the country was increasingly being pulled in two directions at once – in one direction by a militant Bush administration with its 'with us or against us' mentality, and in the opposite direction by France and Germany, increasingly acting like 'Core Europe'.

It was an environment in which the Franco-German 'Core' was beginning to look like the nucleus of a coming global power – particularly when joined on specific issues by Russia. Its first outing on the world stage in the January 2003 UN battle over Iraq had been a success, for in the opinion of many the judgment of its leaders, certainly compared with those of Washington and London, had been vindicated. Then, in March 2004, the pro-Bush Spanish government of Jose Maria Aznar lost the election. The new left-of-centre 'pro-Core' administration that took over in Madrid tilted the whole balance of power in Europe and the EU. Virtually overnight the Spanish announced a new European alignment, and, in effect, expanded 'Core Europe' to over 200 million people, improving the Franco-German hand immeasurably. One immediate result was the re-emergence of the EU's new constitution. This constitution, unlike Britain's own, was a written document, and had been drawn up as a response to the EU's historic enlargement into a continent-wide economic power of 25 nation-states. It represented an attempt by Europe's leaders – principally France and Germany – to make a potentially unwieldy economic superpower more effective by streamlining its governance. The Aznar government had joined Poland in putting the constitution 'on ice' as the two countries refused to accept Franco-German led proposals for new voting powers. But with Aznar gone the new socialist government in Madrid immediately abandoned the Poles, and Warsaw then lifted its veto.[31]

The defeat of Aznar was a serious blow to Europe's pro-Bush forces and to Blair in particular. With Spain now in the Franco-German column, Blair's only major pro-American friend left in Europe was the volatile populist conservative Italian Prime Minister Silvio Berlusconi. In the early spring of 2004 Blair – and with him the American hopes for a divided EU – was looking extremely isolated. It seemed as though the next two years would see a burst of Franco-German-led European integration as the new constitution was constructed and ratified – with Britain having to take it or leave it.

In April 2004 British Prime Minister Tony Blair returned to London from a spring holiday in the West Indies and made a surprise announcement: that his country would hold a referendum, rather than a parliamentary vote, on whether to ratify the new European constitution. Blair had always said that he supported the constitution, and had been anxiously ruminating for months about how best to ratify it: by parliament or by a vote of the people. The decision was a tricky one, to date the most difficult of his career. If he gave the decision to parliament he would stand accused of ignoring the voters and would hand the Tories a big card to play in the coming general election. But if he opted for a referendum he ran the very real risk that it might be voted down as voters were heavily influenced by the anti-Europe media.

The news of the referendum was initially greeted by Britain's jaded media with a large dose of cynicism. After all, the commentators could be forgiven for remembering that the very same Prime Minister had promised a referendum on Britain's future in Europe before – in the 1997 election, on the defining issue of the country adopting the single European currency – and that seven years later the country was still waiting for the vote. Blair's motives were questioned. Was he offering, yet again, a referendum so that he could dish the Tories in the coming election and then drop the idea later? Was he, yet again, stalling for time, calculating that another country would come to the rescue by voting 'no' well before the British referendum?

Yet, by the end of June 2004 it was becoming clear to the journalists and politicians of Britain's political class that this time it really was different. For a start – unlike in the Euro debate – there was a firm deadline. The constitution was agreed by the heads of government in June 2004, and each country was given two years in which to ratify it. At home in Britain this deadline concentrated minds wonderfully. Unlike the decision on the Euro, this new constitution could not be put off – it could not be treated like other awkward political issues and simply be 'kicked into the long grass'. This time, Europe's leaders had provided Britain with no opt-out clause, no special position, and the country, just like all the other member states, would be forced to say 'yes' or 'no' to the whole package within a couple of years from the signing. It was beginning to dawn on an unsuspecting British public that this new constitution was more than a routine tidying up exercise. Rather, it was beginning to look very much like a 'defining act' – and for Britain, the decisive moment in its long, awkward relationship with the continent. It was clear that the European powers were now determined to go ahead and forge a superpower with or without Britain. And, should the 'no' vote win in Britain, then, instead of Europe simply abandoning the whole constitution (as the strict legal position would dictate) the 'yes' countries would simply go ahead – perhaps even by signing a new treaty – leaving the rejectionists, including Britain, outside of the club.

Blair himself had begun to paint this chilling picture. He put it carefully, but typically dramatically, when he told the interviewer David Frost that should the British reject the constitution the country would be in the 'ante-chamber next to the exit'.[32] Many believed that the real position was even worse – that, following a 'no' vote the country would be facing not just the 'ante-chamber next to the exit' but 'the exit' itself. Britain would, in effect, be on its way out of the European project. After 30 years as a full member of the EU the country would, in all reality, cease to be a member state of the union. It might remain in the single market; but it would be outside any further economic integration, outside the Euro-zone, outside the Schengen agreement ('*Europe sans Frontiers*'), outside the new governance of the constitution. It would, in effect, become a 'Norway without the oil' – like Norway, having to abide by Europe's laws without any say in them, in other words, subject to 'taxation without representation'.

By the summer of 2004 there was a real head of steam building both behind a 'no' vote and a willingness to contemplate British withdrawal from the union. Just days before the 'signing' ceremony in Brussels, the British people, in the EU parliamentary elections, voted in surprisingly large numbers for an avowedly anti-EU and 'withdrawalist' party, the United Kingdom Independence Party (UKIP). UKIP secured as many votes as the Liberal Democrats and polled ahead of Labour in four key regions of the country – the East Midlands, the Eastern region, the South East and the South West. They had many supporters and sympathisers within the Conservative Party and their electoral success (and penetration of the Conservative base) put serious pressure on the Conservative Party and its leader, Michael Howard, to change his Eurosceptic policy into outright withdrawal. Whilst mainstream politicians were issuing dire predictions about life outside the EU, UKIP's leaders were sanguine. One of the leaders brushed aside fears by arguing that Britain would fare well outside of the EU, would not be alone or powerless in the world – the country was, he argued, 'the fourth largest economy in the world', and the 'mother country' of a huge English-speaking world'.[33]

Many commentators were, though, predicting that the issue facing Britain was not whether it would withdraw from the union, but whether it might actually be kicked out. They were beginning to ask a killer question: why should the countries that had said 'yes' (many after bruising campaigns) give up on the constitution simply because Britain said 'no'? They might be willing to give a rejectionist Britain one more chance to say 'yes' (although Britain would be in no mood to try again!); but, ultimately, surely they would go ahead without us?

Looking at all this from the vantage-point of Britain's pro-Europeans, it was a frightening prospect. Should Britain reject the constitution and enter the EU's 'exit chamber', then the country would find itself in a highly dangerous geo-political position. A thousand years of British history would have ended up not with a grand reconciliation with the continent and a hopeful new future for the British people within the European home. Rather, the country would be isolated and alone. It would be lost. Outside of an integrating Europe it would have little alternative than to further subordinate itself to the United States and its foreign policy.

By early 2005 there was amongst pro-Europeans a real fear that the British public was going to say 'no'; and that a year's hence Britain would be on the way out of the EU. There was a sense that New Labour's chickens were coming home to roost: that the state of British opinion was the clear result of a near decade of lukewarm governmental support for Europe. Having come into office in 1997 as a fervent supporter of Britain's joining the Euro, Blair had quickly reverted to traditional fears that Europe would compromise the country's world role. Indeed, from the vantage point of many pro-Europeans in 2005, Blair's premiership had represented more than a missed opportunity: it had wrecked the European cause. Whilst Murdoch and the Eurosceptics had campaigned with flair and persistence, sharpening their ideas and their methods, the Blair government not only avoided taking a decision in favour of the country joining the Euro-zone, but avoided both campaigning for Europe and creating a strong pro-European message. And then, after 9/11, when the chips were down, he had chosen the US connection over that with Europe. The symbolism of the British Prime Minister on the early afternoon of the 11th September 2001 abandoning the TUC conference, and the opening of a campaign for the Euro, to rush back to London to stand 'shoulder to shoulder' with the USA said it all.

But in May 2005, as Britain teetered on the brink of a referendum campaign that might well cause it to leave the European Union, the country was to be saved from itself by the unlikely intervention by, of all people, the French electorate. On the 30th May 2005 the French people voted by 55% to 45% to reject the constitution. Britain was no longer going to be put on the spot as the only rejectionist state. The whole of Europe went back to the drawing board and the European cause in Britain could live to fight another day.

In early 2007 as Chancellor Angela Merkel, awaiting the French Presidential election, was working on the new European constitution, Britain's leadership was still unsure of the country's future direction. Ten years into the Blair era, and a decade and a half since the end of the Cold War, Britain's role in the world remained unresolved. The awkward relationship with Europe remained. In London, with Britain and the USA jointly mired in Iraq, Washington still took precedence. For many the 'special relationship' was an anchor in dangerous waters. For others it was undignified. Whatever it was, dependence on America was very hard to shake off.

2. Dependence: Subservient Bulldogs

'There is no source from which we can raise sufficient funds to enable us to live and spend on the scale we contemplate except the United States'
John Maynard Keynes, August 1945

The Origin of Dependence

Exactly when Britain became a dependent of the United States is difficult to pin down. But sometime during the Second World War would be as good a guesstimate as any. Certainly, post-war Britain was not the same country as the one that had entered Hitler's war. For many on the then-ascendant left this was a very good thing – and the good news could be summed up in two words: 'empire' and 'class'. For the fact was that the war had finished off the British empire, and the demise of empire meant social change at home, particularly the slow erosion of the stubborn British imperial class system.

But, in another sense, the war was an unmitigated catastrophe. It saw Britain's economy devastated and its power in the world seriously diminish. In the historian Correlli Barnett's arresting metaphor, British power sank 'like a ship of the line going down unperceived in the smoke and confusion of battle'.[1] Britain's war leader Winston

Churchill himself recognised the magnitude of the country's changed circumstances when, in a poignant commentary at the very end of the war, he ruefully suggested that his life's work of defending the empire might have all been for naught. He also worried that his victory over Nazi Germany might have been bought at the price of allowing a new tyranny, the Soviet Union, to dominate Europe.[2] Soviet Russia did indeed become the pre-eminent European power in post- 1945 Europe – a stark fact that led most western European governments to welcome the other new superpower as a balancing force. And it was this looming Soviet presence, and the Cold War it unleashed, that was to persuade a generation of British political leaders that Britain's fate lay in sheltering under Washington's umbrella.

In fact, Britain's entry into the American-dominated sphere had been going on for some time. Britain's decline and the USA's rise had been almost a century-long story. In 1870, at the height of Victorian power and prosperity, Britain's share of world manufacturing exports was 45%; by 1950 it had fallen to 26%; and by 1989 to only 9%. Britain's share of manufacturing output reached 22.9% of the world level in 1880; by 1913, on the eve of the Great War, it was 13.6% and by 1938, on the eve of World War II, it was 10.7%. In 1890 Britain was second only to the United States in iron and steel production (producing 8 million tons of pig iron) but by 1913 the country was ranked third (producing only 7.7 million tons of steel, compared with Germany, 17.6 million, and the USA, 31.8 million, who were ranked second and first respectively).

One reason for Britain's rather swift fall from economic pre-eminence was that its Victorian economic performance, though solid, was not that impressive. Britain's economic growth in the nineteenth century was, by today's standards, relatively slow; investment rates were fairly paltry – particularly in education and training. As late as 1870 the average number of years of schooling for male workers was as low as 4.3, and the share of the GNP invested in machinery and equipment never exceeded 2%. As the economic historian Nick Crafts has pointed out, the basic enterprise in the growing Victorian economy was 'small-scale family capitalism rather than the joint-stock multi-divisional corporations which were to give the United States its great capitalist boost in the twentieth century'. Americans pioneered the development of the large corporation with the associated investments in highly trained management this required 'whereas in Britain managers continued to be poorly trained and recruited from a narrow social elite'. In the new century, the conditions needed for economic success were changing, and in ways which were not good news for Britain: 'a much higher level of investment, more skilled workforce and more sophisticated management' were becoming the order of the day.[3]

On the eve of the First World War Britain still possessed a high per capita income amongst the great powers, second only to the United States. Yet the writing was on the wall. Indeed, in 1913 – when national economies still had meaning – Britain was slipping well behind its competitors in a whole range of industrial sectors. It was first in rail and shipping, but third in textiles, fourth in alcohol and tobacco, and, crucially, way behind in many of the lighter industries which were to dominate the new commercial age (eleventh in chemicals, twelfth in cars and aircraft, thirteenth in books and films, fourteenth in bricks and glass, fifteenth in wood and leather and eighteenth in electricals). And, a startling fact: in 1918 Britain was dependent on the US for 80% of its supplies of raw materials, and a weakened empire supplied only 2% of global production.[4]

Britain and its oil companies had managed to keep the United States out of the Middle East during the 1921 post-Ottoman oil carve up between Britain and France in Mesopotamia (now Iraq). But under fierce American pressure, at the 1927 'peace agreement' at a Scottish castle in Achnacarry, the British buckled, and Standard Oil of New Jersey owned by the Rockefellers was admitted to the global oil cartel known as the 'seven sisters'. During the 1930s the Americans made further inroads into the Middle East. And in 1933 SOCAL (The Standard Oil Company of California) made its move in Saudi Arabia and signed the fateful sixty-year concession over the Eastern Province. After 1956, and the Suez imbroglio, the Americans moved to fully supplant Britain in the region.[5]

As with oil, so with money. For during the 1920s New York bankers, particularly J.P. Morgan, began to challenge the supremacy of the City of London. Wall Street and the City of London found themselves locked in bitter competition around the world and the American banks were gaining pre-eminence – not least because, as Wall Street lawyer John Foster Dulles, later to become Secretary of State, calculated, Britain and other allied powers owed the USA over $12,500,000,000 at 5% interest in war-debt repayments. And, intriguingly, as American economic and financial power supplanted Britain, it did so under a protectionist umbrella. Britain continued to hold an almost ideological belief in free trade.

By the turn of the century – from nineteenth into twentieth – Britain still possessed something akin to a world-wide empire, but it was becoming a strung-out and somewhat ungainly, rickety affair. As early as 1884 the writer J.R. Seeley saw a future in which 'they [Russia and America] will surpass in power the states now called great as much as the great country-states of the sixteenth century surpassed Florence'.[6] Some of Britain's more acute political leaders, like Tory Prime Minister Lord Salisbury, sensed this growing weakness, and could see the writing on the wall well before the First World War. Joseph Chamberlain also saw the fragility of the empire and believed Britain's imperial decline to be unavoidable unless the empire could be transformed into an imperial preference system – a trade bloc – that would compete with growing American economic power. And his son Neville, Prime Minister from 1937-40, constructed a whole foreign policy based upon an assumption of British imperial weakness; his strategy of appeasement was a forlorn attempt to save what he could of the resources of the empire.[7]

For most of the first half of the twentieth century, though, imperial propaganda was pumping out a different message – particularly to the young in the elite educational system. In 1921 the South African General Smuts told the British that they had emerged from the Great War 'quite the greatest power in the world'. As one young public school boy, educated to run the empire, later recalled, 'we believed in the greatness of Britain and the permanence of the Empire'.[8] Greatness; and goodness too. In the 1930s schoolchildren were being informed that 'We're all subjects and partakers in the great design, the British empire...The British empire has always worked for the peace of the world. This was the job assigned to it by God'.[9] The empire was 'all that was noble and good', and 'was the best thing that ever happened to mankind'.[10]

This kind of moralising universalism was a result of the influence of evangelical Christianity in late nineteenth and early twentieth century England – and its use as a justification for the imperial mission. This mixing of Christian morality and enduring global power was central to the educational culture of many of the leading public schools of the time. It was potent stuff. And through the influence of these schools on the broader elite culture it set a view of the world, England's place in it, and a moral and moralistic tone that was to last. It has dominated foreign policy thinking for well over a century. And, arguably, its echoes can still be heard in the twenty-first century in the Blair government's revival of 'liberal interventionism'.

Yet, by the late 1930s these ideas of enduring British greatness were co-existing with a real world in which Britain was not simply losing her power but also losing her independence. From its pre-eminence amongst world powers at the height of empire some seventy years previously, the country had fallen so far and so fast that once war had been declared in 1939 the country became dependent – for its very survival – upon another nation: the USA. Many in the English ruling groups understood all too well that war would lead to the British empire being supplanted by the USA – a power many of them saw as unlikely to have Britain's interests at heart. When Prime Minister Neville Chamberlain on the 3rd of September 1939 declared war on Germany this was the same man who only two years previously could write to his sister Hilda that 'the Americans have a long way to go before they become helpful partners in world affairs'.[11]

There were two phases in this unfolding dependence. The first began when the country's rearmament programme became reliant upon American industry and technology. American machinery was needed to equip British industry for the production of tanks, aero-engines and weapons. Britain also needed American help in providing steel, the essential ingredient for war-making. By 1940 Britain was effectively bankrupt. As the Chancellor of the Exchequer reported in February 1940 'we are in great danger of our gold reserves being exhausted'.[12] By the end of 1940, with the Luftwaffe over the skies of England, the reserves had gone, and Britain started its slide into debt – with the US as creditor. The British cabinet had a 'confident expectation of abundant American help'.[13] It was already clear what the war had wrought. The relationship between Britain and the USA had changed forever. As Barnett put it: 'in that summer of heroic attitudes…when the English scanned the skies for the Luftwaffe and the sea for the German army…England's existence as an independent, self-sustaining power was reckoned by the government to have just four months to run'.[14] Britain went bankrupt in December 1940 when the gold and dollar reserves ran out.

And after 1940, Britain's war effort – particularly the output of guns and aircraft – would become dependent on the American machine-tool industry: the country's domestic machine-tool industry was simply too inefficient and unskilled to produce the quality and output of guns and aircraft needed. The design and manufacture of British tanks (particularly the Covenanter) remained a problem, and by the summer of 1942 the famous British Eighth Army was equipped with almost twice as many American (Grants and Stuarts) as British (Crusader) tanks. Even in the sensitive and crucial radar industry Britain became reliant upon North America for sophisticated parts – such as magnetrons for the airborne interception radar for night fighters. It was estimated in 1943 that annual imports of radio components and equipment from the USA equalled four-fifths of British production. As with other war technologies, British inventive and theoretical science was first rate, but production and design were often below the standards of allies and potential competitors.

Britain also became reliant upon American financial goodwill. British reserves had run out by the early spring of 1941 and the country was in no position to repay America for war supplies. However, the 'Defense of the United States Act' – otherwise known as 'lend-lease' – was passed by Congress in March 1941 and thenceforth, for the rest of the war, Britain no longer needed to wage war within her own means. She became as dependent upon American strength as a patient on a life-support machine. Correlli Barnett described the dependence as being on a 'heart-lung machine'.[15]

By 1944 the United States had hundreds of thousands of American troops in Britain, and had become the only sizeable foreign army to be stationed on British soil since the Norman invasion. It was soon clear that Britain would be unable to prosecute a second front without the United States; and this new subordinate position was soon confirmed when an American, General Eisenhower, became the supreme allied commander. In such circumstances the idea – central to the ideology of the English ruling classes – of Britain as an independent, 'sovereign' nation was extremely difficult to sustain. At the height of war Winston Churchill boldly stated that 'I have not become the King's first minister in order to preside over the liquidation of the British empire'.[16] And at the end of the war he proclaimed that the empire had emerged 'safe, *undiminished* and united from a mortal struggle'.[17] The truth was that the empire was over. And with it went British independence. The historian John Charmley summed up Britain's situation in 1945. He suggested that 'Churchill stood for the British empire, for British independence and for an anti-socialist vision of Britain' (and he could have added a fourth – that Churchill also stood for eliminating or weakening the Soviet Union). Charmley then suggests that 'by July 1945 the first of these was on the skids, the second was dependent solely on America and the third had just vanished in a Labour election victory' (and he could have added that Churchill's anti-Soviet vision had also just vanished, for the result of the war meant that the Soviet Red Army was now right at the heart of Europe).[18]

Churchill and Bevin: Subservient Bulldogs

Churchill was marginalised by the Americans virtually from the first day that US troops arrived in Britain. He was a minor player at the wartime conferences of the big three at both Teheran and Yalta; his idea for invading Germany through the 'soft underbelly' of Yugoslavia was vetoed, as was his vision of a bold forward thrust following D-Day; and his attempt to secure an agreement with the Soviet Union on Poland before the Red Army arrived there was ignored. The Americans, both Roosevelt and Truman, saw Churchill's various manoeuvres during the war as trying to secure a British sphere in the post-war settlement. The Americans, quite naturally, were keen to secure *their own* interests which they saw as best being pursued in Europe through a post-war American-Russian condominium.

Churchill saw all this. He was no innocent. And, out of dire necessity he accepted this new reality – and became the architect of Britain's 'junior partnership' with the USA. As the country stood on the brink of defeat in 1940 he, and the country, famously stood alone. Churchill's strategy of survival was based upon a gamble that eventually the US would come into the war on Britain's side. But as things stood in the late summer of 1940 with France overrun, the defeated and defeatist French politicians of Vichy took the opposite gamble: that the future was with Germany, that America was endemically isolationist, that the German-Soviet pact would hold, and that if it didn't, either Germany would win or, after some fighting, there would be a deal between the two totalitarian powers.

Churchill's great 'gambler's throw' was the one that came off; and Britain did not fall under Nazi control. The country had been saved by its own efforts in the air war of the Battle of Britain. But, even after this victory, the country might still have fallen. Hitler's decision to invade the Soviet Union and then, later, to declare war on the United States (following the Japanese attack on Pearl Harbor) brought both the Soviet Union and the United States into the European war. It was the Soviet armed forces who broke the back of Hitler's armies in 1943-4 and thus Germany's military strength. And it was America's armed forces that made D-Day possible and thus limited Soviet hegemony over Europe (and Britain).

The war may well have been 'our finest hour'. But it also saw the end of Britain's independent sovereign ability to defend itself – for the country had been saved by forces and resources outside of its control. It had, in effect, become a dependent of the new superpower in the west. For Churchill, and for most of the British, such dependency was a price well worth paying. But it was a price nonetheless. And as the war dragged on, in decision after decision, Churchill was overruled by his American allies. He was called 'the Last Lion' by Churchill's American biographer William Manchester and his reputation in the US was unsurpassed (and has remained so). Yet this great lion of a man was, on policy matters and geo-strategy, effectively tamed. As power passed to the Americans during the war, Churchill's wartime Foreign Secretary, Anthony Eden once plaintively asked 'can we not have our own foreign policy?' And he further believed that 'the common language should not delude the British into believing that the Americans also had common interests'.[19]

After 1945 Churchill continued to represent an image of British power and greatness when, in fact, he had presided over Britain's defeat – if defeat is to be defined as losing the independent ability to defend oneself and conduct an independent foreign policy. For Churchill it was, as Charmley argues, truly the 'end of glory'; and Churchill knew it – and said so in his own words in the very title of his war history – 'triumph was tragedy'.

Yet, long after the war, establishment British historians were continuing with the story not just of British resolve and heroism but also of the myth of Churchill and the British as being 'victorious'. The approved narrative was that Churchill, not the Americans or Russians, 'saved' the country. Even the contrarian historian AJP Taylor in his work *English History 1914-45* described Churchill as 'the saviour of his country'.[20] It was an image that was to become a great source of post-war pride, but also a great source of illusions about the country's true place in the world.

Devastated in war, and with the US the clear 'winner' and the new superpower, it is hardly surprising that, following the conflict, Britain drifted deeper under America's sway, indeed further into America's sphere of influence. American troops left the whole of Europe – including Britain – very shortly after the armistice, and commentators could be forgiven for thinking that, maybe, with America gone, Britain could regain her independence and reclaim her 'sovereignty'.

It was not to be. For in the first few weeks of peace, post-war Britain was to be reminded of her new, reduced, status. On the 21st of August 1945 Washington announced a surprise decision to bring Britain's credit facilities in the lend-lease deal to an abrupt end; and to do so without even consulting the British government. According to historian John Dickie the US action amounted to a 'diktat', which caused even in the timid-looking Prime Minister, Clement Attlee, an unlikely well of public rage. In London, Washington's post-war treatment of her great ally was seen as hugely unfair. After all, during the war Britain had borne a far greater burden than had the US in the common cause of defeating Hitler. British casualties were over twice the American figure, and those killed and missing were three times more; Britain's losses in external investment were a huge 35 times greater than those of America; and Britain's total expenditure on the war was 50% greater than that of the USA. The British felt that such abrupt treatment was shabby, and even Churchill made a complaint about American high-handedness. In a rather forlorn and unusually critical statement the great man summed up Britain's new position: he said he found it difficult to believe that 'so great a nation...would proceed in such a rough and harsh manner as to hamper a faithful ally'.[21]

Britain needed a new loan to survive, and John Maynard Keynes summed up the country's humiliation – and optimistic aspirations – when, as chief UK negotiator in the loan negotiations with the US, he argued that 'the conclusion is inescapable that there is no source from which we can raise sufficient funds to enable us to live and spend on the scale we contemplate except the United States'.[22] Britain secured the loan, but at a huge price. The terms set by Washington as it flexed its new geo-political muscles were stiff – and they required of their wartime ally the full implementation of the long-held

American strategic goal of ending Britain's imperial preference trading system.[23]

Ernest Bevin, the British Foreign Secretary, told the cabinet that he was 'reluctant to agree to any settlement that would leave us subject to economic direction from the US'. But he did agree – using the argument that 'were we to reject these terms' it would mean even 'further sacrifices from the British people'.[24] Again, as with Churchill before him, Bevin reckoned he had 'no alternative' but to accept the terms of American leadership.

Bevin, though, had one great advantage over Churchill in his dealings with the Americans. He had fewer sentimental ties, and fewer illusions. During his time as a trade union leader Bevin when travelling in the States met fellow unionists – the working men and women who mostly hailed from non-Anglo backgrounds, the Irish-Americans, Italian-Americans and the like. He quickly came to understand that America was not England – certainly not the England of the great houses and country lawns of the American Anglos whom Churchill would have known. Bevin came to understand during his early time as Foreign Secretary that the new superpower pursued her own interests, not Britain's – and that in Washington's approach to Britain sentiment played a very small role indeed. And, in return, calculation, not sentiment, governed his attitude towards America.

Whilst Foreign Secretary, Bevin had some tough fights with the US administration – particularly over his opposition to the establishment of the state of Israel (Britain abstained in the UN vote setting up the Zionist state). But his overriding preoccupation in the early postwar years was to oppose Soviet power in Europe, and he did so by taking the lead after 1947 in creating NATO and bringing the power of America back into the European continent. He was Britain's top cold-warrior and as such he could be little other than a supporter of American power in the world.

Ernest Bevin was also a patriot. A 'Great Brit' nationalist who, with Attlee, took the decision to build the British nuclear bomb, he was, as Hugo Young put it, 'the only man in the Attlee cabinet who faintly resembled Winston Churchill'.[25] He was, in all senses, a big man – at ease with himself, confident, steadfast, direct. But in his relations with the Americans he was – for understandable reasons – another subservient bulldog. He knew that in the Cold War Britain survived and prospered only by courtesy of American power.

Marshall Aid and NATO

By 1949, and the arrival of Marshall Aid and NATO, the structures of the post-war world were erected. And the Cold War face-off between the USA and the Soviet Union brought the divided Europeans under one or other of the newly-constructed strategic umbrellas. In this new superpower contest Britain found itself in a weak, but intriguing position. The country was firmly under the US umbrella and, as such, continued in a subordinate role; but, at the same time, it could argue that, although a junior partner to Washington, it remained, in European terms, a leading nation – indeed America's top strategic asset in Europe. And as such Britain's foreign policy class may have accepted the indignity of being presented at court in Washington – but the country was, without doubt, the *leading* courtier.

This was a role – soon dubbed 'the special relationship' – which, although often difficult for London to swallow, could, just about, serve to appease Britain's elite sensibilities and pride, at least for a while. Britain's foreign policy establishment told itself that the country, though less powerful than the United States, had become 'Athens to America's Rome'. This excruciatingly patronising vision was first proffered by Lord Halifax when, as Ambassador in Washington during the loan negotiations, he gave of the opinion that 'it's true they [the Americans] have all the moneybags but we have all the brains'.[26] The result of the negotiations did not, as it happens, tend to reflect these supposed relative intellectual capacities.

This idea of 'Britain as Athens' could not, though, obscure the fact that in the immediate post-war years Britain remained utterly dependent upon the United States: as much so as during the war itself. Whereas the wartime dependence could at least be justified as a temporary emergency, the Cold War dependence, it seemed at the time, was open ended, even permanent. As the Cold War unfolded, and the Soviet threat took on a nuclear dimension, Britain was forced to rely for its ultimate defence upon the strategic nuclear deterrent of another nation state some 3,000 miles away.[27] In 1949 Whitehall's Permanent Under-Secretary's Committee chaired by William Strang set out the strategic basis of the country's foreign policy and concluded that Britain had 'no option other than reliance on the United States'. Churchill's vision of British foreign policy resting on three concentric circles (the Commonwealth, Europe and the United States) was a nice idea, but this committee came to the stark conclusion that the Commonwealth and western Europe between them were simply not powerful enough to deter the Soviet Union.[28]

During the late 1940s and early 1950s Britain adapted quickly to her new role of junior partner to the USA – so much so that during the Korean War the British Labour government not only increased defence spending to new heights (a development even criticised by opposition leader Winston Churchill) but also sent British troops to the peninsular. The British government became so supportive of the American Korean effort that it stretched its resources to the limit. 'This great expenditure' argued Prime Minister Attlee in the House of Commons 'represents the maximum we can do...without resorting to the drastic expedients of a war economy'.[29]

In January 1951 John Strachey, the British Minister of War, and other ministers including Aneurin Bevan, argued for a show of British independence during the Korean War, but were overruled by the cabinet, particularly the very pro-American Hugh Gaitskell, who argued that if Britain supported an anti-American resolution at the United Nations it could lead to the break-up of the alliance and the Americans leaving Europe. This theme – of Britain needing to support America in order to have influence – was echoed across the parties and even in some surprising quarters. Left-wing socialist MP Richard Crossman supported increased defence spending by arguing that 'if we want to influence American policy we have to contribute to the defence of the west'.[30]

Labour's junior partner role was even more evident during the 1951 Abadan crisis when the Iranians nationalised the Anglo-American oil company, and the British Labour government seriously considered using force. However, Britain backed away from a confrontation when it became clear that the United States had determined that no force should be used. It was a seminal moment at the fag-end of empire; and in a story later told to Anthony Eden, Egyptian leader Colonel Nasser remarked to a friend of Eden's: 'you British from that moment no longer retained any respect. If Mossadeq [Iran's Prime Minister] could do that to you, why couldn't the rest of us?'[31]

Only Flirting With Europe

By the time Labour left office in October 1951 the building blocks of the 'special relationship' were all in place. Marshall Aid was flowing, NATO was formed, British troops were alongside American in Korea, and Britain was easing herself, somewhat awkwardly into the new junior partner role. And it was London's commitment to this new role that kept Britain from any serious involvement in the initial stirrings of unity across the Channel. The country essentially stood aside from 'Schuman's Europe'. In May 1950 the Schuman Plan, with French and West German support, was launched 'as a first step in the federation of Europe'. It called for the coordination of iron and steel industries and – incredibly to contemporary ears – for a European army. Britain, though, was to play no part in the Coal and Steel Community when it was set up in 1952; and it essentially subverted the European army project, the European Defence Community, in 1954 when Eden refused to commit sufficient soldiers to the idea – giving France a way out. In August 1954 the French National Assembly shelved the ambitious idea.

Yet pro-European sentiment, and federal ideas, were not absent from the highest rungs of British political life. Both before and after the Second World War the list of leading Britons who saw European federalism as the way forward was peppered with luminaries: including the founder of the welfare state, William Beveridge, the socialist Harold Laski, the Editor of *The Times* Wickham Steed, Lord Lothian, Arnold Toynbee, LSE academic Lionel Robbins, and – intriguingly – the greatest classical liberal thinker of the twentieth century, Friedrich von Hayek, a professor at the LSE. As Hugo Young could write 'federalism was not the obsession of some irrelevant cranks' corner of British public life'.[32]

Winston Churchill too was a European enthusiast – of a sort. In a speech in Zurich on the 19th September 1946 – which he conceded would 'astonish' his audience – he advocated a 'United States of Europe'. It was a task he suggested that 'we must begin now'.[33] There was just one catch – in Churchill's view it should not include Britain. Churchill's sense of the sweep of history led him both to envisage a future united Europe, and to see the post-1945 era as the time to achieve it. Yet, he remained too much of a British imperialist to be able to accept the radical idea of a federal destiny for Britain. For him, Britain's best position was to welcome a united continental power but to stand offshore from it – retaining Britain's global links through association with American power.

This, too, was the ultimate logic behind the foreign policy of Britain's other bulldog, Ernest Bevin. Bevin too had initially flirted with some kind of European super-state. He argued as late as January 1948 that he could envisage the creation of a 'European third force' which 'was not merely the extension of US influence but a real European organisation strong enough to say "no" to both the Soviet Union and the United States'.[34] But as NATO began to take form, with the US central to its design and very much its leader, Bevin, like Churchill, backed away from the idea.

These two post-war giants, who effectively ran British foreign policy from 1945-55, held very serious cards in the developing European game. Presiding over Europe's leading nation at the time, and with Washington in favour of European unity, they had the leadership of Europe for the asking. They could have formed and founded the post-war European settlement and, crucially, have designed it in Britain's interest. Instead, they left the founding to the Franco-Germans (essentially to Schumann, Monet and Adenauer). It was a lost opportunity.

Intriguingly, it was not the United States that blocked Britain from playing a full role in immediate post-war European development – in fact, the US administration was in favour of Britain leading a more united Europe. Rather, the rejection of a European future was the British elite's own decision. It was based upon the geo-political assessments and predilections of Bevin and Churchill. But it was also, at bottom, about identity. As Anthony Eden was to say to an American audience in 1952 about Britain joining a European federation 'this is something which we know, in our bones, we cannot do'.[35]

3. A World Role: Pretence and Pomp

'Only the English-Speaking peoples count: that together they can rule the world.'
Winston Churchill, State Department Dinner, April 1954

When Winston Churchill returned to power in 1951 the very first decision that was taken was to abort the de-colonisation process set in train by Labour. Under Churchill's influence the Conservatives in opposition had voted against the independence of India and Burma, and now, back in power, were not about to see any more imperial losses. Churchill had stated bluntly during the war that 'I have not become the King's First Minister in order to preside over the liquidation of the British empire' – and he stuck to this position right up until leaving office in 1955.[1] Although there were rumblings amongst the progressives in the Tory party (from the youngish Rab Butler in particular), Churchill remained an imperialist to the end.

This decision was eloquent. For it perfectly represented the inability of the post-war British governing classes to adjust to their diminished world role. Edmund Wilson, the perceptive American man of letters, who visited Britain soon after the end of the war, noticed this unreconstructed mood. His encounters with the top people of the period surprised him, as they were, in his view, completely 'unreconciled to the post-war diminishment of Britain'.[2] In 1947 it certainly seemed for a while as though the British Labour government was withdrawing from its world role. In February Bevin gave notice that Britain would be handing the Palestine issue over to the UN; shortly following this the government decided that British aid to Greece and Turkey was not to be renewed; and in the same year it was announced that Britain would be ending the imperial control of India and Burma by June 1948. Yet, as it turned out, this, for the moment, was to be the extent of withdrawal. And it was a withdrawal that was forced on Labour by the exigencies of its economic and political position, rather than by a real change of heart.

Ernest Bevin's biographer, Alan Bullock, set out what was later to become a central charge against the post-war politicians. 'Instead of straining to keep up the part she had played as a leading power since the eighteenth century, so the argument runs, Labour should have taken the opportunity to withdraw from all overseas commitments in the shortest possible time and concentrate the country's energies on rebuilding her economy and foreign trade.'[3]

It was not to be. And, with Churchill's Conservatives back in office there emerged for a time a cross-party consensus about the need to keep some kind of truncated world role. As the British elite looked at their position in the very early 1950s they saw a Britain that may well have been diminished, but they also saw a Britain that could preserve something of its former greatness. The country was a permanent member of the Security Council of the UN, still had an empire in Africa and a powerful presence, with bases, East of Suez. The trick was to accept the 'junior partner' position to the US that was on offer, but use it to bolster this retrenched imperial role. Britain would piggy-back, on the US.

And, following the foundation of NATO, with the American connection now firmly established, Britain's leadership could set about constructing its new, updated, and virtual, world role. By the mid 1950s the three key institutions which would both embody and sustain this great pretence of a 'world role' and 'world leadership' were in place, and are still there today: the Queen, the Commonwealth, and the bomb.

The Queen, The Bomb and The Commonwealth

This great post-war pretence went on full display in the early 1950s with the pomp and pomposity surrounding the new Queen's reign. King George V died in February 1952 and the new Queen's coronation came in the summer of 1953. The coronation was to become a seminal moment for defining the country and its role in the post-war world. It was to be a lavish imperial event, and was relayed to both the British people and around the world by the new medium of television. On the eve of the coronation, at 11.30 on the morning of 29th May 1953, the imperial 'world leadership' role was nicely reinforced by the news that Edmund Hillary (with loyal Sherpa Tenzing Norgay at his side) had reached the top of Mount Everest. The newspapers talked of a 'new Elizabethan Age' and it was obvious, as Harold Wilson was to argue over a decade later, that 'Britain's frontiers lay in the Himalayas'.

An estimated 20 million people – huge for its time – watched the coronation on the new medium of television. The new Queen, as the BBC put it, 'took the coronation oath and is now bound to serve her people and to maintain the laws of God', presumably, though not necessarily, referring here to the laws of the United Kingdom of Great Britain and Northern Ireland. The coronation displayed a Britain that still – for all the reduced circumstances of war, and all the egalitarian changes under Labour – saw itself as an imperial, global, power. It was as though the empire was in full swing and the country was crowning an empress, and an 'empress' who derived her authority from God. In her coronation oath the British Queen took an oath to 'uphold the laws of God' and in a medieval ceremony was anointed with consecrated oil by the Archbishop of Canterbury. She also solemnly promised in the oath to 'govern' the peoples of far flung states from the United Kingdom to Canada, Australia, New Zealand, South Africa, Pakistan, and Ceylon 'and her possessions and other territories according to their respective laws and customs'.

The young Queen herself and her court played into the pomp of this global role as though to the manner born. She proclaimed herself 'Queen and Head of the Commonwealth' and would later show a continuing personal resolve to stress the importance of the newly-created 'British Commonwealth of Nations' and to place her headship of the organisation at the centre of her view of her constitutional role.

The coronation introduced to a wider public this new concept of a 'British Commonwealth' as a successor to, and subtle continuation of, the empire. The idea of some sort of 'Commonwealth' had been around well before the Second World War. It had first been mooted by Lord Rosebery in 1884 when he introduced the idea as a means of prolonging the empire by binding the white dominions, which upon independence might well consider totally breaking with Britain. 'There is no need for any nation, however great, leaving the empire', he stated 'because the empire is a commonwealth of nations'.[4]

Later, Lord Milner's so-called 'kindergarten' of bright young imperial thinkers from Oxbridge, brought together to reconstruct South Africa after the Boer War, had also re-thought the contours of empire with a view to prolonging it (including toying with outlandish ideas like an 'Anglo-Saxon world state' which would encompass the white dominions and North America). Lionel Curtis's 'Project of a Commonwealth' was published in 1915 and an odd grouping known as the Round Table, which included such notables as Lord Lothian and Geoffrey Dawson, took up the idea. At the Imperial War Conference of 1917 the notion of the dominions as autonomous nations within something called an 'Imperial Commonwealth' was formally floated. In 1921 the Prime Minister of South Africa, Jan Smuts, had echoed the views of other white dominions that the empire's days were numbered and that 'it will no longer be an empire but a society of free and equal sister states'.[5]

The idea that a white 'Commonwealth of Nations' could be adapted to include non-whites was floated during the inter-war years. That quintessential British imperial figure, Lawrence of Arabia (T. E. Lawrence), put forward the idea of creating 'brown dominions' and, under Curtis's influence, the concept of a 'multiracial Commonwealth' began to be propagated. And the present multiracial 'Commonwealth of Nations' was indeed born when India, Pakistan and Ceylon joined in (Burma refused). As Kathryn Tidrick, in a most perceptive analysis of the British and empire, put it the Commonwealth 'gracefully combined the idea of imperial unity with that of national autonomy'.[6]

Yet there was a big story behind all this, for all these British pioneers of the idea of a Commonwealth (white or multi-racial) – every single one of them – sought not to end, but to continue, Britain's global role, but with much looser, more indirect relationships. In official Britain there was not even any suggestion that Britain should bring to an end its global reach and become a continental power.

For Attlee's post-war Labour government the idea of a new multi-racial 'British Commonwealth' was a godsend: for it could serve to square the growing moral opposition to colonialism within the British left with the continuing desire for British global grandeur (seemingly contradictory instincts often carried within the same British breast). British post-war left-wing internationalism always had a large tinge of moralising globalism about it. Labour left-wingers Fenner Brockway and Michael Foot were serious exponents of decolonisation – but they also genuinely believed in British global leadership by moral example (for instance by adopting unilateral nuclear disarmament).

With this imperial mentality still redolent, it was not surprising that Britain's post-war establishment should also unite behind the need for Britain to possess 'the bomb'. The decision that Britain should become a nuclear power was taken in January 1947 by Prime Minister Clement Attlee together with Ernest Bevin and only four other ministers (and without even a reference to the cabinet); and the British bomb was announced to the world by Churchill in February 1952 with the first successful test taking place in October of the same year.

The British felt that as British science had played a leading role in the creation, through the Manhattan project, of the American atomic programme that led to the bombs unleashed on Japan in 1945, they had every right to belong to the nuclear club. But, more importantly, they were convinced that possessing a nuclear weapon was the key to the country remaining at 'the top table' and continuing with an independent global role, no matter how minimal. There was, intriguingly, much talk at the time, in late 1946, of the need for the bomb as a symbol of British independence (from the USA). Lord Portal, the wartime Chief of the Air Staff, had declared that 'we could not afford to acquiesce in an American monopoly of this new development'.[7]

At one of the preliminary meetings which approved the bomb Bevin declared that it was necessary so that future British Foreign Secretaries would never be treated in the way he had just been by US Secretary of State James Byrnes. Hugh Dalton and Stafford Cripps were opposed to building the bomb on grounds of cost, but Bevin won round his colleagues by reportedly declaring 'I don't mind for myself, but I don't want any Foreign Secretary of this country to be talked at by a Secretary of State in the United States as I have just had [sic] in my discussions with Mr. Byrnes'. Bevin insisted that the bomb be built and that 'we've got to have the bloody Union Jack flying on top of it'.[8]

Yet these concerns for independence from the USA did not last. Bevin's outburst against Byrnes was to amount to little more than a spasm, a blowing off of steam. And Attlee himself later argued that when the decision for the bomb had been taken he had not been worried so much about Britain controlling its own bomb, but rather about America reverting to isolationism and leaving Britain high and dry. 'There was no NATO then' he had declared to interviewer Kenneth Harris.[9]

Any idea of Britain developing a truly independent nuclear system was soon to be stopped in its tracks. During the 1950s Britain's delivery systems became a major problem. The original V-bombers, and the missiles (Blue Steel, Blue Streak) became progressively redundant; the delivery problems were only solved by the country's 'independent deterrent' becoming utterly dependent on American technology. It was during Harold Macmillan's premiership that Britain ceded effective control over Britain's nuclear weapons to the USA when the Prime Minister arranged a deal with President John Kennedy for Britain to use the US Polaris system. Ever since then the country has been dependent upon the US guidance system for its targeting. But this key deal was fine for a British political class only interested in the appearance, and not the reality, of global power. By comparison the French nuclear weapon systems have remained genuinely independent.

By the mid 1950s as Churchill handed over to Anthony Eden, the word from the heart of the post-war British establishment – from the Queen, her court, from war leader Churchill and the opposition Labour Party – was clear: there was to be no radical re-adjustment to a new role in the world, or a new view of ourselves, our standing or our power. The myth of British global power was to continue its fateful grip. And, on the face of it, for a broader public looking at life through newspaper headlines, post-war movies and the new medium of television, Britain was indeed still a great world power. The Churchill era may well have ended with the great war victor leaving Downing Street, but his successor, Anthony Eden – the wartime Foreign Secretary and a man totally associated in the public mind with Churchill and great power politics – still looked the imperial part. And was soon to act upon it.

The Imperial Mind at Mid-Century

This lingering sense of empire was – as we shall see – widely shared throughout British post-war society, but it was most keenly felt within the country's political and ruling classes. Most countries' foreign policies are still dictated by relatively small groups, and Britain's foreign policy at mid-century was no exception. What was remarkable, though, was the tightly-knit social background, and the consequent uniform ideology of this elite. The country's Foreign Office, its intelligence services, and its governing political class were all drawn from an exceedingly narrow social background – overwhelmingly peopled by ex-public school boys educated at a very small number of elite institutions. And so tightly drawn was this class that over the period 1918-50 over 80% of all Tory cabinets were populated from public schools and almost 50% from two – two! – such schools: Eton and Harrow. By 1960, fifteen years into the post-war peace, an incredible 83.2% of top army positions, 65% of top civil servants and 82.6% of ambassadors came from public schools.[10]

This small dominant class which governed the country in the 1950s was an imperial class. Many of their number had direct experience of empire for they had, after all, been young men in the early part of the century, some before the First War. Others were imbued with imperial mentality in the 1920s and 1930s when the empire was still a going concern. Indeed, almost all of them had had an education specifically designed for an imperial ruling class – a training that it was considered would equip them to deal with the exigencies of ruling and administering a far-flung empire. This 'education for empire' had been designed in late nineteenth-century English public schools, and carried over into the public schools in the new century. That its influence lasted well into the late twentieth century may well be due in part to the sheer rigour of its earlier application. Correlli Barnett went so far as to argue that: 'except for young Nazis or Communists no class of leaders in modern times has been so subjected to prolonged moulding of character, personality and outlook as British public school boys in this era'.[11] Katherine Tidrick echoes essentially the same sharp point: 'the public school system worked to produce Fuhrers on the wholesale principle' and these schools developed so that 'the imperial demand for leadership met with an unfailing supply' and also 'operated to rivet upon the British political system a governing class through which the leadership ethos was thoroughly diffused'.[12]

Of course, these young men, as they came to power in mid or late life in mid-century Britain, had lived through some shattering events – particularly the Second World War – which had sapped Britain's power and wealth. And they had also seen this power pass to other countries, like Russia and the USA whose support for Britain during the war had ensured that she did not go under. Yet, even so, this generation never truly experienced overt, unadorned defeat: the sharp, total experience of loss and impotence felt by the people on the continent. And even the obvious emergence of the USA as a world power, and its growing supplanting of the British empire, did not undermine the confidence of the class. Indeed, it had a rub-off effect. The English elite could – and did – claim pride of authorship of this newly powerful nation on the other side of the Atlantic. In the immediate post-war period, during American world supremacy, the levers of power and culture in the USA were still largely controlled by anglophile white Anglo-Saxon protestants – in the hands, that is, of the 'cousins'. And, by the late 1960s these 'cousins', although themselves still very anti-colonialist, were beginning to see the value to themselves of the remnants of Britain's empire east of Suez, and, ever so subtly, were encouraging the British to stay.

An Imperial People
The wider public was also still smitten by empire. Although, as H.G. Wells could assert in *Mr. Britling Sees It Through* that '...the middle class and most of the lower class knew no more of the empire than they did of the Argentine republic or the Italian Renaissance', this would also have been true of their knowledge of much of their own government.[13] A direct experience of ruling an empire was not necessary in order to feel part of a great nation which had conquered a third of the globe, and to feel, no matter how inchoately, superior culturally and racially to lesser breeds, and to believe that England and Britain was the centre of the world.

The depth of popular support for the empire can be gauged by the interesting fact that before World War II no section of British life ever turned decisively against the empire – not the Scots, the Welsh, the English, the industrial proletariat, the middle class, the nineteenth century Conservatives or Liberals, and incredibly, not even the

Radicals. There were votes in social unity imperialism and in imperial preference. And there was no serious anti-colonial protest movement in the country until well into the second half of the twentieth century, not until after the Second World War made the empire economically redundant. Indeed, the empire possessed a popular constituency right up to and beyond the Second World War. The Conservatives remained the party of empire right up until Winston Churchill died, and neither the Liberals nor Labour (nor even the socialist intellectuals before the Second World War) attempted any systematic rejection of the principle of empire.

And after 1945 the empire remained a constant source of images and tales in the mass popular media. Messages about the innate superiority of white Englishmen were produced and recycled in educational texts and popular newspapers right up into the 1960s. And in the working class areas of the cities – after the large council house building programmes of the 1930s – the Pretoria Avenues, Khyber Crescents and Mafeking Roads acted as a constant reminder of British imperial superiority. Through association with empire the working classes could feel superior to others – the black and brown races.

These mid-century British lived in a world in which the map was still painted red, in which Africa, Asia, the Middle East, and even parts of Latin America, were still run from London. They also inhabited a national culture which was still pumping out its imperial messages – particularly to the young. And even in the mid 1950s and 1960s it was impossible to think of Britain without thinking of the empire – secondary schoolchildren throughout the country were still assembling for 'Empire Day' to be told that they were the inheritors of a world power. It was a point massively reinforced by the imperial culture and trappings of the British monarchy in the new mass television age.

Two Wars

It was also underpinned by the story the British began telling themselves about their role during the Second World War. Although the World Wars had drastically reduced Britain's geo-strategic position, for many people these great conflicts simply served to renew the country's greatness. The fires of patriotism, and nationalism, were re-stoked as war reinforced the sensibility of not only a separate but also a virtuous English and British identity.

The sheer nationalistic fervour of 1914-18, when millions volunteered to fight (and die), is, to much contemporary thinking, still inexplicable. Yet it was very real. And so too was the full engagement in the war effort of the country's ruling class youth. Quite simply 'the Great War' against Germany saw the English 'public school gentlemen' go to war *en masse* – thus precluding a re-run of the eighteenth-century radical taunt that the upper classes were unpatriotic. And the 'classlessness' of this sacrifice may help explain why the ineptness and bungling of many within the senior officer corps during the carnage of the trenches provoked very little anger once the war was over.

World War II also served to revive national, and nationalist, sentiment – particularly from its low point when pacifism and internationalism suffused the culture during the inter-war years. Britain came out of Hitler's war very well. The country faced, alone for some time, a clear, unambiguously evil, enemy. And 'unlike France' it successfully repelled an invasion. Also, 'it won the war', thus providing the country and, through the glamorous lens of the burgeoning film media, the wider world, with British heroes. The Churchill 'bulldog' and the handle-bar moustached R.A.F. fighter-pilot type became world famous as 'victors' and 'winners' – hardly the stuff of a declining empire.

The month of May 1945, with the economy in ruins and its world role draining away, nonetheless provided an image of a country of power and greatness. Field Marshall Bernard Law Montgomery was an Ulsterman, but could easily pass – by accent and bearing – as an archetypical public school Englishman. And on the 5th of May, commanding the 21st army group, he presided over the surrender of all German forces in north-west Germany, Holland and Denmark. Three days later, Winston Churchill – the ultimate symbol of warrior Englishness – appeared alongside the royal family on the balcony of Buckingham Palace to salute 'Victory in Europe'. The British people could be forgiven for believing that the country had not just survived but prevailed; that it had pulled it off yet again; that it was still the most powerful nation under the sun; and that the culture of Englishness, personified in the 'English bulldog' personality of Winston Churchill and the decent 'English reticence' of King George VI, would resonate around the globe as emblems of a democracy to be copied.

Indeed, following the war a major myth-making industry did emerge to feed the illusion of British centrality in the defeat of the

Germans. To some extent national myths can serve the function of hiding bitter and awkward truths. Britain played an important though subsidiary part in the Battle for Normandy in 1944; and Normandy itself was a secondary front. The 'turning point of the war' was more likely located in the 1942 battle of Stalingrad. Yet, the post-war British media vastly exaggerated the British contribution, as they did the role of Winston Churchill – who, as his own records more than abundantly testify to, was very much the junior partner to Roosevelt throughout the last three and a half years of the war. Churchill's post-war standing, particularly in America where he became a statesman hero (and rivalled the posthumous popularity of Roosevelt), did wonders for the country's reputation as a 'winner' and as a great power. The American media was still referring to the 'British empire' as a world player as late as the 1960s.

Superiority and Race

Yet the 'victory' in two wars only confirmed, and continued, the unbroken culture of imperialism. Had the country been defeated and occupied it might have been a different story as the British may well have been able to put the imperial past fully and finally behind them. As it was, they weren't so able. And the values and prejudices of empire marched on well into the late part of the twentieth century.

Two prejudices of empire stand out and can help explain why, by comparative standards, a particularly exceptional type of nationalism endured in Britain. The first is a superiority complex that is different in kind from that of most other people in developed countries. Other nations have a narrative of exceptionalism, and the British certainly continued to believe they were an exceptional people. But an empire controlling a third of the world on which the sun never sets is heady stuff. And the British came to believe they were a superior people too. In imperial experience British and English contact with 'foreigners' was always minimal. The English did not mix, they conquered, and then they ruled. So the colonial experience – though technically an internationalising phenomenon – hardly encouraged cosmopolitan instincts amongst the rulers.

Lord Hugh Cecil, English landowner, imperialist, and High Tory, is a perfect representative of this English sense of superiority – class, national, and racial. In 1912 he proffered a view of the English mission which perfectly represented the sentiment of his fellow rulers during the height of empire. In what was the very stuff of the ideology of Englishness he argued that 'our vocation in the world... [is] to undertake the government of vast, uncivilised populations and to raise them gradually to a higher level of life'.[14]

And another imperialist, Rudyard Kipling, revealed a similar mental framework in his famous poem:

> Take up the White Man's burden--
> Send forth the best ye breed--
> Go bind your sons to exile
> To serve your captives' need;
> To wait in heavy harness
> On fluttered folk and wild--
> Your new-court sullen peoples,
> Half-devil and half-child.

Thus English superiority was not simply cultural; it was racial as well. And the era of empire saw the emergence in England not only of a general prejudice in favour of English and white racial superiority (Lord Hugh Cecil's views would have received near-universal support) but also of strains of literary racism (in, amongst others, the works of H.G. Wells) philosophic racism (exemplified by the works of G.K. Chesterton), even systematic, scientific racism (of which Stuart Houston Chamberlain was a leading exponent.)

General theories of race – like general theories of politics – did not catch on amongst the English, and scientific racism became unacceptable to the political class following the experience of the 1939-45 war and Nazism. However, a profound basic racial prejudice remained. As one contemporary theorist has put it, '...with or without a theory of biological racism, whether derived from the work of Count Gobineau (1915) or some other source, a deep-seated unrefined belief in racial difference in performance, and in standards, probably owes its origin to the colonial relationship between white master and black subordinate...The white man's civilising presence, the need to develop backward nations, the missionaries' vocation to convert the heathen acted as powerful justification for continued imperial domination. Such ideas deeply penetrated the culture of the British population and survive to the present day'.[15]

Winston Churchill, the country's last unashamedly imperial leader, possessed a decidedly racist side – one shared at mid-century by many of his contemporaries in the higher reaches of English public life. The historian Andrew Roberts writes of Churchill, in a passage worthy of quoting at length, that his 'views on race did not spring up fully formed when he regained office in 1951, but were held consistently during his long political career. By the standards of today – and possibly even of his own time – Winston Churchill was a convinced racist...For Churchill Negroes were "niggers" or "blackamoors", Arabs were "worthless", Chinese were "chinks" or "pigtails", and other black races were "baboons" or "Hottentots", Italians were "mere organ-grinders"...As the great tribal leader of 1940 his [Churchill's] speeches were peppered with references to the British race...Sir David Hunt, one of his Private Secretaries during his 1951-55 period of office, recalls "Churchill was on the whole rather anti-black. I remember him sending a telegram to [South African President] Dr Malan and asking me whether he should say 'My dear Mr. President, *Alles sal rect hom* [all is well]. Keep on skelping the kaffirs!'" "Blackamoor" was also a term in normal upper class usage – indeed was used by another prominent figure of the fag-end of empire, Elizabeth Bowes-Lyon (later "the Queen Mother").'[16]

This kind of 'unrefined' racial superiority existed in Britain well into the late twentieth century, and was revived by the arrival of mass third world immigration into the country, a process begun in the late 1950s. And notions of racial and national superiority at the heart of imperial Englishness were complemented by a mild and understated anti-semitism. Victorian English society developed a certain tolerance for very rich Jews like the Sassoons, the Rothchilds and the Oppenheimers (as its 'practical-man' persona tolerated big money from any quarter). Yet, a disdain for Jewish people still surfaced regularly amongst English leadership groups. Even as late as 1959 the then British Prime Minister, Harold Macmillan, could claim that 'the Jews, the planners and the old cosmopolitan element' were playing 'no small part in the [European] Commission'.[17] A standard view, even as late as the 1970s would be that 'everyone knew very well that there was a gaping chasm between them and us' and that although Jewish people are 'not really Jewish here in England...of course they're not really English either'.[18]

Yet, superiority had its obligations. The imperial version of Englishness, conscious that it was the English role to administer large tracts of the globe, and 'the vast uncivilised populations', developed a cult of rulership. Englishmen would be trained in the arts of leadership. They would be trusted. And, like the feudal nobility, in return for the loyalty of their subjects, they would rule paternalistically – over both the brown and black races and the domestic whites. They would be 'firm but fair' – incredibly, as late as 1974 a paternalistic election slogan of the Conservative Party in the February general election. This idea of rulership, of *noblesse oblige* leadership, still produces faint echoes in political language well into the twenty-first century: as in 'leading in Europe' and 'giving a lead to the world'.

And this notion of rulership would often involve leading by example, and the setting of standards of behaviour for lower ranks and lesser orders to follow. This idea that rulers needed to lead by personal example had been present earlier in English history, but came into its own during imperial rule in India – when the needs of administration coincided with the rapid growth, at home, of evangelical religion. And the British governing class of India 'owed much of its character to evangelical religion' particularly its concept of authority which 'was rooted in the evangelical cult of personal example'.[19] Some aspects of this imperial culture of rulership can be seen in contemporary thinking about 'humanitarian' or 'liberal interventionism' which surfaced under the premiership of Tony Blair.

4. No End of a Lesson

'I think Suez, more than anything, punctured the Great Power illusion once and for all.'
Joe Garner, Permanent Under-Secretary Commonwealth Office, 1981

'I want to tell you that in the Middle East our great enemies are the Americans.'
Enoch Powell to Anthony Eden, sometime in the 1940s

Anthony Eden: An English Gentleman's World Role

In April 1955, Anthony Eden became Prime Minister of Britain. Churchill, the unapologetic aristocratic imperialist was succeeded by no less a child of empire and aristocracy – though from a somewhat lower ranking than his illustrious predecessor. Born into minor aristocracy in 1897, the family home, Windlestone near Durham, was surrounded by only 8,000 acres, a smallish holding by the standards of the time. Eden had the full establishment education. He went to preparatory school in Surrey, thence to Eton, then saw service in the Great War (described by a biographer as 'selfless, courageous and modest'), and then went up to Oxford University at Christchurch College (then often dubbed 'Eton by the Cherwell').[1]

Not surprisingly the young Anthony Eden had all the orthodox attributes of English superiority, separateness and standoffishness. There was some slight radical dissidence in him – qualities of sensitivity, asceticism and intellectuality that led him to think beyond the narrow confines of his upbringing – but, at root, like all those destined to secure political influence in the Conservative Party in mid-century Britain, he was thoroughly imperial in mindset, brought up and immersed in the power and superiority of his class and country.[2]

Eden had become Churchill's Foreign Secretary – and heir apparent – when the Conservatives returned to office in 1951. The Conservatives, Churchill aside, had difficulties in settling into the new junior partner relationship. The British, and particularly Eden, still saw something of an independent role for themselves – based upon Churchill's formulation of the country being at the centre of 'three concentric circles' – the Commonwealth, America and Europe. From the American point of view the Cold War was now the overriding issue, the 'western world' through NATO was in a struggle that demanded unity, and the US was the only country that could give leadership to the west. Britain's role was to be supportive in the struggle.

Washington believed it would be helpful to have Britain as a European sidekick willing to advance its interests both in Europe and through its residual imperial position East of Suez. And in the early 1950s Washington was also warming to the idea of a united Europe as a potential strategic ally. The US administration was constantly urging Britain to join in early moves towards European unity. After 1952, the new American administration's Secretary of State John Foster Dulles was so keen on European defence integration that he threatened to change US policy if unity in Europe should lose momentum. 'If the European Defence Community should not become effective; if France and Germany remain apart' he said, 'that would compel an agonising reappraisal of basic United States policy'.[3]

Anthony Eden did not agree. He had delivered a speech at Columbia University in New York in January 1952 on British foreign policy. There was much speculation at the time about the creation of a European Defence Force (an idea later ditched by the French National Assembly) and even of a new European federation – an idea being pushed by the Eisenhower administration. Yet, in two grandly dismissive sentences Eden ended speculation that British policy under the Conservatives would take a serious European tilt. 'Speaking of the frequent suggestions that the United Kingdom should join a federation on the continent of Europe...this is something which we know, in our bones, we cannot do.'[4] Here he was essentially echoing Churchill's September 1946 Zurich speech in which the war leader had advocated a 'United States of Europe' but one which Britain, though supporting, would not be a part of. What exactly it was within 'the bones' of Eden and Churchill that would not allow them to contemplate Britain being part of a new European enterprise was never spelt out.

The historian D. R. Thorpe has argued that 'many in Britain felt themselves to be on a different level from the principal continental countries' and that Eden, a 'man of his times' was one of them.[5] This 'different level' was operating when the continentals, pulling themselves up from the failure of the European defence treaty, began negotiations for the setting up of a common market. Invitations were issued to come to Messina. And whilst other continental states sent full ministers, Eden sent a mid-to-upper level civil servant – a Mr. Russell Bretherton. British hauteur was on full display at the time when Eden's deputy, Rab Butler, talked grandly and dismissively, and typically, of Messina as the product of some 'archaeological excavations'. These 'archaeological excavations' ended up creating the Treaty of Rome – the Common Market and the European Union.

Suez and Humiliation

In the early post-war years Anthony Eden had paid obeisance to, but had not truly digested, the real role of Britain in the Anglo-American 'special relationship'. The new unspoken rules set by Washington were clear: that Britain could, if it wanted, posture on the world stage, but it could not act – except, that is, in concert or agreement with the new leaders of the western world in Washington. Anthony Eden was to fall foul of these rules when, as Prime Minister in 1956, he reverted to an older mode – the leader of an independent imperial power. On 26th July 1956 Egyptian leader, Colonel Nasser, nationalised the Suez Canal company. Eden saw this action as a threat to Britain's security, but after a series of international initiatives no agreement could be secured. In his full pomp and in an extraordinary outburst of suppressed imperialism, the British Prime Minister decided to invade Egypt.

Having decided to act with France against Nasser, Eden, at a secret meeting outside Paris, fixed up a deal with the Israelis that they would attack Egypt and thus give Britain and France the excuse to invade the third world country under the guise of separating the combatants and securing the canal. On 29th October 1956 Israel invaded the Egyptian controlled Gaza strip and Sinai peninsula.

After an ultimatum to both sides to withdraw Eden ordered the invasion of Egypt and 'Operation Musketeer' got underway. A bombing campaign started immediately and was followed up by the invasion itself on 6th November . The invasion bitterly divided British public opinion. It was opposed by many Commonwealth countries. And the United States not only publicly opposed the invasion but also used its economic leverage over Britain to put pressure on the Eden government to withdraw from the Canal. This Britain did by December. It was a humiliating retreat for Eden, who resigned from office in January 1957.

Eden's 1956 war seriously offended the Americans on several fronts. He launched an invasion of a sovereign Arab country without US agreement. He fixed up a 'secret plan' with the Israelis for the invasion behind Washington's back. He then carried out the Anglo-French-Israeli conspiracy and invaded Egypt without informing the Americans – the US administration first heard about it from a leak by an anti-Eden minister only a few days before. And all this on the very eve of the 'senior partner's' Presidential election.

Eden was no novice. He had been at Churchill's side as the wartime leader had assumed the junior partner role in the transatlantic alliance; he had supported Labour's lopsided post-war 'special relationship', and fully supported Churchill's post-war pro-American line. Yet, all the time Eden had had a pent-up hankering after an independent world role – and perhaps a belief that the 'special relationship' could actually allow for real independence of action. Indeed as one of Eden's biographers put it Eden throughout his premiership 'found it difficult to adjust to the fact that Britain would inevitably have to play a secondary role alongside America'.[6]

This hankering after independence was one reason for Eden's prickly relations with America's post-war leaders. Reportedly he tended to patronise President Eisenhower – partly because 'Ike' was 'no gentleman' but also because during the war the American President had, technically at least, been below him in the allied hierarchy.[7] He got on

4. No End of a Lesson

even less well with the new American Secretary of State, John Foster Dulles. But this antipathy was mutual: Dulles disliked what he considered to be Eden's contrived old world good manners; and Eden hated Dulles's new world tactile over-familiarity and was also irritated by Eden's 'fey' ways such as his constant use of the term 'my dear' in addressing men.

In any event, Eden's behaviour over Suez was proof positive that the British political establishment had not adjusted to the new power relationships in the western world, and the American reaction to the Anglo-French-Israeli invasion – clear, strong and swift – came as a huge shock. In refusing to support sterling unless Britain abandoned the invasion, withdrew its troops from Egypt and handed the problem over to the UN, Washington was laying down the law. And by forcing the British – and the French – to pull out of the Canal in such a public manner, Washington humiliated the British establishment and the Tory party in particular. Later, Eden, whilst in retirement, was to ruefully recall a conversation he had had with Enoch Powell sometime in the 1940s when Powell had said to him 'I want to tell you that in the Middle East our great enemies are the Americans...' Looking back Eden remarked 'You know, I had no idea what he meant...I do now'.[8]

The political upshot of the imbroglio was stark. America had shown its opposition to Eden, Eden's policy failed, and after a decent interval Eden resigned. The diplomatic historian, David Carlton, has argued that by 1956 British dependence on Washington had become so marked – and Eden's burst of independent action so delusional – that the US was in a position to organise what amounted to a cabinet coup against Eden. He tells the extraordinary story of how the President of the United States ceased to have any direct dealings with the British Prime Minister and 'set about humiliating him'. He recounts how Eisenhower suggested to his ambassador in London that he go behind Eden's back in a clandestine move and encourage members of what amounted to a pro-American cabal in the British cabinet – Harold Macmillan, Rab Butler and Lord Salisbury – to replace the elected British Prime Minister. So sensitive were these manoeuvres that the President felt he had to talk to his ambassador in code – almost in the manner of a spy novel. Carlton reproduces from US government sources Eisenhower's exact words to the ambassador as he indicates the identity of his potential American collaborators.

'Eisenhower: You know who I mean? One has the same name as my predecessor at...university [Eisenhower meant Rab Butler] the other was with me in the war [meaning Harold Macmillan].'[9]

To interfere in the politics of a major ally in this way in order to secure a change of Prime Minister was not dissimilar to a Moscow-inspired coup in an eastern European satellite regime. And it revealed the new power relationship between Washington and London. More surprising perhaps was the willingness of British politicians – in this case Macmillan, Butler and Salisbury – to be part of this palace coup, an enterprise that can be interpreted, in old-fashioned classical terms at least, as near-treasonable.

The leader of this pro-American cabal, Chancellor of the Exchequer Harold Macmillan, had originally taken a tough line against Nasser, but later softened. He took Eden's place in Downing Street and then immediately sought to restore relations with Eisenhower and Dulles.

During the crisis the Labour opposition leadership was also in league with the Americans. After initially supporting the anti-Nasser rhetoric of Eden, Labour's new leader Hugh Gaitskell not only opposed Eden's invasion but openly campaigned against it in rallies throughout the country. He also, controversially, went on national television at the height of the crisis, whilst British troops were in action, to denounce the invasion. This extremely contentious move – denounced as 'traitorous' by Tories and Tory media – was, though, a calculated risk. Gaitskell was extremely close to the Americans and the US Embassy, and his actions could only have been carried off with the sure knowledge that Britain's great ally in Washington supported his position.

With Eden's fall, so fell any notion of an independent British foreign policy. Some Conservatives, not least the aged Churchill himself, continued to believe that should Britain have ignored the pressure from Washington, and kept its troops in the Canal, then the country would have faced down American pressure. 'Who could have got us out?' asked some die-hard Tories. Others in and around the Tory party – the Suez group of Tory MPs and the supporters of the League of Empire Loyalists – toyed with a break with Washington. But the Macmillan Tory cabinet quickly reasserted the 'special relationship' and within a year it was almost as though no breach with Washington had occurred. All again was sweetness and light across the Atlantic.

British leaders seemed to learn lessons from the Suez humiliation. The country's leadership continued to seek a 'world role' through the junior partnership. But never again – in the half-century since the invasion – has Britain taken a foreign policy action in express opposition to Washington. Permanent Under-Secretary at the Commonwealth Office, Joe Garner, later reflecting on the Suez affair, spoke for many when he argued that 'I think Suez, more than anything, punctured the Great Power illusion once and for all'.[10] Anthony Nutting, one of two Tory ministers who resigned over the crisis, entitled his book on the crisis *No End of a Lesson*.

Yet was it? Or was it to be, in the other meaning of Nutting's clever double entendre, no end *to* a lesson?[11]

5. 'Greece to Rome' and the Atlanticists

'We are the Greeks in this American Empire.'
Harold Macmillan, North Africa, 1942

Harold Macmillan

When Harold Macmillan became Prime Minister in January 1957 the Tory leadership was shaken. It was a stark time. A Prime Minister had resigned following a foreign policy failure and a breakdown in relations with the country's main ally. A new, pro-American Prime Minister had been installed (without an election). Washington had flexed its muscles, made clear who was boss, and had even engineered Britain's humiliation. A picture of the end of empire could not have been more colourfully drawn. Britain, whether it wanted to or not, was finally entering its post-imperial phase.

In one sense the premiership of Harold Macmillan had the potential to represent something of a break. In Tory terms Macmillan came from the commercial, not the aristocratic, class. He was not overly invested in the imperial sensibility, his foreign experience being administration in war-time North Africa, not India or the colonies. And his defining political issue – the unemployment of the 1930s which he witnessed as Tory candidate for

Stockton-on-Tees – gave him something of a leftist instinct for the need for change.

When Macmillan made his 1960 application for Britain to join the Common Market many took this as a sign that the British political class, still smarting from Suez, had taken the big decision to abandon its obsessive search for a global role and become a European power. But contemporary historian and acute observer of Prime Ministers, Professor Peter Hennessey, sees the application in a different light. Hennessey believes that Macmillan had not given up on the 'world role' – and that he sold the idea of EEC entry to the cabinet as a way of harnessing the economic dynamism of the EEC to Britain's still global aims.[1]

Harold Macmillan was an actor. And he liked acting, above all, on the world stage. He was to give many good performances, and one such was on display during his highly-publicised visit to Moscow in February 1959 when he tried to act as a go-between for President Eisenhower and Chairman Khrushchev over the question of nuclear weapons. The British Prime Minister – still, but only just, thought of around the world as one of the 'big three' – made next to no difference on any big international issue during this trip. Yet, wearing a white fur hat as he padded down the aircraft steps in Moscow, he was the picture of a world statesman – and was to be dubbed 'SuperMac' by the British cartoonist Vicky.

A global actor, though, needed a global organisation, and during Macmillan's time in Downing Street the British political class began to formulate the idea of an updated and reformed 'British Commonwealth of Nations' as the way forward. Macmillan had argued as late as 1952 for 'the development of the Empire into an economic unit as powerful as the USA and the USSR'.[2] This echo of Joseph Chamberlain's earlier idea of a British superpower based upon imperial preference was not, though, a serious runner in the 1950s – not least because the USA, having dismantled the earlier version, would not tolerate its return. What was possible, though, was a loose – non-economic, non-political and non-military – club of ex-colonial countries which, as the 'British Commonwealth of Nations', would create a forum for discussion and co-operation, and which, crucially, would allow Britain's politicians to head up a world organisation – a kind of mini UN. It was an idea that appealed to the British Queen who, as head of the organisation, would find a continuing role for herself.

Macmillan's Tories, after the Churchill interregnum, had restarted Labour's decolonisation programme – with independence for, among others, Ghana (in 1957), Nigeria (in 1960), Sierra Leone (in 1961) and Kenya (in 1963). Alongside this decolonisation, the 1950s saw the arrival of 'non-alignment' and 'the third world', and the idea that any new Commonwealth would need to be multicultural and multiracial. Thus, the Tory government accepted that the unreconstructed apartheid state of South Africa would need to be cut adrift. Macmillan started this process in his famous speech in Cape Town on the 3rd of February 1960 when he argued that: 'the wind of change is blowing through this continent, and, whether we like it or not, this growth of [African] national consciousness is a political fact'. Macmillan's aim was not the end of the Commonwealth. Quite the opposite: it was to bring into being a reformed, multi-cultural world body – the British Commonwealth – through which the British political class (headed by the Queen) could continue to play a global role.

'Greece To Rome'

But for Macmillan, unlike for Eden, it was clear that the road to a world role ran through Washington – and that it was the 'special relationship' which allowed him to 'walk the boards' on the world stage.

And the 'special relationship' was becoming more necessary all the time. During the Macmillan premiership the stark facts were that Britain was falling more and more into the American orbit. The full extent of Britain's increasing security dependence on the United States became apparent as problems emerged in the delivery system for the British nuclear deterrent. In February 1960 Britain decided to abandon its own Blue Streak missile and buy instead from the USA the Skybolt missile – which could be fired from an aeroplane thus avoiding the problem of fixed land sites.

This deal was arranged between Macmillan and Eisenhower at Camp David, and the quid pro quo was the controversial decision to allow the Americans to use Gareloch on the Clyde for a new American Polaris base – a base containing nuclear warheads, and therefore subject to Russian targeting – near the large population centre of Glasgow. In a sign of Britain's subservient position within the alliance, Macmillan tried several times to persuade Eisenhower not to push for a nuclear base on the Clyde – he offered instead the more remote base at Loch Linnhe – but Eisenhower insisted, and the President got his way.

Another sign of British dependence was the character of the sub-sequent Polaris deal between Washington and London that was concluded in December 1962 at Nassau between Macmillan and President John Kennedy. Macmillan sold himself as the youthful Kennedy's wise old uncle, but, in reality, he was a supplicant. Britain's own nuclear bomb was built, originally by the post-war Labour cabinet, as an attempt to retain some independent influence and to keep a seat at the geo-political 'top table'.

There was considerable opposition in Washington to Britain retaining a nuclear force partly because – an argument that might have been disingenuous – of the problems it would cause for the French. The Americans also balked at anything 'independent', offering initially to provide the British with the missiles on condition they were 'assigned' to a NATO multi-lateral force. Macmillan finally got an agreement that stated that the British Polaris system would indeed be assigned to NATO except in a 'dire national emergency'. Yet, the truth was that the British bomb's delivery system became progressively dependent upon American technology and goodwill (Polaris needed an American guidance system and regular upgrading in the US). If nuclear independence was a test of national independence, then France – which under De Gaulle insisted upon a genuinely independent and self-sufficient nuclear system – remained an independent nation much longer than Britain.

This Nassau agreement was yet another piece of British vainglory – and counter-productive at that. For, far from retaining the ostensible prize of an independent nuclear deterrent the British government remained dependent on the US, and at the same time managed to sour relations with the French, the result of which may well have led to De Gaulle's veto – one month after Nassau – of British membership of the Common Market.[3]

Britain as 'junior partner' to the USA in the Atlantic Alliance was, though, still difficult for many Conservatives to swallow. And to appease these sensibilities, and indeed Macmillan's pride, a new line of reasoning entered into the discourse. It amounted to an argument that Britain, if not strong and powerful, was 'wise' and 'prescient'. The comforting image was drawn of Britain as 'Greece' to America's 'Rome'. Harold Macmillan himself had suggested this role when, during the war when in North Africa, he had written to Richard Crossman. 'We are Greeks in this American Empire' he had argued, and 'we must run the Allied Forces HQ as the Greeks ran the operations of the Emperor Claudius'.[4]

Peter Riddell in his excellent account of the Anglo-American 'special relationship' reports Harold Macmillan as understandably irritating some American policy-makers with this 'Greeks and Romans' comparison. Riddell calls it a 'patronising implication that the wise and experienced British could guide and educate the crude, though powerful, Americans' and suggests that 'while not expressed publicly after the 1960s, this thought still persisted in the minds of some British politicians and diplomats for a long time afterwards'.[5]

Alec Home: America's English Gentleman

Macmillan was succeeded in 1963 by Sir Alec Douglas Home. Home, unlike Macmillan, was the Tory real McCoy – a large landowning aristocrat from the Scottish borders. A classic imperialist in his younger days he had supported Neville Chamberlain's geo-politics aimed at all costs towards maintaining the British empire. And he had come to power in a very imperial and aristocratic way. He had 'emerged'. In 1963 the Tory party did not elect its leaders. And when Harold Macmillan resigned there were no procedures in place to hold an election for his successor. Instead, a Ruritanian system of 'soundings' of opinion took place. In full view of the new democracy of the media age a small cabal of senior Tory leaders, together with the Queen, held discussions following 'soundings' of opinion amongst Tory MPs, Peers and activists.

As in the manner of a Papal cabal – though with no formal voting as in the Vatican – the new Prime Minister was suddenly announced to a waiting world. Lord Home, a member of the House of Lords, suddenly appeared waving on the steps of Downing Street having been commissioned by the Queen to form a government. It was a procedure worthy of Gilbert and Sullivan – and it was to be bitterly denounced by Tory MPs Ian Macleod and Enoch Powell when they later complained about a Tory 'magic circle' that with effortless superiority, and not bothering about democracy, had hand-picked the new Prime Minister. What the 'senior partners' in Washington felt about this method of selecting a British Prime Minister was not reported in the British press.

In foreign policy Alec Home – as he came to be known – was a natural and consistent anti-communist. As Neville Chamberlain's

Parliamentary Private Secretary before the war he had supported Chamberlain's anti-Soviet geo-strategy of which appeasement of Hitler was a part. In the Cold War years he became very pro-NATO and pro-American, and, understanding the new power relationship between America and Britain, had come to loyally accept British subordination to US leadership. His administration only lasted for a short period, and took few important foreign policy decisions; but the mere presence in the democratic age of a fourteenth Earl in Downing Street provided cartoonists with a nice – and misleading – image of the 'Greece to Rome' 'special relationship'. Home became the traditional 'English gentleman butler' – poorer but wiser – to the nouveau American LBJ who had all the power.

Hugh Gaitskell

During the Macmillan years, the American cause in Britain was greatly enhanced by the Leader of the Labour opposition, Hugh Gaitskell. He had shot to prominence as a fierce opponent of Eden's attack on Suez in 1956, and his eloquence at this time had burnished his radical, anti-establishment credentials. Yet, at the same time, many in the Labour Party saw him in a different light – as an upper crust, public school-educated Tory. Indeed, like many Tories of the time, he was a son of empire – literally so, as he was born in India into a colonial civil service family during the Imperial Raj. He went on to public school in England and thence to Oxford.

This imperial background was hard to slough-off, and it led him naturally to the kind of 'world role' thinking of his class; indeed, Gaitskell believed the Commonwealth to be hugely important for Britain's future and saw Common Market restrictions on imported goods from the Commonwealth as a major reason to oppose British entry. And in his emotional conference speech against British entry in 1962 he sounded as 'imperial' as any traditionalist as he rhapsodised about Britain's world role, evoking 'a thousand years of history' and imperial Anzac connections of 'Vimy Ridge and Gallipoli'.

Yet, appearances to the contrary, Gaitskell was no traditionalist. He was an atheist and a republican (who, for prudential reasons as Leader of Her Majesty's Loyal Opposition, kept his republicanism quiet). He was a 'Wykemist' (a term for those who attended the intellectually up-market public school of Winchester) and, like many on the left, was guided by reason rather than tradition. He was in essence a European social democrat with cosmopolitan tastes. And he wanted to change Britain. He believed the country's still strong class system – and sense of class – disfigured society, and he disliked the still strong racist attitudes permeating society, not least the upper class English. His campaigning organisation, The Campaign For Democratic Socialism (CDS), openly confronted bigotry and anti-foreigner sentiment, arguing that 'an inward looking re-orientation would encourage the conservative and not the progressive forces in Britain. Those who are most suspicious of foreigners are most nervous of change'.[6] He married a German Jewess and took his holidays in Yugoslavia (often as a guest of Marshall Tito). All this was hardly the stuff of Tory imperial traditionalism.

Whereas many in Britain's traditional ruling class were resentful and hostile to America, and used the 'special relationship' as a cover for pursuing a world role, Gaitskell, on the other hand, was a true believer. He was, literally and lavishly, pro-American – an ideological fellow-traveller. Britain's 1960s Labour social democrats saw America, then the land of Kennedy and Johnson and Martin Luther King and the civil rights movement, as 'the new frontier' and 'the great society'. They saw the American republic as more classless and egalitarian – socially if not economically – than stuffy old Britain, and, as meritocrats, they warmed to the more open and democratic atmosphere of the US. Also, the Labour leadership had few imperial hang-ups and, unlike many of their Tory counterparts, did not suffer from nostalgia for empire. Many of them positively welcomed American power in the world, and America's supplanting of British imperial influence.

The late 1950s and early 60s was the height of the Cold War, and Gaitskell was the archetypal cold warrior – what Americans would call a 'liberal cold warrior'. Often difficult to comprehend today, the atmosphere of the times was dominated by the east-west conflict, and, for many in the Labour Party, a deep political commitment to social change at home went hand in hand with seeking to defend the west against the spread of communism. Gaitskell saw the USA as the undisputed leader of the western system, and opposed any weakening of the relationship with Washington. He supported NATO against the left in the late 1950s, a campaign that culminated in his famous 'fight, fight and fight again' speech opposing unilateral nuclear disarmament at the party conference in 1960. Interestingly, he was undogmatic about keeping the British bomb – determined primarily to keep NATO nuclear.

Hugh Gaitskell liked Americans, so much so that he formed close American friendships. One such was with the CIA's Joe Godson. Godson, who had met Gaitskell during the opposition leader's many visits to Tito's Yugoslavia where he, Godson, was a US embassy official. Godson was a bright and funny life-force, and Gaitskell took to him. Over the years he became a more than welcome guest in Gaitskell's circle and was in and out of Gaitskell's office, so much so that Gaitskell was warned by political friends that it would be judicious to lower Godson's profile.

Hugh Gaitskell died prematurely in January 1963 at age 59, and subsequently came to symbolise British social democracy for a whole generation. Yet he was to leave a discordant note amongst his band of loyal followers when, in 1961-2, in the last year of his life, he opposed British entry into the Common Market – and in such a high-profile manner.

Many of his younger supporters, like Roy Jenkins and Bill Rodgers, were wounded by his visceral opposition to entry, and even years later could not fully understand the reasons for it. Yet, like many surprising political moves, there were a number of contributing factors all coalescing at the same time. One was that in 1961-2 Gaitskell had just come through a bruising contest with his left wing over unilateral nuclear disarmament and opposing Common Market entry was one way of restoring party unity – as well, that is, as out-manoeuvring Macmillan – ahead of a general election. Another reason may well have been purely personal: Gaitskell's wife Dora was a fervent opponent of joining.[7]

Missed Opportunity

The Macmillan-Gaitskell years (1957-64) were good years for the Anglo-American 'special relationship'. They saw transatlantic relations recover from their rupture at Suez and then go on to reach a new stability. They were years which also saw the American-led western post-war boom get fully underway. Britain's living standards were slowly improving, a middle class was beginning to appear (based upon the greater availability of consumer durables) and trade unions, though powerful, were not militant.

But commentators and analysts argued, both at the time and later, that these were Britain's 'locust years' when a fateful complacency set in. It was a time of growing competition from Japan and the European neighbours – principally Germany; and Britain was beginning to fall down the economic league tables as its economy remained largely unreconstructed. As did its political and constitutional system – as the Byzantine 'selection' of Lord Home as Prime Minister in 1963 stood testimony to. In the early 1960s a small head of steam was building up on the left, around ideas of modernisation – many of them linked to Europe – but the predominant ethos was one of complacency. Britain's security rested under the American defence umbrella, and the American-led consumer boom put off thoughts of change and adjustment. It was a period in which long held illusions about the British way of life and British power were simply reinforced.

On the face of it Harold Macmillan's decision in 1961 to apply for entry into the Common Market was a surprising sign of change – of a new clear-eyed appreciation of reduced power and a willingness to abandon global illusions. And questions still remain about why this generation of post-Suez Tories made the application. The contemporary historian Martin Holmes argues persuasively that, rather than a change of course based upon a new realism, it was the same old tune: 'he and his generation of Conservatives wanted to find a way in which British power could be rekindled, a way in which our influence could continue to spread beneficially beyond Britain's borders'. Holmes argues that Europe was seen by Macmillan and his circle as nothing more than a 'substitute for empire'. He suggests that they said to themselves: 'why not join the European Community?'. 'If Britain could join Europe then our diplomatic experience, our skills in negotiation, and our special relationship with the United States...could provide the Europeans with political leadership'.[8]

If Holmes is right in this Macmillan's application was not real, certainly not wholehearted. It was a contrivance. The longing for a world role still dominated. The three most influential political figures of the immediate post-Suez era – Harold Macmillan (Prime Minister from 1956-63), Alec Douglas-Home (1963-4) and Queen Elizabeth – saw themselves as worldly-wise, realistic statesmen and women; yet none of them, even in the aftermath of the Suez humiliation, truly sought to adjust policy and abandon the 'world role' and the 'special relationship' in favour of a more realistic and modest foreign policy in Europe. In any event, President De Gaulle vetoed Macmillan's application in 1963 – he believed that if Britain joined it would become an 'American Trojan horse' inside the Community.

6. The 'Declinists' and Europe

'One of the preoccupations of reasonable men and women across the world – in Washington, in the Commonwealth countries, in the European capitals – is the question: Will Britain Flounder?'
Professor Alistair Buchan, in *The Times*, January 1976

Harold Wilson

Harold Wilson's government, elected in 1964, initially saw itself as a modernising administration, set to sweep out the dead wood of 'the establishment'. The Tories were painted as out of touch traditionalists from another age. Britain's 'upstairs-downstairs' class system was singled out for attack. Wilson described his 1964 election opponent, Alec Douglas-Home, dismissively as 'The Thirteenth Earl', and he sought an end to what he called 'the gentlemen and players' society. Wilson's rhetoric was all about the need for sweeping reforms, and he pledged that Labour would modernise Britain by embracing 'the White Heat of the technological revolution'.

A flavour of these 'reforming' times can be captured by reading a little known but highly influential book published in 1959. Called 'The Establishment' it was edited by the historian Hugh Thomas (later to be made a peer by Margaret Thatcher) and included essays from both Labour and Tory contributors. It was written with a radical verve and passion, and included ideas and sentiments (for instance, about public schools and the army) that, for their times, were revolutionary. Most every British institution – bar the monarchy – was savaged. Thomas himself declared that 'to those who desire to see the resources and talents of Britain fully developed and extended, there is no doubt that the fusty establishment, with its Victorian views and standards of judgement, must be destroyed'.[1]

In this book Simon Raven (army captain and book critic for *The Spectator*) attacked the officer corps in the British army. 'I found a caste rooted in its own conception of superior, God-given status' he wrote. John Vaizey (later to advise Labour minister Tony Crosland whilst he was Education Secretary) argued that the public schools which 'lie at the root of the establishment...stand condemned'. Thomas Balogh, Oxford economist, later to be in Harold Wilson's inner circle, made a systematic critique of the amateur in Whitehall in 'The Apotheosis of the Dilettante'. The stockbroker Victor Sandelson wanted the City of London open to 'talent from whatever class or education'. Former Tory MP and Assistant Editor of *Punch*, Christopher Hollis, pointed to the way in which 'the establishment' had neutered Parliament through the two-party system. And *Daily Mail* columnist, Henry Fairlie, who is reported to be the first person to coin the term 'the establishment', made a searing attack on the 'baleful' influence on British life of the BBC for 'brainwashing' the country with a patronising 'attitude to life and thought'.[2]

This modernising impulse had its effect on the foreign policy of Wilson's new government – for it reinforced the 'special relationship'. The US was seen – socially and technologically – as the fount of modernisation. Wilson came to Downing Street after John Kennedy was assassinated but had made a point, whilst Leader of the Opposition, of modelling his style – progressive, young, modernising – on that of the fallen President.

Labour saw the US Democrats as a progressive force to copy, and Wilson borrowed from Kennedy the idea of using the 'first 100 days' to set the agenda for reform. For many of the incoming Labour MPs in the class of '64, America's classlessness and 'go-ahead' attitudes were going to replace those of fusty old Britain. Labour was going to arrest Britain's decline by becoming more like America. Indeed the connections across the Atlantic between some of the coming influential Labour politicians and the USA were strong: Denis Healey had spent time in the Rand Corporation, and Tony Crosland, Tony Benn, and the young David Owen, who stood as a candidate in 1964 and entered Parliament in 1966, had married American women.

But within two years this radical-inspired optimism had dissipated, and the Wilson government had hit the buffers. It was becoming clearer by the month that Britain's economy was in very serious trouble, and in 1969, with the defeat by the trade unions of Wilson's 'In Place of Strife' trade union reform proposals, there appeared to be no way out. Wilson had little idea what to do. And his governments were soon consumed by the growth of trade union militancy and the emergence within the party of extreme socialism.

In foreign policy Wilson fought a rearguard action. He stuck to the 'special relationship' as best he could. But the growing left, in and out of the Labour Party, were placing the American action in Vietnam in their sights – with big demonstrations and sit-ins. Wilson, and his very pro-American Foreign Secretary, Michael Stewart, continued to give support to US policy, though they were careful, and unlike Tony Blair some decades later, refused to send British troops to support the American forces.

In the late 1960s the idea of decline – of irreversible decline – was beginning to set in. Indeed the sense of decline had been the prevailing national mood ever since Britain began to slip down the economic league-tables in the late 1950s, a slippage that had become a theme of the politics of the late 1950s and early 60s. Harold Wilson himself had made vivid this theme by constantly reciting the figures of Britain's low economic performance in his attacks on what he described as the 'complacent' Tories. For some, this idea of decline was powerfully reinforced by the fall-out from the Suez affair – clearly proving that Britain was no longer the power, domestically and internationally, that she had been earlier in the century.

Cecil King's diaries covering the period 1965-70, and published in 1972, revealed the sheer alarm at the country's position held by many top people in Britain following the failure of Wilson.[3] And this sense of alarm was to grow even stronger during the early 1970s when the country was engulfed in the three-day week and the bitter disputes between government and miners – bringing home the acute nature of Britain's crisis. In December 1973 the Chancellor of the Exchequer, Anthony Barber, could state that 'over the past week or so many have described the situation which we as a nation now face as by far the gravest since the end of the war. They did not exaggerate'.[4] In 1976, just before the IMF was to visit London, Professor Alistair Buchan in an essay in *The Times* in January 1976 could write 'one of the preoccupations of reasonable men and women across the world – in Washington, in the Commonwealth countries, in the European capitals – is the question "Will Britain flounder?"' and went on to suggest that the British, unlike intelligent observers abroad, 'hold their peace because they are afraid'.

This sense of heightened or acute crisis pushed to the fore a lively debate about British decline, the reasons for it, and how to recover from it. It was so pervasive a debate that it was dubbed 'Declinism'. And the mid to late 1970s became a period of 'High Declinism'.[5] In 1972, the same year as the publication of the Cecil King Diaries, one of the classic so-called 'declinist' books of the period, Correlli Barnett's *The Collapse of British Power* was published. It was a poignant and powerful analysis in which Barnett argued that Britain's decline took place during the first half of the twentieth century – with 'the decay of British power between 1918 and 1940' and 'its collapse between 1940 and 1945'.[6] And it did so because of a fatal combination of 'imperial overstretch, moral pretensions and inadequate education, particularly technical' – attitudes fostered in establishment minds by the ruling culture of the late nineteenth-century public schools (he singled out the Rugby of Dr Arnold for particular scorn). By educating England's future elites in the wrong way – attempting to create moral character, 'all that was noble and good', rather than hard-headed realism – a whole generation of twentieth century leaders were infused with the wrong values. It was a withering critique that could at least help explain why Britain's post-war leadership (from Churchill to Blair) were to lack strategic vision and grasp and could not properly identify Britain's real position and place in the world, constantly overstating and overselling the power of the country.

Barnett put it all down to hubris, moralism and complacent 'overstretch' during the height of empire in the late mid nineteenth century. 'Just at the time when we were beginning to congratulate ourselves – 'we have the secret, we are absolutely tremendous' – other nations were thinking hard how to catch up with us'.[7] Barnett was educated in state school in Croydon and he went to Oxford in the late

1940s where he developed his critique of the educational system, specifically of 'Britain's unquestionable backwardness in education generally, and particularly technical education'.[8]

It was a time of feverish introspection, but also one – unusual for the British – that was largely lacking in complacency. Professor Andrew Gamble has suggested that 'it is hard to think of a major public intellectual who has not contributed to the decline debate'.[9] And in 1974 he himself argued that 'if capitalism is to survive some new relationship has to be worked out with the trade unions'.[10]

All kinds of explanations for decline were bubbling, some of them under the surface, only reaching the light of day in later books and articles. There were those who put it down to cultural factors (like Martin Weiner whose 1981 book *English Culture and the Decline of the Industrial Spirit* became a vogue work: he put Britain's decline down to anti-industrial values of a people in love with England as a rural arcadia). Others suggested it was primarily to do with the predominance of the City of London and finance over manufacturing (a part of the analysis of Labour MP Stuart Holland and of futurologist, James Bellini). Others yet placed the blame on institutional failures such as the lack of state-led modernisation (a view of the politician and writer David Marquand). Yet underlying all these explanations was a fundamental geo-political analysis: how imperial overstretch and complacency, and two wars, had decisively diminished the nation's power.[11]

'Decline is not Inevitable'

So dominating did the debate about decline become that in the 1970s a defeatist aphorism did the rounds in Westminster and Whitehall. It went something like: For Britain 'decline is not the problem, decline is the solution'. And the crisis improved the position of Britain's political extremes – the Bennite left of the Labour Party and the Thatcherite right of the Conservative Party – as they both rejected the 'unpatriotic' idea of 'decline as the solution'. On the socialist left there was a view that Britain had a unique capitalist crisis – an analysis outlined most cogently in a host of articles and essays in *The New Left Review* in the early and mid 1970s. *The New Left Review* was edited and written by neo-Marxist socialist writers such as Perry Anderson, Robin Blackburn, Tom Nairn and Peter Gowan, and the thrust of their argument was that there was nothing inevitable about decline, and nothing that could not be put right by an 'alternative strategy'. This alternative would transform Britain by transforming the capitalist economy into a socialist one, thus causing an 'irreversible shift of power to working peoples and their families'.

Prominent in this campaign for a socialist 'alternative strategy' was Ken Livingstone, the Leader of the Greater London Council from 1981 to 1986. In the early and mid 1970s Livingstone was the unofficial leader of a small band of Marxist-inspired socialist GLC councillors but was regularly out-voted by the majority of the GLC Labour group. I was Chairman of the GLC's General Purposes Committee at the time and saw the young aspiring 'Ken' at close hand. Unlike many of the puritanical leftists then making their way in constituency Labour parties, Livingstone was a likeable colleague who, no matter political differences, even sharp ones, was always good for a laugh. Yet, underneath this sociable persona he was developing a serious-minded left alternative to the Labourist social democratic regime that ran County Hall and then, after 1974, Westminster. After he became the Leader of the GLC, following his breath-taking ouster of John Macintosh, he further polished this 'alternative' socialist strategy and sent it into war against Margaret Thatcher – who returned the favour by abolishing the GLC in 1986.

The 1970s radical left developed a 'foreign policy' – of a kind – as part of their more general alternative socialist strategy. It amounted to a moralistic and ideological rejection of both American capitalism and what was called Soviet 'state capitalism'.

For them a 'socialist foreign policy' amounted to a romantic role for Britain as a neutral power in the world allied with non-aligned nations, particularly 'socialist' Cuba. Its heroes were the anti-colonialist radicals like Che Guevara and Franz Fanon. It was an approach to Britain's role in the world that sat uneasily alongside the more realistic hard-line 'neutralism' (often shading-off into pro-Soviet sympathy) of the trade union activists who were making headway in the Labour Party during the 1970s. Yet both types of leftists could, however, agree on the issue of Europe and Britain's application to join the EEC – they were both against it. Indeed the Livingstone left and the trade union left both made great headway within the Labour movement in these years because they opposed entry into the Common Market. They could also paint the Labour leadership of those years as defeatist and 'declinist' compared to the left who saw national revival as possible should socialist policies be adopted.

The Tory right, too, rejected the idea that 'decline' was inevitable. During the 1970s Tory economic thought was becoming increasingly 'dry', a term introduced to distinguish them from the more left-wing Tory 'wets'. And Tory politicians were falling under the influence of neo-liberal economists from the USA, Milton Friedman and the Chicago School chief amongst them. These Tory 'drys' believed that the rigours of the market would solve the problem of decline and lead to a rebirth of Britain. Indeed Margaret Thatcher herself, when Leader of the Opposition and Prime Minister, made a point of attacking the notion that decline was inevitable. She turned what she saw as the cynicism of the decline debate into a powerful political weapon. 'At the heart of a new mood in the nation' she argued 'must be a recovery of our self-confidence and our self-respect. Decline is not inevitable'. Rather than accepting it she sought to reverse it. And Winston Churchill was called in aid: 'it is given to us to demand an end to decline' she said 'and to make a stand against what Churchill described as the long dismal drawling tides of drift and surrender'.[12]

Ian Gilmour

By the mid 1970s the Tory 'dry' faction was gaining ascendancy in the party and was promising radical right measures as the only way forward to national revival. And these 'drys' were becoming irritated, and more, by the still strong Tory 'wets' who wanted to avoid what they saw as extreme, and counterproductive, solutions. The intellectual leader of the 'wets' was Tory cabinet and shadow cabinet minister Ian Gilmour. Many of the younger Thatcherites saw him as a shadowy and dangerous character, the *éminence grise* of defeatism and 'declinism'. On the face of it Ian Gilmour was an almost perfect caricature of the old English pre-war political establishment. A scion of wealth and land, this thin, tall, languid, 'wet' Tory was not, though, quite what at first blush he might have seemed. A member of the gentleman's club, White's, he was seemingly at home amongst the county, 'huntin, shootin and fishin', rural, shire fraternity. Yet, he was, in fact, not at home at all. An intellectual in a philistine culture, he possessed a detached wry humour, wide sympathies, and a very un-Tory-like politically serious disposition.

Gilmour's approach to the crisis of the 1970s was to try and limit what he saw coming – a right-wing reaction to national failure that would involve the introduction of radical, rampant economic neo-liberalism. He was dismissive, almost contemptuous, of Thatcher's proposed solutions – they were, for his taste, far too extreme, or, as he called them 'ideological' and 'dogmatic'. His fear was that the developing Thatcherism he saw around him would, if implemented, weaken the social fabric of the country and lead to another extreme, this time socialist, or worse, counter-reaction.[13]

I was surprised one morning in 1979, on the eve of the announcement of the 1979 general election, to receive a call from Gilmour. 'Well' he said 'the election is upon us. Please try and persuade your friends Johnson and O'Sullivan (leader writers on the *Daily Telegraph* and advisors to Thatcher) to stop Thatcher going round the country saying she will dismantle the welfare state'. Later, after Thatcher had won the election, and I was a young Labour politician on the GLC, I was shocked to stand in the bar at White's Club, as a guest of Gilmour's, surrounded by a circle of her new Cabinet ministers (Jim Prior and Willie Whitelaw particularly) who, in private, adopted a tone fluctuating between ridicule and serious concern about their leader's 'ideology' and about where she wanted to take the country. Indeed, so worried was Gilmour about the future under the Thatcher government – he believed market solutions were so dividing the country that the seeds for a left-wing takeover were being planted – that he actively sought to aid Labour's social democrats as a means of strengthening the political centre. A close friend of Roy Jenkins, Gilmour took a behind-the-scenes interest in the formation of the Social Democratic Party (SDP) which he saw as helping to give expression to the majority 'social democratic constituency' in Britain and thus blocking the growing left-wing threat in the Labour movement.[14]

Declinists for Europe
Gilmour's 'declinist' school of thought served to introduce into British politics a new factor – a sober and realistic assessment of Britain's new place in the world. The charge that 'declinists' were in some sense cynically seeking or wanting national decline was an unfair depiction – for personal wants or needs aside, for these 'declinists' it was a question of accepting, and working within, the limitations which decline placed on British power. And that, in turn, meant that a difficult truth needed to be faced – that there was in fact no 'national road to recovery' available. Academics Elizabeth Meehan and Marie Theresa-Fay were later to argue in a perceptive

analysis in 1981 that 'it may not be valid to speak of a *national* road to recovery in the British context' because both 'sub-national features' as well as 'trans-national sectors could invalidate discourses of *national* economies (and therefore much of the debate on British national decline)'. They set the whole thing in a European, not British, context.[15]

For Gilmour and many in the mainstream centre of British politics the only real solution was not a British one at all, but lay in Britain's full integration into Europe. Whatever was wrong with Britain could not be solved by Britain alone. And trying to solve Britain's problems in isolation – outside of the European context – would be a hopeless venture and only lead to further division, trouble and poverty. It amounted to a strategy of 'ever closer union' or bust!

This radical approach often 'dared not speak its name': for, by arguing that Britain could not solve its problems alone – that it should not and could not have a 'sovereign' political future – it would lay itself open to charges of not being patriotic, even of being treasonous. But, even so, the idea that Britain needed to integrate with others in order to save itself, remained the guts and soul of the drive in the 1970s for Britain to join the European Community.

By contrast, the growing voice of Thatcherism saw Britain as able to solve her own problems. Thatcher, like her left-wing socialist opponents, believed fervently in the national road to survival and recovery. The irony here was that these neo-liberal market solutions were also solutions that could only be effected through an international context – through, as it turned out, merging Britain into the increasingly globalised economy and in close, 'ever closer', association with the United States. Thus it was that in the depths and fog of the national crisis of the 1970s the two alternative geo-political futures for Britain – 'ever closer' relations with Europe, or alternatively an 'ever closer' 'special relationship' with America – began to emerge and clarify themselves.

Wilson moves towards Europe.
The Tory 'wets' were not the only grouping to see no national road to recovery, and to see Britain's only realistic future as lying in Europe. So too were many of the younger members of the 1964-70 Wilson government and parliamentary party. MPs such as Roy Jenkins, Bill Rodgers, John Macintosh, David Marquand, and future leader John

Smith were amongst those who saw entry into the Common Market as the only way for the country to revive its economy and halt its decline. For them, the Common Market was a success story as were the continental economies and societies with their social democratic and social market traditions. And when in May 1967 Harold Wilson's government – out of the blue – reactivated Britain's application to join the Common Market, they supported it with relish.

At this time, George Brown, the Deputy Prime Minister, was the *de facto* leader of the pro-Europeans in the Labour Party (and he was to remain so until Roy Jenkins became Chancellor of the Exchequer in December 1967). Brown, like his hero Ernie Bevin, hailed from a trade union, working class background and was self-educated. And he was able to give to the European cause a straightforward, populist flavour at a time when the Common Market was beginning to be tarred with the elitist and bureaucratic brush. Yet in the European movement Brown was always surrounded by Oxbridge-educated social democrats and was never able to put a popular stamp on the pro-European campaign – which in the view of the wider public often seemed to be the preserve of meritocratic young men and languid power brokers.

George Brown was in awe of what he believed to be the superior social and intellectual prowess of the other European movement leaders, Roy Jenkins, Shirley Williams and David Owen. He was even somewhat insecure with me and my lecturer friends in the Social Democratic Alliance, Roger Fox and Douglas Eden. On one occasion the full extent of the British class problem was on display when, at his flat in Notting Hill, he confessed that he 'had the ideas' but 'simply didn't have the words like them...and like you guys'. He was not being disingenuous. He meant it. Here was the former Deputy Prime Minister and Foreign Secretary whose powerful speeches I had listened to from afar, confessing his insecurities and supposed inabilities. When the 'gang of four' formed the SDP they left Brown out of the central leadership. I considered this a mistake. Every one of the leaders of the new party were Oxbridge graduates and I tried to bounce George Brown on 'the gang of four' – to turn it into the 'gang of five' by simply announcing it to the press. Roy Jenkins, who thought very highly of Brown was in favour, but 'the four' collectively would not agree to it.

Brown, again like Bevin before him, was at heart a Cold Warrior – it was the centre of his political life. He would therefore never be overtly anti-American, although he was often critical, like many European enthusiasts, of aspects of American policy – particularly US policy in the Middle East. Even so he did not warm to the 'special relationship' and tried to tilt British foreign policy in a more European direction. He was the moving force, with Roy Jenkins, in getting Wilson to apply for Common Market entry in 1967.

But, like Macmillan's application seven years earlier, Wilson's, if not Brown's, 1967 move towards Europe seemed a contrivance – born out of the need to be seen to be doing something, and devoid of positive geo-strategic vision. Wilson's application was a very guarded affair – again hedged around with qualifications, concerns and worries. Also like Macmillan's it would certainly not have been attempted if it had cut across the 'special relationship'. In fact the United States was all in favour, and had been pushing Britain to become more engaged in the European enterprise. President Nixon's foreign policy guru, Henry Kissinger, had made a cutting complaint about needing 'a single European phone number' to ring in case of a crisis. And the whole US political leadership wanted Britain in Europe in order for them to have a place at the top table of European affairs.

So determined were the Americans that Britain should join the Community that, during the 1975 referendum campaign they placed a committed European federalist, Cord Meyer Jr., as CIA Station Chief for the duration of the campaign. According to the former MP Richard Body he was told 'to do what it takes' to secure a 'Yes' vote.[16]

Wilson may have successfully secured Britain in the Common Market – outmanoeuvring the anti-Market forces by calling a referendum and then winning it – but he had done so at a huge long-term cost to the European cause in Britain. Wilson himself had been half-hearted about the whole thing – 'I am not throwing my hat in the air about it' he had said – and he gave Britain's European future no vision or colour, and set out none of the big arguments for Europe. In the campaign the issues got bogged down – to the long term disadvantage of Britain's pro-Europeans – in small, niggly issues of trade standardisation and Commission incompetence and bureaucracy.

7. The Radical Government of Edward Heath

'It was not that he was anti-American...[but he believed] that the special relationship was an obstacle to the British vocation in Europe'.
Henry Kissinger on Edward Heath, 1979

Edward Heath entered Downing Street in June 1970 and, like Wilson before him, was an instinctive moderniser. And, again like Wilson, he was classless. A grammar school boy from Kent he was the first Tory leader not to go to a public school and, incredibly, the first to be elected (in a formal ballot of MPs). His lack of interest (if not disdain) for old-fashioned English privilege was displayed when he took the historic step of abolishing hereditary peerages (they were brought back by Thatcher). And his classlessness also showed in his attitude to industry and commerce – for although his government was marked by hostility to the trade unions he was also a fierce opponent of its mirror image, the out-dated 'old-boy network' in British management.

Heath was also the first truly post-imperial Prime Minister. By the time he came to office, the last serious British imperial military presence – the forces East of Suez in the Gulf – had been abandoned. And, crucially, Heath shared none of the nostalgia or pretensions for a 'world role' that had infected every one of his post-war predecessors. He was simply uninterested in a grand role on the world stage, and consequently playing junior partner to Washington also left him cold. He had been Tory Chief Whip during the traumatic months – for the British establishment – of the Suez affair, and that searing experience had led him to a clear-eyed understanding of Britain's true position in the world – and in the world according to Washington. For Ted Heath, Britain's 'glorious past' was just that. Its present and future was that of a medium-sized country off the coast of Europe desperately in need of social and economic modernisation.

Heath's original fervour for European unity may, like many of his generation, have come from his experiences during the Second World War – leading him to view European unity as the only way to avoid future European wars. But during the 1960s as he witnessed governments grappling with the British disease of union militancy and backward management he came to the conclusion that the much needed modernisation could only be made by an irreversible immersing of the country in the new Europe.

But a European future for Britain was a revolutionary idea – particularly for Conservatives. Heath had initially largely avoided the European issue by launching his premiership on the back of a domestic programme of free-market change – the famous 'Selsdon Park' manifesto, named after the hotel at which the plan had been drawn up. He had called for a 'silent revolution'. And although he was known as a keen European, Heath had not stressed Europe in the general election campaign. Yet, chance now took a hand and only days after Heath had taken over in London the new French President Georges Pompidou made it known that he was prepared to lift De Gaulle's veto against Britain's EEC application. Heath immediately headed off to Paris and a deal was done: negotiations for Britain to join the EEC started on the 30th June 1970, just twelve days after Edward Heath entered Downing Street.

Heath signed the Accession Treaty at the Egmont Palace in Brussels and Britain entered the EEC – together with Ireland and Denmark – as a full member on the 1st January 1973. This historic and revolutionary act had, though, been achieved very much against the grain of British politics and tradition. Indeed, in securing British entry Heath had taken few prisoners. He forced a parliamentary vote on a three-line whip, using all the resources of persuasion at a Prime Minister's command. And, even then, his victory was only secured because 69 Labour MPs defied their own party whip to vote with the pro-European Tories.

It was this revolution that led Heath towards yet another revolution: for it soon became clear that as Prime Minister he would be placing the European connection – and future – ahead of the 'special relationship' with the USA. To this day he remains the only post-war British Prime Minister to do so. In 1970 the European Council had established the 'European Political Co-operation' procedures for foreign policy; it was an unprecedented step and was hailed at the time as the beginning of a European foreign policy – and Heath took it seriously. Whenever possible he tried to side with his major European colleagues. At his December 1971 summit with President Nixon, Henry Kissinger reports that 'Heath pursued his favourite theme of European unity and assured the President [Nixon] that it would be competitive not confrontational. It was an interesting and *not entirely reassuring* formulation, a considerable step away from the automatic cooperation taken for granted by our own twin-pillar Atlanticists in the 1960s and by all of Heath's predecessors'.[1]

This new alignment in Britain's foreign policy was on display in British policy in the Middle East. During the Middle East war in October 1973 President Nixon decided to provide Israel with military equipment and asked the British government for overflying rights so that the Jewish state could be resupplied from North America. Heath refused, and the US was forced to use the Azores instead. Criticised for supporting the French in calling for Israel to implement UN Security Council resolution 242, Heath bluntly stated, in words unthinkable from a British Prime Minister before or since: 'The day when the voice of the United States automatically prevailed over each of its individual partners has passed'.[2] At the Tory conference he called, again in terms unusual for a British Prime Minister, for a 'common European policy towards our principal ally, the United States'.[3]

Henry Kissinger said of Edward Heath that 'of all the British leaders Heath was probably the least committed emotionally to the United States. It was not that he was anti-American...[but he believed] that the "special relationship" was an obstacle to the British vocation in Europe'.⁴ This did not stop Heath getting on with America's leaders. He and Nixon however, did not hit it off personally. 'Like a couple who had been told by everyone that they should be in love and who might try mightily but futilely to justify these expectations... the relationship never flourished.' Heath, like Nixon, was shy and awkward. In his biography *The White House Years* Kissinger, who witnessed the Nixon-Heath get-togethers, offered a shrewd assessment of Heath, proof of his negotiator's eye for an opponent: he wrote that Heath 'rose from modest beginnings to lead a party imbued with Britain's aristocratic tradition. The ruthlessness necessary to achieve the ambition did not come naturally...he was a warm and gentle person who anticipated rejection and fended it off with a formal politeness...He had a theoretical bent closer than the rest [British PMs] to that of the continental Europeans'.⁵

Nixon outlasted Heath in office by a few months. Heath lost the general election of February 1974 after a year of bitter industrial disputes which were exacerbated by the sheer bad luck of the huge oil price inflation set off by the 1973 Middle East war. He was to lose, just, the subsequent general election held in October 1974; and a year later he lost out to Margaret Thatcher as Leader of the Conservative Party.

Heath's short-lived and turbulent administration represented a real break with Britain's 'world role' fixation and hence with the 'special relationship'. To attempt to solve Britain's problems in a European context and to secure the country's future as part of Europe was radical stuff. Ultimately, it was too ambitious. It went against several grains. It challenged the post-imperial 'Atlanticist' foreign policy consensus that placed the USA at its heart – and it did so, in the 1970s, at a time when the Cold War dictated American leadership of Europe. Also, it went right up against a nationalist culture – with its myths of 'independence' and national 'greatness' that were still well embedded.

Heath won the battle over Europe: Britain became a full member of the EEC. But he may well have lost the long-term war. For the bruising nature of the campaign to secure this radical break with British tradition and culture still resonates. Heath and the Europeans were, after all, challenging some basic myths and a deeply felt identity.

Roy Jenkins

Heath could not have secured his pro-European mission without the decisive help from Labour's pro-Europeans. In the key vote in parliament which ratified Britain's accession to the EEC 69 Labour MPs voted against their own leadership on a three-line whip. The vote – historic by any standards – represented a deep schism within the Labour Party – a split that was never truly healed. In one sense this split led directly to the overhaul of the British party system which occurred some eight years later when Labour broke up, the SDP was formed (by the 'gang of four' all of whom were numbered amongst 'the 69') – and the split on the left wounded Labour for 15 years. It was this division that was crucial in allowing the Thatcherite revolution to get under way.

This historic revolt was led by Roy Jenkins, and it remains his great 'moment' in British parliamentary history – arguably much more important than his earlier role as a liberal Home Secretary. Jenkins was a convinced European. He first came to prominence as a young Gaitskellite MP when he went to the rostrum at the Labour Party conference in 1962 and broke with his mentor and hero, Hugh Gaitskell following Gaitskell's anti-Common Market 'Vimy Ridge' speech. After he became Chancellor of the Exchequer in 1967 he became Labour's leading pro-European and during the debates on Europe in the 1970-2 period he formed an unspoken alliance with the new Prime Minister Edward Heath. In 1975 he joined with Heath as the effective co-leader of the 'Yes' campaign in the referendum on the Common Market in June 1975, which was won by a 2 to 1 vote.

The origins of Roy Jenkins's Europeanism were in no way anti-American. Like many Labour right-wingers (particularly Hugh Gaitskell, Tony Crosland, Roy Hattersley and David Owen) he was fascinated by American politics. He wrote a book about Harry Truman and, with Arthur Schlesinger, wrote a book on Franklin Delano Roosevelt, and he also penned short biographies of Joe McCarthy, Adlai Stevenson and Robert Kennedy. But he became convinced – partly due to wishful thinking whilst active in the European cause in the 1960s during the Vietnam imbroglio – that American power was waning, and he wrote an essay poignantly entitled 'Twilight on the Potomac' to make the point.

Jenkins was, unusually for a top rank politician, an historian – a student of contemporary history and a biographer whose subjects, as well as Roosevelt and Truman, ranged from Asquith to Churchill. This historical bent equipped him with a detachment from everyday politics that allowed him to set the country's problems in a wide context. And his cosmopolitan habits, and his contacts and friends abroad, particularly amongst his continental contacts and the Kennedy generation of Democrats in the United States, added to his ability to view his country from outside the narrow perspectives of Westminster.

He was in fact the only major politician (other than Edward Heath) of this crucial generation which came to power in the 1970s that had truly ingested Britain's reduced role in the world, and thus saw clearly the continuing global pretensions of many of its leaders. And he could warm to the depiction of the middle class Britain of his day as being 'smug with not much to be smug about'. It was in large part this recognition that led him so early in the post-war years to embrace the cause of Britain in Europe.

His last signal service to the European cause was to come a few years after the victory of the 'yes' campaign in 1975. Jenkins was appointed by Jim Callaghan to become President of the European Commission in 1976 and found himself out of British politics at a crucial time of change. His own Labour Party was veering wildly to the left and in 1980, after Michael Foot became Leader, it adopted – only five years after the resounding 'yes' vote in the referendum – a policy for outright withdrawal from the Common Market. British politics was becoming highly polarised and the security of British membership of the EEC could not be guaranteed.

It was in this atmosphere that Jenkins, whilst still President of the Commission in Brussels, made his overture to return to British politics by founding a new party. I had been campaigning for such a break with the Labour left for some five years and had always hoped – against hope – that Jenkins would lead such a new breakaway party. I had raised the subject with him in 1975 in Reg Prentice's office when Prentice was Education Secretary, and he had deflected the issue spending most of the time trying to get Reg Prentice to sign up for the coming 'yes' campaign. I was therefore somewhat surprised in 1980 to receive an invitation from Jenkins to come to his London flat in Ladbroke Grove, Notting Hill Gate, for a private chat about it all. He said he could do little actively whilst still President of the European Commission, but that he had made his mind up to confront the Labour left. He agreed that a new party was necessary and he further acknowledged that any big split on the left might well help the Tories; but the stakes were too high. I suspected that although we had talked about the threat from the extreme left in the Labour Party, for him it was all about Europe, always had been about Europe.

It was an extraordinary meeting: and I came away with the real belief that he was going to do it. And he did it! In 1981 the new party was set up. It did not win – although in the 1983 general election it came within two percentage points of beating Labour's total vote tally. Subsequently, it did not even 'break the mould' of two-party dominated politics as Jenkins wanted. But it did succeed in marginalising Labour for a generation and destroying extreme socialism. Britain stayed in NATO, and Britain stayed in Europe – although awkwardly so.

Roy Jenkins was always an unlikely candidate for this kind of divisive and populist political operation – going directly to the electorate to create a new political force. For many years he had appeared as one of nature's Westminster insiders; and he had developed an undeserved reputation for only enjoying the good life – made famous by his supposed love for claret. A Labour MP once quipped that 'the only thing Roy will ever fight for is a good table in a smart restaurant'. But, in forming the SDP, he showed an energy and a resolve that surprised many of his critics. He went outside the system, over the heads of the party establishments, and set up from scratch a new party that had a real impact on the future course of the country. If Heath was the architect and statesman of the European cause, Jenkins was its tribune.

But he was a very strange, out of time, kind of tribune. He certainly had the background for such a role – the son of an influential Welsh trade union official who had gone to prison for his trade union activities. But, under the influence of his mother, he seemed more ashamed than proud of these roots, and, following his time in Oxford, like many of his contemporaries who were also victims of the restrictions and humiliations of the British class system, he completely transformed his personality. By the time he entered Parliament all traces of any Welshness or Celticness he had possessed had gone, and he had so changed his accent and manners that he came across as an English upper class fop. Somewhere along the line he had cultivated a weird Bertie Woosterish accent – he was, seemingly purposely, not able to pronounce his r's. One Labour MP suggested that he spoke in a manner that had not been heard in England since the 1920s.

In many respects this throwback personality, almost as much as his views, made him something of a fish out of water in the left-moving, proletarian-conscious Labour Party of the time; those who opposed him politically, and some who supported him, made fun of this social pretension. Canvassing on behalf of the Labour Party in the early 1970s he had knocked on the door and in his plumby voice had enquired as to whether he could count on their vote. 'No, we're Labour here' had been the reply. In early 1981 I had arranged a transatlantic conference in Milton Hall near Oxford which brought together European and American political and foreign policy people. Jenkins spoke at the conference on his 'twilight on the Potomac' theme and delivered his remarks in his usual way, probably putting on even more affected speech for the American audience. At the end of his speech Ed Feulner, the President of the conservative Heritage Foundation came over to me and said 'so this is your great Roy Jenkins. What a weird man. A bit fey?' His good living, particularly his fondness for wine, was also mocked. *Claret and Chips* was the title of a book about him and the SDP. Yet for the most part he seemed to take this kind of ridicule with good humour.

It was this manner above all that led many on the left to completely misread Roy Jenkins. He was often depicted as an establishment-minded 'Tory toff'. In fact, nothing could be further from the truth. He was in no way a socialist, and was never at home in the Labour Party. But, in essence, he was an old-fashioned British radical who had been influenced in this radicalism by both his quasi-Celtic upbringing and by the quirky liberal radicalism of the Mark Bonham-Carter circle in which he moved as a young politician. He was determinedly anti-Tory all his life. And it was his anti-Toryism that fuelled his life-long campaign for electoral reform which he always argued would, if ever implemented, consign the Conservative Party to the dustbin of history. And his anti-Tory instincts were also at work in fuelling the cause of his life – for he saw Europe as the way of civilising the reactionary nationalism of Tory Britain which he hated.

Yet, like Edward Heath before him, his cause may have prevailed in the short-term, but he was not able to give it a lasting popular rationale. His party (the SDP) and his cause (Europe) was always seen by the wider public as too remote and too elitist. By the 1970s it was quite clear to most British people that Europe was not going to experience any new wars, so the great pro-European theme of his generation was in essence redundant. And ever since, the pro-Europeans in British politics have been struggling manfully to give a reason – a gripping, overwhelming reason – for the British to support the European adventure. By comparison, the status-quo – with the country within the EEC but with its 'special relationship' intact – seemed more acceptable. And particularly so when Britain would no longer be viewed by its own people, as it was in the 1970s, as in long-term decline, the sick man of Europe in need of radical surgery.

1974: Atlanticism Renewed: Callaghan and Crosland

Heath's breach in the Atlanticist wall was not to outlast him. For with his defeat, and the return to office of Harold Wilson in February 1974, the Atlanticists were back in power – and the 'special relationship' was firmly reinstalled.

Of course, completely ditching Atlanticism was never a real option, at least in the 1970s. The imperatives of the Cold War saw to that. Most everyone, including fervent Europeans, believed that any serious breach in Atlantic unity would damage NATO and bring aid and comfort to the common adversary in the Kremlin. So, after Heath's brief interlude Britain's top political leadership fell back into the certainties of the Atlantic relationship and the comforting role of junior partner.

In 1975, Wilson had managed to secure Britain's membership of the EEC by presiding over a referendum in which the British people voted by 2 to 1 to remain within the Common Market. However, although the 'yes' forces carried the day this was in no way a prelude to Britain moving closer to Europe strategically and weakening the 'special relationship'. In fact, exactly the opposite. Wilson's successor in Downing Street, Jim Callaghan, was ideologically more distant from Europe even than Wilson. He was something of a traditionalist – with a reactionary tinge – and his 'Little Englander' instincts resisted too close a relationship with the continent. At the same time, with the Cold War 'hotting up' around the world as the Soviet Union expanded its influence (following the American defeat in Vietnam) the British government felt it needed the 'special relationship' more than ever. And Callaghan was reinforced in this

Atlanticist instinct by his fellow social democrat German Chancellor Helmut Schmidt. The West Germans in the mid 1970s, conscious of being on the Cold war frontline, were pursuing a 'special relationship' of their own with Washington. Schmidt's administration, although a 'good European', was somewhat wary of France on security matters – and sought to persuade Callaghan to continue with the British nuclear system in order that France would not become the only European nuclear power.

Callaghan's instinctive Atlanticism was on display in January 1975 when the British Labour government – in an echo of Ernie Bevin – took a crucial decision to extend the life of the Polaris submarine fleet and the British nuclear bomb. Wilson and Callaghan acted in secret to approve the 'Chevaline project' to update the British nuclear deterrent. 'Chevaline' was a new missile system which had been developed largely in the USA and, again, made Britain highly dependent upon US goodwill. 'Chevaline' became operational on the submarine HMS Renown in 1982. This project was kept secret by Wilson and Callaghan from government, parliament and people, and was only announced to the public some seven years later – by Thatcher's Defence Secretary Francis Pym. In the post-1974 'social contract' between government and trade unions drawn up by Wilson and Callaghan, the union leaders had a say over a wide range of domestic policies, but the government was specifically shielded from trade union involvement over foreign policy and defence.

Callaghan's detachment from Europe was repeated when in 1978 Britain took the decision to stay out of the newly established forerunner of the Euro, the Exchange-Rate system. And his premiership was in one very real sense the death-knell for any further British integration in Europe. He opened the way for Thatcher's 1980s revolution – with all the consequences for Britain's future foreign policy and alignment.

Callaghan was Prime Minister during the International Monetary Fund's visit to Britain in 1976 when the country needed a massive loan to stabilise its currency. The result was that the Labour government was forced to seriously limit the growth in public spending – as Anthony Crosland put it at the time: 'the party's over'. Callaghan himself then began to turn the corner onto a new route. As Prime Minister he publicly embraced monetarism in a famous speech – allegedly delivered under the influence of his son-in-law Peter Jay – to the trade unionists assembled at the Labour Party conference in

1976. In reviewing the historical importance of this speech the economic columnist William Keegan has reported Robert Hormats, a former White House economist, as saying that 'that speech...demonstrated to us that the UK had changed course. Without that speech it would have been difficult to obtain support in the US'.[6]

Even before the votes had been counted in the 1979 election Callaghan was predicting that the country was embarking upon a major change of course. He said 'there are times, perhaps once every thirty years, when there is a sea-change in politics. It does not matter what you say or what you do. There is a shift in what the public wants and what it approves of. I suspect there is now such a sea-change – *and it is for Mrs. Thatcher*'.[7]

Thus did the last representative of the great post-war consensus give way to the neo-liberal revolutionary. And, in foreign policy terms, the Eurosceptic gave way to the Europhobe. After its flirtation with Europe in the 1970s the country was to continue with what Stephen George has termed an 'awkward' relationship with Europe (both Community and Union).

Tony Crosland

The very embodiment of English awkwardness about its role in Europe, and a near-perfect exemplar of Labour's approach to its global role, was the leading social democratic theorist of the post-war years, Tony Crosland. Crosland's 1956 book *The Future of Socialism* became required reading for a whole generation of Labour moderates, and it remains the key post-war text on social democratic theory. Crosland became a member of the first two Wilson administrations, and then a senior Labour figure in the 1970-74 opposition, and when Labour came back to power in 1974 he ended up as Foreign Secretary under Jim Callaghan. He died prematurely aged 58 in February 1977.

As a social democrat Crosland was a natural pro-European. He saw the European mixed economies as attractive and he had many European socialist friends. But he was also something of a 'Little Englander'. His social democracy was always very domestically determined providing domestic solutions for domestic problems. Highly theoretical and analytical, and not at all geo-political, he rarely set politics in its global context. Like so many of his generation he saw Britain as big enough to control its own destiny and to sustain his social democratic vision.

By the time – the early 1970s – that the gnawing issue of Europe began to seriously impinge on Labour politics, Tony Crosland was advancing within the politics of Labour. He saw the European issue as an unwelcome intrusion into his political world, and was quite open and honest about not wanting to put what was by then his seriously rising career at risk by taking sides on the issue. During the early 1970s my friend, the historian David Carlton, and I were regular visitors to his house in Holland Park (I was a Chairman on the Greater London Council and was thinking of hitching myself to his rising star). We became unofficial policy and 'career' advisors. We had admired Crosland as one of the few British intellectuals-cum-politicians (what Americans call a public intellectual); but we wanted him to become less remote and more 'political'. His intellectuality and Plymouth Brethren background had left him with a strong residue of political austerity and fastidiousness. And – particularly as it was becoming apparent that he was a possible future Prime Minister – we wanted him to lighten up and become more 'flexible'.

To our constant surprise he warmed to our promptings. He was obviously starved on straight talk about ambition, and warmed to strategising about how he could become Prime Minister. So Carlton and I would turn up to gossip with him – and sometimes his American wife Susan – over a drink. We would invariably ask for bourbon whiskey and, playing on the name, would drink to the 'bourbon know nothings' who were all around us in the Labour Party.

One upshot of his campaign for the leadership was his vacillations over Europe. He was thought of in the party as one of the committed right-wing pro-European revisionists. But, during the big debates on Common Market entry he made some speeches that placed him more in the centre of the party and he echoed some of the objections to Europe being put forth by the Labour left. On the historic vote when 69 Labour MPs rebelled against their party line he abstained. Crosland was distancing himself from the Jenkins-led Europeanists who would later break from the party.

This move by Crosland was in part also to do with his life-long competition with his contemporary and rival Roy Jenkins. Jenkins – always the more politically sensitive and intellectually flamboyant of the two – had moved ahead of Crosland in the career stakes when Jenkins became Chancellor of the Exchequer under Wilson. But Crosland (and James Callaghan) believed that Roy Jenkins had misread not only British but crucially Labour opinion on the European question and had put himself too far out on a limb; and that he, Crosland, had an opportunity to best his rival and overtake him by a more ambiguous policy.[8]

Crosland continued to row a left-of-centre course which was neutral, almost Eurosceptic, on Europe and he allied himself more and more with Jim Callaghan. In the Leadership contest of 1976 he got 17 votes only on the first ballot and then threw his weight behind Callaghan on the second ballot. Once Prime Minister, Jim Callaghan made him Foreign Secretary. In the party, on the big issue of the IMF loan crisis of 1976, Crosland continued this left-of-centre stance and led the faction in the cabinet that opposed overly-swinging cuts in public expenditure, and he even proposed the semi-protectionist policy of import controls. By this time I was attacking Labour's move to the left, had helped form the party faction the SDA, and worked for a break up of Labour and the formation of a new party. There were no more 'bourbon' sessions with Tony Crosland, who was set on a course that would keep him at the top of the party and en route for Downing Street. We had gone in different directions.

Yet, for all his latter-day careerism, Tony Crosland had, ultimately, stuck to his intellectual guns. Amidst the upheavals of the 1970s he had remained a classic social democrat. On the other hand, Roy Jenkins and his supporters ultimately responded to the crisis with a clear and definite move to the right. Jenkins ultimately formed the SDP. His colleague and fellow cabinet minister, Reg Prentice, actually joined the Conservatives.

Almost from the first day he joined the cabinet in 1974 Reg Prentice wanted to bust up the Callaghan government, and Roy Jenkins was constantly flirting with the idea. Downing Street insiders later told me that every time Wilson or Callaghan would see a picture in the papers of Prentice and Jenkins together they would shudder at the thought that between them they had the votes to bring down the government. Sometimes they would become extremely anxious. On one occasion Harold Wilson lashed out at us from the Labour Party conference platform (in 1974) for 'leaking our smears to an ever ready press'. And on another occasion Tony Crosland, acting as an emissary from the Prime Minister Callaghan, appeared unannounced on David Carlton's doorstep in Great Peter Street – just round the corner from the Foreign Office. Crosland knew that we were advising the Cabinet Minister Reg Prentice who was threatening, with colleagues like MPs Brian Walden and Neville Sandelson, to end Labour's majority. Carlton, determined not to meet him, let the bell ring and pretended not to be home.

Tony Crosland, though, remained convinced that Britain's deep economic crisis of the mid 1970s could be handled in such a way that extremist solutions – whether of the socialist or Thatcherite kind – were not necessary.

Many on the left have naturally speculated about what would have happened if Tony Crosland had lived. What kind of Prime Minister would he have made? And, in 1981, would this archpriest of social democracy have broken with Labour and, like so many of his friends and colleagues help set up the Social Democratic Party (SDP)? Most Labour insiders tend to think that he would have been a truly hopeless political campaigner but, potentially, a great left-of-centre Prime Minister. From the record of his last years, it would seem that he would probably not have joined in the SDP adventure: for the new party would have been too pro-Europe and too anti-trade union for his tastes. In the great split he would most likely have stayed Labour.

The late 1970s though was a time when Labour was on the way out for a whole generation. The social democrats had failed to keep the country on a centrist course. The centre could not hold and power was passing to Thatcher and the Thatcherites.

8. 'Little England' Versus Americanisation (and the Modern World)

'After the detour of empire, the Saxon is now back ploughing his field.'
Tom Nairn on Enoch Powell

When the new Prime Minister Margaret Thatcher stepped into Downing Street on the 4th May 1979 the country was, on the face of it, slowly becoming reconciled to a European future. Britain had entered the Common Market some six years earlier and this historic act had been validated by the 2 to 1 victory in the subsequent referendum. And when the new Conservative Prime Minister took over it seemed that she would continue the European policy inherited from her Tory predecessor. She had excellent pro-European credentials having taken a leading role in the 'yes' campaign in the 1975 referendum.

Yet, even though the public had spoken in 1975, Britain's relationship with its European neighbours was not to run smoothly. The campaign to secure British membership had left much bitterness and resentment, and there was still considerable opposition to life in the Common Market. In Stephen George's well-known phrase Britain remained an 'awkward partner' in Europe.[1]

Also, British entry into the EEC had not led to the country ditching her 'special relationship' with Washington. Seen from London during the years following the referendum, Britain had in no real way settled for a European future. She saw her Common Market membership as enhancing, not diminishing, her global role; and as strengthening, not weakening, her 'special relationship' with Washington. Inside the Common Market Britain was in a stronger position to develop her role as America's 'Trojan horse'; after all, it was Washington that had been pressing Britain to join.

In the 1980s Europe was certainly becoming an economic force in the world (and the country needed to be a part of it), but the US remained the dominant western power. For Britain to attempt anything more in Europe – and muscle in on the Franco-German relationship, or even attempt to align with France – might place the primary alliance in jeopardy, and was not worth the candle.

Cultural Invasion: Americanisation
This dominant 'Atlanticism' in British thinking was not, though, the simple product of a geo-political assessment. It was also the result of the much-proclaimed deep roots of kinship and language – indeed of the old idea of 'cousinhood'. For most Britons, these Anglo-American pieties beloved by the Pilgrims Society and the transatlantic British elites, were, though, rather theoretical. Few ordinary Britons had actually met an American before the GIs arrived in early 1942, and not very many were to get to know Americans after they went home in 1945. And, during wartime Britain, with thousands of British husbands and sons abroad, and rationing at home, tensions between locals and the well-provisioned newcomers were widespread. Yet, at the same time, many Britons saw the 'Yanks' as friends and allies, as generous, and as bringing a breath of fresh air to the country; and around US bases, particularly in East Anglia, relationships were often warm and friendly.

During the war, the military rivalry between British and American forces was a real fact, but the allied victories on D-Day and beyond served to solidify the idea of the US as a staunch, if somewhat overbearing, ally – but an ally nonetheless. It was, though, in the early post-war decades that British attitudes towards the US began to cohere. There was something of a difference based upon class. Amongst the 'middle classes' there was a decided jealousy of the US based upon resentment at the upstart power which had overtaken Britain as a world leader and – a view held amongst Tories – had actually subverted the empire.

But this resentment was a minority sport, more than balanced out by popular views of America induced by the massive post-war Americanisation of the country. During the 1950s and 1960s Britain underwent what amounted to a cultural revolution. The old world of class, of deference to one's betters, of snobbery and exclusiveness, was slowly being replaced by a new world which was more open, democratic and egalitarian – and American. This cultural makeover had started in a serious way back the 1940s when large numbers of American troops, and then, later through the Marshall Plan, large amounts of American money, flowed into Britain. And in the heyday of post-war affluence and optimism (the 1950s and 1960s) the American challenge turned into a great cultural contest – a battle in which the ideal of 'Englishness' (essentially built around the traditional image of 'country life' and 'the gentleman') had to compete with American culture and 'the American Dream' (of prosperous property-owning families inhabiting a mass consumer society) in its own backyard – for the minds and loyalty of the British.

American movies, television, mass catering, clothes, even many aspects of American music, literature and art, engaged provincial class-based 'Englishness' in fierce competition, and 'the American Dream' won. Hands down. It was hardly surprising. 'The American Dream' had some powerful advantages over an England still recovering from wartime restrictions and still suffused by an outdated class system. American culture was democratic. It was not exclusive: it said to anyone who would listen and aspire that they too could participate, that 'you too' can be like this. By contrast 'the English ideal' remained purposely elusive, a life (a male life!), which certainly allowed itself to be admired, but was available only to a few. It reduced the broader population to onlookers.

In Britain, the increasingly odd – by world standards – idea of royalty set the ultimate social standard, and could not, ever, and by definition, be emulated. Whereas 'the American Dream' of 'rags to riches' upward-mobility had universal appeal and provided an accessible and attractive ideal of suburban life, the ideal of 'the English gentleman' or of English royalty was far less accessible and

115

far more provincial. And this 'American Dream' also had the financial and technical power of the US economy and the propaganda arm of Americana, Hollywood, behind it. And as new information technologies took advantage of the new post-war mass market, mass-circulation newspapers, paperbacks, magazines, movies and, finally, television, brought this 'alternative' American culture to millions.

This American influence on British 1960s popular culture was so pervasive that Stephen Amidon has suggested that in the 1950s and 1960s 'Great Britain' became so Americanised that it 'became a 51st state of mind', without, he argued fancifully, 'ceding her national identity'. The late Arthur Marwick, in his influential work on contemporary Britain, *Culture in Britain since 1945*, also outlined the power of American culture in Britain during these times, and argued that it was part of a broader, including indigenous, popular cultural change.[2]

In the 1950s and 1960s the arrival of popular music amounted to a social revolution. On one level it was a revolution in public taste; but on another it was a revolution in sociology, as the previously dormant social category of 'the teenager' was discovered, and a mass market for this new social group was created. Both the United States and Britain (primarily in New York and London) became world centres for this new, highly commercial popular art form. Yet, at the same time, much British popular music was essentially a derivative of a slightly earlier American experience. Arthur Marwick argues that British popular music's origins 'lay solidly in America, with black rhythm and blues, transmitted to Britain by the white imitators and adaptors, principally Bill Haley and Elvis Presley'.

The list of British popular musicians who owe much of their inspiration to American artists is impressive. Marwick suggests that the American artists Little Richard and Chuck Berry gave birth to the British artists the Rolling Stones, while 'the great Chicago bluesmen' – and other blues singers – were the inspiration for Eric Burden in Newcastle and for the very popular British singer Eric Clapton. He sees the British bandleader Ted Heath as but a (poor) response to the American swing bands, and Vera Lynn – the 'wartime forces sweetheart' – and the crooner Donald Pears as essentially imitative of the American crooners and ballad singers Bing Crosby, Guy Mitchell and Doris Day. Also, Keith Richard in London, it is argued, modelled himself on the guitar-playing of such rock 'n' roll stars as Chuck Berry.[3] Charlie Gillett has suggested that Britain's most successful popular music group, The Beatles, were 'derivative of two American styles which had not previously been put together', the hard rock 'n' roll style like the singers Little Richard and Larry Williams, and the soft gospel call-and-response style of the Shirelles and the Drifters.[4] And, apart from any direct American influence on British popular music taste in the post-war years, the propensity of generations of British pop singers to adopt American accents in their performances is another tribute to the power of American popular music.

Post-war American literature was also extremely influential, both as an inspiration for many British writers and directly with the public. American novelists, most notably Saul Bellow and John Updike, have inspired a generation of British writers. In popular literature, and the seemingly English preserve of detective stories, the American Hank Jansen catered to a huge British audience, and even Peter Cheyney 'who was English to the core...' had his characters speak the weirdest kind of pidgin American.[5] And in the theatre the great post-war British genre of the 'angry young man' lent heavily on some of the works of Arthur Miller and Tennessee Williams.

In painting, a host of American Abstract Expressionists and 'pop artists' have inspired a whole generation of British painters, most notably David Hockney, who left Britain to live in the United States. And American influence upon the built environment was also pronounced. Many of Britain's most prominent architects spent considerable time in the United States, where they were influenced by modernism and 'high tech' architecture.

Yet it was in the world of film – the movies – where American culture scored its greatest success with the British public. Cowboy films (heroes like John Wayne, Randolph Scott, Gary Cooper and later Clint Eastwood) provided a new frontier for the imagination of Britons. American detective characters, like Philip Marlow (created by Raymond Chandler) or Perry Mason, and even some of the early gangster movies, possessed for the post-war British a certain romantic charm. American musicals (such as *Annie Get your Gun*, *Oklahoma* or *West Side Story*) were huge box office hits.

The Hollywood star system provided role models for British youth and for many British women the female roles in American movies – many of them strong and assertive – proved attractive and, to some extent, subversive of the lowly role assigned to women by the 'gentlemanly' ideology of Englishness. It also provided role models for some of the best British actors. In the land where the profession of Shakespearian actor still held sway, 'Albert Finney's hard man monologues in 1960s *Saturday Night and Sunday Morning* have a lot more to do with Brando and the "Method" than they do Lawrence Olivier and the Royal Shakespeare Company'.[6]

Intriguingly, British movies produced no real heroes or role models from amongst the 'blue-collar' working class majority. In the post-war British movie industry Britain's largest social group were assigned the roles of 'chirpy cockneys' or the role of joker, loyal deferential (who blurted out 'gor bless ya guvnor' as he went over the top in the First World War trenches), or bitter young talents who turned into 'angry young men' as they railed at the establishment and the system. Nor were British women assigned particularly strong roles in the new mass medium of film – a reflection of the dominance of male life in the national culture. It was not surprising that 'the world of Ealing and Norman Wisdom was swept away when a new generation of film makers such as Tony Richardson and Karel Reisz, weaned on American directors such as Sidney Lumet and Elia Kazan, came to the fore'.[7]

With this huge cultural invasion it is little wonder that an Americanisation of the English language used in Britain took place. American English increasingly interpenetrated English English and British English. Greetings such as 'Hi', words such as 'hike', 'wise', 'sure', 'guy' entered British English. An Englishman, Captain Marryat, travelling in the US in 1838, singled out a number of American English words with meanings strange to the British English ear. Few of them are unfamiliar any longer. Amongst them were: 'reckon', 'calculate', 'guess' (colloquial synonyms for 'think' or 'believe'); 'clever' (for 'good natured'); 'smart' (for 'clever'); 'fix' (for 'repair'); 'mean' (for 'ashamed'); 'great' (for 'fine' or 'splendid'); 'stipulated' and so forth. Other American words or phrases now in common use in British English are: from the wild west – 'poker', 'saloon'; from the Gold Rush 'bonanza' – 'pan out', 'strike', 'hustler'; from the railroad era – 'in the clear', 'make the grade', 'right of way', 'off the rails'; from Mark Twain – 'take it easy', 'get over', 'a close call', 'giltedged'; from German Americans – 'check', 'delicatessen', 'ecology', 'fresh' (meaning impertinent), 'hoodlum', 'kindergarten', 'yes man', 'no way', 'will do', 'let it be'; and from American Jewish – 'enjoy' and 'I should worry'.

The twentieth century wars created some common words between the Americans and the English: such as 'barrage', 'camouflage', 'going over the top', 'digging in' and the like.[8] With the arrival of mass television (a process largely complete in Britain by the mid 1960s), American influences upon the culture of the post-war British became ever more potent. Also, North American ownership of the mass culture industry helped propagate American cultural forms and attitudes.

In one sense this American influence on the culture of Britain in the 1950s, 60s and 70s could not properly be called 'Americanisation'. 'Modernisation' might be nearer the mark. For 'modernisation' – a term describing the growth of cultural social and political democracy and the spread of consumerism – may well have been taken forward in the USA but was, in fact, a product of broader western industrialism and liberalism, much of which had gravitated to North America from Europe (particularly Britain).

The seeds of 'modernisation' were, thus, European in origin. And this would help to explain why in the 1950s and 1960s those western societies most self-conscious about their national identity and most resistant to 'Americanisation' nonetheless ingested large doses of Americana. In truth, British Conservatives who railed against American influences were in fact raging against their own history of liberalism. And in 1960s France, the centre of anti-Americanisation sentiment, many of the malign cultural aspects that chauvinist Frenchmen thought they had adopted from the New World were, in reality, indigenous to France. French accusations of materialism, social conformity and status seeking were always a caricature of America, and as French cultural analyst Robert Kuisel has written 'these faults were as inherently French as they were native to America'.[9]

Enoch Powell: 'Little England' Throwback
In Britain during the 1960s and early 70s resistance to modernity was not, though, primarily about resisting Americanism. Rather, it was about a reaction against the end of empire and the loss of British sovereign independent power. During the Macmillan-Wilson years, whilst Britain's leaders were, with varying degrees of success, adjusting to the new realities of the country's place in the world, a stark, romantic, and sometimes frightening voice was stalking the British political scene. John Enoch Powell made his entry into British

politics in opposition to Edward Heath's immigration policies when in April 1968 Edward Heath sacked him from the shadow cabinet for the 'racist' tone of a speech in Birmingham. Talking of the growth in immigrant communities he forecast growing violence. 'Like the Roman' he said 'I seem to see the River Tiber foaming with much blood'. For a while Powell became the most popular politician in Britain and, although not himself a racist, he certainly played 'the race card' in a series of speeches in the late 1960s.

His primary, overwhelming, belief, though, was in British independence and he became a vociferous opponent of Heath's pro-European policy and one of the leaders of the anti-Common Market campaign leading up to the referendum of 1975.

Powell was a classic nationalist. He operated from a belief in the continued reality of British 'sovereignty' and independence – and the threat which both Europe and the United States posed to it. He saw the legal sovereignty question as fundamental; during the 1975 EEC referendum debates he based much of his campaigning on the 'supremacy clause' of the EEC – the clause which made European law supreme over British law, should they clash. He saw Britain, as in the days of empire, acting as an independent power, and as a broker able to manoeuvre between America, Russia and the continental countries. He saw British membership of NATO as constraining British independence. He was, in fact, bizarrely but logically, a supporter of an alliance with Soviet Russia. He once told me, during a lunch organised in the spring of 1976 by a mutual friend, the Tory historian and journalist Michael Harrington, that 'Russia', as he insisted on calling the Soviet Union, was no threat to Britain. Over chops and his favourite brandy snaps in Stone's Chop House in Soho, he lent forward to say that he shared this view of Russia with 'those lefties in your party'. And with a broad smile declared 'So I'm a fifth columnist too'.

Intriguingly for a British nationalist of the time, Powell, unlike many of his fellow Tories, had broken mentally with empire. He had certainly been a romantic imperialist as a young man. But by the 1960s, unlike many on the right, he had ingested the news that the empire was over. And he saw the 'British Commonwealth' as essentially a fraud, without real meaning. At a meeting of The Radical Society in 1987 he argued to a hushed audience that the key to understanding the 'false idea' of the Commonwealth could be traced all the way back to the 'shock and terror' of the British ruling classes at the time of the American war of independence when they had to face the 'loss' of the American colonies. So devastating was this loss that they had never truly come to terms with it. And over time, as other losses added to the trauma, they created 'the fiction' of the 'British Commonwealth' and 'the dominions' in order to keep a psychological link to the imperial past.[10]

As well as being a nationalist, Powell was an early advocate of the neo-liberal free market that was to form the core idea of Thatcherism. He had resigned on the question of public spending and was a huge influence on Keith Joseph and Margaret Thatcher as, in the early 1970s they began to challenge the Keynesian orthodoxy of their party. Powell was enough of an intellectual to appreciate that the universalism of market ideology ultimately clashed with national sovereignty. He had to choose. And he did, famously, arguing that he was a British nationalist first.[11]

Powell was a throwback to an earlier age. He was a romantic Tory in the age of the modernisers. The 'British nation' was the mega and omega of his existence, and pursuing 'British interests' was his cause. With his bowler hat, formal pin-stripe and moustache there was something of the 'last Englishman' about him. He was not romantic about empire, although he had once been so; but he recognised it was now over. He believed, though, that in this new post-imperial world Britain could still retain its independence. There was simply no need to fall under the sway of either Europe or America. In the coming world, Britain, no matter its status as a medium-sized power, could make it on its own. Powell was, in effect, an early 'Little Englander'.

The Idea of 'Little England'

The term 'Little England' first came into use in 1963 when John Mander's book *Great Britain or Little England* was published.[12] 'Little Englander' perfectly caught the idea of a very definite type of Englishman of the time. In the 1960s and 1970s they were seemingly everywhere. In essence, they disliked change and foreign influences. There was little that was unpleasant, brutal or even particularly ideological about them – they were, though, decidedly narrow in outlook. And they were worried about how the modern world was diluting the idea they carried in their minds about what it meant to be English – about 'Englishness'.

In the late 1950s and 1960s, the comedian Tony Hancock played aspects of the 'Little Englander' part well, as, somewhat later, did some of Peter Cook's and Dudley Moor's comic characters. The best exemplar in the political world of 'Little Englandism' was the unlikely figure of Douglas Jay. A serious-minded socialist intellectual, Jay rose to become President of the Board of Trade in the Wilson government of 1964-6 and then, later, to become one of the country's leading parliamentary opponents of Britain's entry into the Common Market. Jay may well have been progressive on questions of social policy and taxation, but, like others on the left at the time, was at heart a nationalist, indeed a chauvinist. He simply did not adjust to the creeping cosmopolitanism of the 1960s. He once confessed to me – somewhat, but not wholly, disingenuously – that 'I don't like foreign food'. There was nothing virulent in his thinking but it was obvious that he simply did not much like foreigners.

He saw English history in very traditional terms as a unique history of liberty. 'Socialists believe in Liberty, political and personal, as firmly as they believe in Equality' he once argued.[13] This view of England as a great and exceptional story of the advance of freedom and democracy – based upon Magna Carta, the Levellers, Britain's parliamentary tradition and the like – has been very powerful on the British non-Marxist left, and Michael Foot was its major advocate. It was, though, an idea that often subtly underpinned much antipathy to the Common Market and to Europe more generally. For the continental political experience was often deemed as deficient in democracy and the structures of European integration – particularly the Commission – were seen to represent this deficiency.

For many English, even as the twentieth century drew to its close, a traditional idea of Englishness, although weakening, was still alive and well. Indeed, national self-consciousness had arguably somewhat intensified with post-1940s political and economic decline. With every passing post-war decade, almost as a feature of decline, the English appeared increasingly interested in themselves, in what Englishness meant in the modern world, in the search for the essence and deeper meaning of their nationality.

There was also a relatively clear view of what Englishness amounted to. In a recent, typical, self-conscious depiction, one writer suggested that 'a group of dinner guests in their thirties' would describe Englishness as: 'A bowl of scented roses on a sunlit table and the muted thwack of leather against willow. Umbrellas clashing on city streets and felt trilbies brim to brim at the races. A cup of tea, or a pre-prandial glass of sherry. The first cuckoo of spring and the first Pimms of summer. Kipling and Just William. Royal Doulton figurines and talking about the weather'.[14]

In a somewhat similar vision of the meaning of Englishness, the 1990s saw the country's Prime Minister – John Major – evoking a nostalgic theme of nationality by quoting approvingly George Orwell at his most sentimental: '...the clatter of clogs in the Lancashire mill towns...the old maids biking to Holy Communion through the mists of the autumn morning...'; and it saw too a leading advertising agency – with a 'voice-over' quoting from Shakespeare's 'sceptred isle' soliloquy – establishing for millions the images of cottage and countryside (set against 'less fortunate lands' with the channel 'defensive as a moat') for a television advertisement for tea.[15]

This Englishness exists for export. It is the 'English product' which is sold around the world, particularly so in North America, but also is aggressively marketed – mainly to upper income groups and to the international super rich – in continental Europe and amongst the third world elite, particularly in the Arab countries and East Asia. Increasingly it is becoming a key ingredient in the broader English heritage industry, which as part of the leisure and tourist industry can be expected to grow in a country increasingly relying upon the service sector. The Conservative Party under John Major recognised its importance when soon after Margaret Thatcher left Downing Street it established a 'Heritage Minister' with cabinet rank.

This 'English' product is primarily about life-style. Englishness is sold as a way of life. One of its flagship publications is *Country Life* (which publishes every week of the year, and can be acquired as an annual subscription in the United States for around $200). *Country Life* tells its audience how to acquire Englishness (at a price of course). And it suggests that the heart of the matter of Englishness is the grand house or country cottage, and the related furnishings (advertisements for which take up almost half of the magazine), the English garden and the English dog, all of which appear in a rural setting. *Country Life* presents 'A Week in the Country' by the Duchess of Devonshire and has even developed a series entitled 'Hero of the Countryside'.[16]

Country Life also presents a highly self-conscious 'how to do it' kind of Englishness. In an article entitled 'How a Gentleman should Dress' the Duke of Devonshire advises the wanabees – 'At Cambridge I wore flannels and tweed. Cavalry twill was just coming in and it was rather laughed at as the Jodhpur in June brigade'.[17] And an 'English look' is presented for parading at the races, Ascot, the Badminton Horse trials, the Royal Windsor Horse Show, Henley, and of course, polo- at 'the events which make up our summer season'.[18]

In promoting this 'English look' diversity is not encouraged – for instance, the men all tend to look like Charles Windsor in corduroys and tweeds, 'dressed in the best British country style' as *Country Life* put it.[19] Similar advice is offered over a range of pursuits from sports cars (normally referred to as 'motors' or 'motoring') to the proper way to picnic – Roy Strong offers in 'A Question of Taste' advice on the traditional English picnic 'before the corporate clients promoted conspicuous wealth'.[20]

This 'stage Englishness' has been so successful that it has caused imitation: the inventing of an 'English' personality. An extreme, and somewhat sad, contemporary example is the amazing career of Stanley Olson. In 1969, at the age of twenty-two, Olson, a Jewish-American from Akron, Ohio left America and set about 'rectifying nature's error: he would create himself anew – live as if born without parents, siblings, family history and religion, Midwest education and cultural trappings'. He moved to London and transformed himself – thoroughly, wholeheartedly, impeccably – into an Englishman.[21] He adopted the accent, the clothes, the mannerisms, indeed the persona of an English gentle-man until, according to his biographer, 'Englishness fit him like a glove'.[22] In his twenty years in London – he died of a stroke at the early age of thirty-nine – he lived the manufactured life of an 'English Gentleman', an aesthete, a man of letters, a social lion with a circle (including, appropriately, the Duke of Devonshire) which he entertained, often lavishly, on the Akron-based Olson family fortune.

Olson's story is not so odd. It is the story of large numbers of Britons too. It is the journey taken by umpteen intelligent and aspiring working class, lower middle class and bourgeois young men from Britain's provincial towns and cities. Faced with so stark a chasm between mainstream British life and the life of an 'English gentlemen', some have engaged in just as brutal a switch of identity as did Stanley Olson. Others have adopted the manners, lifestyle and ideology of Englishness more naturally and less abruptly. Even so, the journey from Akron to Englishness is hardly any further than the journey from Bristol or Birmingham or Manchester.

In any promotion of Englishness, of the 'English product', the upstairs-downstairs image needs to be catered to. Upstairs is covered by lashings of royalty – royal tittle tattle primarily. And downstairs also makes regular appearances, though normally bathed in ladles of condescension and bordering on the kitsch. Identikit servants and 'loyal working folk' appear in the pages – under the title of 'Living National Treasure' a hayrake maker, a basket maker, a gypsy caravan restorer and, inevitably, a housekeeper have been profiled.[23]

Of all the icons of theme-park heritage Englishness the most exalted must still be the game of cricket, particularly village cricket. No aspect of Englishness induces such sentimentality as the 'leather on willow' images: 'When the late squire of Crowcombe, Major Thomas Trollope Bellew, was buried last year, he was escorted to his grave not only by uniformed hunt servants, but also by his cricket team in their whites. The image of village cricket is enduring and endearing: it has its stock characters, its folklore, its champions, its literature and its idyllic settings – the green, with the church behind, and the pub somewhere handy.'[24]

This kind of rhapsodising is, of course, not really about the game of cricket. Those who play the game, and take it somewhat seriously, are often oblivious to its mystical cult status – for many of them it remains a game like any other, though more intelligent and competitive. Rather, the game – and its 'Englishness' – has in reality become a metaphor for the celebration of the English village and rural nostalgia. It has other attributes which make it attractive as an icon of nostalgic Englishness. Of course, it was invented in England, and is largely played by Englishmen and those considered 'honorary Englishmen', from the ex-colonial lands, thus restricting it to the old imperial family (continental Europeans and Americans do not play the game).

It also, particularly in the three, four or five day game, and to a lesser extent at league or club level on Saturday and Sunday afternoons, exhibits and encourages a range of supposedly 'sturdy'

'English' qualities: perseverance, patience, team spirit (although in truth cricket, unlike football, is not much of a team game, involving at its heart a contest between bowler and batsman only) and, of course, 'fair play'. It is a measure of the extraordinary success of cricket as an English ritual and totem of national character that, more so than the real national game (in terms of popular support football would qualify for this prize), so much of the terminology of the game has entered into the mainstream of every-day usage in the language of contemporary British English. 'Sticky Wicket', 'end of play', 'stumped me', 'hit for six', 'straight bat', 'had a good innings' and the like are 'very English' phrases.

This contemporary theme-park Englishness also embraces a notion of English national character. According to the standard self-image promoted during the twentieth century the essence, the 'quintessentialness', of the Englishman and woman involved very prosaic qualities. The stereotype had it that English people were essentially practical and not overly-bright (certainly not, in the national phrase which mocks intellectualism, 'too clever by half'). Yet, at the same time, they were loyal and trustworthy ('sturdy' again suffices to describe the attribute). By contrast, foreigners (and 'foreigness'), particularly continental Europeans, are altogether more exotic: they were theoretical and – particularly southern Europeans – emotional, given to grand gestures and ideas, qualities which can easily make for instability.

Paul Addison has argued that it was Britain's role during the Second World War that induced this particular self-image of national character. He argues that 'on all sides publicists proclaimed that the key to victory lay in the native genius of a people who were sturdy, industrious and unimaginative – not very clever in fact – but moved by an inner spirit that expressed itself in such things as patriotism, a love of the countryside and a love of liberty'. He suggests that so powerful is this stereotype in the films and literature of the post-war period – the product not simply of Dunkirk, the Blitz and the subsequent mass media legends, but also deriving from the English elite's reaction to French revolution and Napoleon – that 'it remains there to this day, a massive chunk of patriotic legend that still defies the best efforts of historians to break it up'.[25]

This notion – that the essence of Englishness combines ordinariness with a 'sturdy' love of liberty (and a concomitant need for privacy) was extolled by two wartime English writers, J.B. Priestley and George Orwell, whose influence on the contemporary image of Englishness was profound. Priestley, both a novelist and playwright, helped make his name by evoking Dunkirk as an obvious example of this English characteristic of sturdy independence. And the essayist and novelist George Orwell virtually exalted the concern for privacy and freedom (particularly from 'bossy' bureaucrats) as a unique attribute of Englishness.

Intriguingly, both Priestley and Orwell, who cornered the market in describing and evoking the life of England in the wartime and early post-war years, are themselves often both depicted as being 'very English'. One writer suggested that J.B. Priestley was so English that he still nestles 'in the nursery wing of the Anglo-Saxon mind'. And George Orwell was described by one of his leading biographers as being 'a specifically English writer and a specifically English character, both in his seeming amateurism...and in his eccentricities...' (a depiction which begs the question as to whether 'a specifically English' writer can possibly be both professional and normal!).[26]

To some extent this may be because Orwell and Priestly added to this contemporary idea of Englishness a certain glorification of English insularity and provincialism – an aspect, too, it is argued, of the works of the less political, though 'most English of writers', Alan Bennett.[27] They were the founders of 'Little England'. For them, England's reduced circumstances were no bad thing. No lovers of empire and the aggrandising imperial mission, they domesticated the idea of Englishness. The true English spirit, they argued, was to be found at home, was provincial and practical – not outward looking, cosmopolitan and full of grand visions.

The domesticity of Priestley's and Orwell's Little Englandism was in part a reaction against the terrors of the grand designs of fascism and communism (and, to some extent, those of American Capitalism too, for both Priestley and Orwell were moderate socialists). Thus, the sheer cosiness of English life, instead of provoking a reaction against its limiting, unimaginative and unproductive qualities, was built into a virtue. And in the process one of the most revered values of Englishness became familiarity. Although current theme-park English images such as 'the muted thwack of leather on willow' or 'the first cuckoo of spring' may have been a little over-ripe for Orwell and Priestley – and also too middle class: for they were both determined to depict Englishness as a phenomenon existing beyond the home counties – they, nonetheless, both prized the familiar. In his famous essay, *The Lion and the Unicorn*, George Orwell was at his sentimentalising best when describing familiar English scenes. 'English civilisation' he argued 'is somehow bound up with solid breakfasts and gloomy Sundays, smoky towns and winding roads, green fields and red pillar-boxes...However much you hate it or laugh at it, you will never be happy away from it for any length of time. The suet puddings and the red pillar-boxes have entered into your soul'.[28]

Little Englanders saw the country not only as cosy, but also as stable, indeed uniquely so. This idea of England as a peaceable island in a troubled world, and of Englishness as a stable pillar of cultural security, has carried itself forward from Orwell and Priestley into the contemporary debate about England's role in Europe. Almost fifty years after the end of the Second World War one of England's, and Englishness's, leading polemicists, the prolific Eurosceptic Paul Johnson, still sees Britain as uniquely stable and continental life as somehow threatening this stability – indeed as rendolent with images from the Second World War, of 'conflagrations' and of Hitler's panzers hurtling with a 'speed and intensity' through France. In a commentary, one which is not unrepresentative of much contemporary English opinion, he argues unexceptionally that 'there is a feeling throughout Europe that democracy is not working and that the gap between what people want and what they are allowed by their rulers is too wide'. But then, in an extraordinary passage he goes on 'that means trouble, and exactly how and where it starts is less important than the speed and intensity with which it will spread. A European conflagration will bring the Channel (as opposed to the Chunnel) back into fashion...as the continent slithers into anarchy – or worse – and we watch the exciting drama from our grandstand seats on the White Cliffs...'.[29]

So powerful is this Little England image of Englishness (stable, cosy, twee) that it has increasingly assumed the proportions of an 'official' idea of Englishness. In the latter part of the twentieth century this theme-park Englishness (with its stage Englishmen and women) has become so dominant that it has forced aside other, more realistic images of Englishness. It remains a mental straightjacket which imposes itself upon the diversity and plurality of the real life of the country and its peoples. And it is, of course, as illusory as any of the other stage nationalisms (Irish, French, German) the English still laugh at.

As with any 'official' culture or ideology Englishness presents us with problems of conformity. Inevitably, there remains a tendency to dismiss as un-English those things which do not meet the standard, approved style or product – even though they may represent the life and culture of millions of people living in the real England. For instance, Priestley himself once observed that the society emerging in England in the mid 1930s – 'clean, bright...factories, palatial cinemas...crowds as rootless as the car which symbolised the age... *wasn't really England at all'*.[30]

This 1960s and 70s Little England idea of national identity formed the basis for a developing anti-Common Market sentiment. And the heart of this anti-European appeal was the powerful idea that English identity needed to be preserved and protected from the threat posed to it by a uniting continent.

Yet, one of the great ironies of the time was that the verities and comforts of Little England, far from being eroded by Brussels, were being undermined from a wholly different direction, from American-led modernisation. This Americanisation however was amorphous unspecific and undefined and involved no obvious institutional or constitutional change. The influence of Brussels on the other hand, though far less pervasive had legal reach into Britain and to the little Englanders this made it a threat to 'sovereignty'.

In consequence it was the European juggernaut in Brussels, and not the American cultural empire, that was to become the target of the new Eurosceptic Conservatives who, in the 1980s and 1990s were to dominate the politics of Britain.

9. Thatcher's American Revolution

'I always feel ten years younger – despite the jet-lag – when I set foot on American soil.'
Margaret Thatcher, 2002

'There are times, perhaps once every thirty years, when there is a sea-change in politics. It does not matter what you say or what you do. There is a shift in what the public wants and what it approves of. I suspect there is now such a sea-change – *and it is for Mrs. Thatcher.*'[1] Thus said the outgoing Prime Minister, the last representative of the old, social democratic 'declinist' order, only hours before the end of the 1979 general election.

Jim Callaghan was an Atlanticist. And on the face of it so too was the new Prime Minister. Yet, Margaret Thatcher was to become much, much, more. In fact, in all but name and manners – and formal nationality – she was to become an American. The incoming Prime Minister gave little appearance of being such a revolutionary. Brought up as a provincial middle class Englishwoman she seemed a typical southern English small town rural-cum-suburban lady. Yet, like so many bright and ambitious young grammar school children of the time she had to adapt to the class bound and 'county' world of the late 40s and 50s in order to succeed. She took the subtle personality-changing first step of taking elocution lessons – and would thereafter sound and appear the almost perfect 'twin set and pearls' English county tweedy Tory. She was, in fact though, very different. And her deeper identity was to come out later.

By the standards of the time the young, aspiring Margaret Thatcher was a fish out of water in the Tory Party. A meritocrat in a party that valued inheritance, a suburbanite in a party still highly influenced by big landed interests, a developing ideologue in a party suspicious of systematic thought, and a woman of strong opinions and principles – who loved a good fiery argument – in a man's club. In fact, there was very little of the Tory traditionalist in her at all. Yet during the 1950s she was to make her way in the party – in the 1951 and 1955 elections she fought the safe Labour seat of Dartford in Kent.

By the time she entered Downing Street, however, it was becoming clear that she was attracted neither to the governing ethos of her own party, nor certainly to the socialist alternative (no matter how meritocratic). Margaret Thatcher had more in common with the values and attitudes of a different country altogether – and that country was America.

Many East Anglians of Thatcher's generation have always had a soft spot for Americans – based upon their formative years in wartime Britain when American soldiers and airmen came into contact with the locals. They liked their directness, their enthusiasm and their optimism about the possibilities of life. Margaret Thatcher herself once wrote that there is 'something positive, generous and open about the people' and that 'I always feel ten years younger – despite the jet lag – when I set foot on American soil'. In any event this American way was, for her, a deal better than what she often saw as the elliptical over-sophistication, hypocrisy and, above all, appeasing, instincts of the Tory governing class.

She had a sense of, as she put it, 'belonging to America'. And, as Prime Minister in the 1980s, she saw herself as struggling, often against the odds, to bring American-style capitalism to Britain. And in the process, she increasingly indentified with America.[2]

A great part of her attraction to the United States arose from the great ideological struggle of the Cold War. Thatcher believed deeply in the reality of the struggle, and of the threat from Soviet power.

In the 1970s *détente* was at its height and there was a sense the west was losing the east-west struggle as Soviet influence was seen to grow around the world, particularly in Latin America and Africa. Thatcher saw America, the leader of the west, as the only bastion against communism. She saw the republic as 'the last best hope'.

In Britain, decline was in the air. The Heath government had, in effect, been defeated by the Miners' Union when it failed to get a majority following its 'who governs Britain?' appeal in the February 1974 general election. And the subsequent Wilson government's 'social contract' was widely seen as a further surrender – both to the miners and to the wider trade union movement. It was a period rife with talk of 'ungovernability' and 'extremism'.

It was during this period, in late 1975, that I first met Margaret Thatcher. I was a Labour member elected to the GLC and Chair of a pressure group called Social Democratic Alliance and she was Leader of the Opposition. She had heard of my outspokenness about the Labour extreme left. Through a mutual acquaintance, her assistant Richard Ryder, later to become Tory Chief Whip, I was invited to her home in Flood Street for a chat. Two things now stand out from that get-together. Something had obviously happened in of all parties, the Tory Party, for I was met by a cultural role reversal. Her husband Denis greeted me, but the husband then remained in the kitchen as the wife, her assistant and I went upstairs to her living room for a chat. Secondly, and very unusually for top Tories of that era, this Tory leader was an enthusiast, almost a crusader – a bubbly woman who was also highly intellectual – in the sense that she was interested in ideas and abstractions. She was dogmatic in her beliefs but also loved argument. What, though, shone through was an Englishwoman who, the moment she talked politics, transmogrified into a replica of an American suburban conservative – without, that is, the religion. She exhibited the kind of political fierceness and commitment – and a disdain for liberals, socialists and communists, which she saw as melding into each other – that I was later also to witness in Reagan's Washington amongst right-wing Republican activists.

She saw 'free markets' as bringing freedom and democracy in their wake, and capitalism as unleashing merit and enterprise around the world. In an echo of American right-wing rhetoric of the time she fervently believed that America had saved the world before (on D-Day) and would do so again; and that the Europeans, particularly the

French, were 'weak sisters', riddled with socialist thinking and bureaucracy. Sometime after she left the premiership Thatcher revealed just how much she actually believed in this right-wing American view of the world. 'In my lifetime' she reflected 'all our problems have come from mainland Europe and all the solutions have come from the English-speaking nations of the world'.[3]

Not surprisingly, Thatcher was to go on to become the most thoroughly pro-American Prime Minister of the post-war era. Her relationship with Ronald Reagan simply solidified her love affair with America. His straight, no-nonsense, folksy approach appealed to her. However, even she was to have a 'Greece to Rome' moment when she reportedly remarked privately about the President: 'poor dear, there's nothing between the ears'.[4] Even so, she came to see that Reagan's simple, straightforward approach was basically hers too, and she soon realised that the 'great communicator's' clear, uncomplicated political messages were necessary for the prosecution of their joint cause.

Above all, though, it was their convergence on western strategy and policy that made the match. Abandoning *détente* was the key unifying point. As Leader of the Opposition Thatcher had developed an anti-*détente* approach that set her aside from governing opinion in the west. She sought a stronger attitude towards the Kremlin; an increase in defence expenditure; and achieved considerable global publicity for her anti-Soviet views when, whilst still opposition leader, the Kremlin dubbed her 'the iron lady'. When she became Prime Minister in 1979 there was a sense that the western guard might be changing, and the American conservatives, mainly gathered around the governor of California, Ronald Reagan, began to court her. The Soviet invasion of Afghanistan in December 1979, some few months after Thatcher had become Prime Minister, brought *détente* to an end and her approach to the fore.

Ronald Reagan became President in January 1980 and his national security team – including Richard Allen and Bill Casey – visited Britain just before his inauguration. As part of their trip Ed Feulner, the President of Reagan's favourite Washington think tank, asked me to arrange a private lunch for them at Brown's Hotel in London to introduce them to a variety of British opinion-formers – and these included Jimmy Goldsmith, television journalists Alistair Burnett and Michael Charlton, and some Tory MPs. It soon became clear that, even before they had taken over in Washington, Reagan's officials were treating Margaret Thatcher very seriously. They were highly conscious that a new phase of the Cold War was dawning, and that the two new leaders could make a real difference.

And, as it turned out, the Reagan-Thatcher Cold War duo did change the global scene – and in the process it gave, for the first and only time, some real meaning to the term 'the special relationship'. For a short time during Reagan's presidency the Anglo-American relationship became something of a two way street, and Britain surpassed Germany as 'first amongst equals' in the ranking of US allies. Thatcher herself in 1985 could say with confidence that 'I feel no inhibitions about describing the relationship as very, very, special'.[5]

The US and the Falklands

Yet, no matter how genuinely 'special', the Reagan-Thatcher relationship was still one of dependence. An early example was the Falklands crisis which broke in the spring of 1982. The Argentine military junta, seemingly out of a clear blue sky, had suddenly invaded the British colony of the Falkland Islands. And the Thatcher government was faced with a furious House of Commons and the prospect, should it be unable to expel the Argentineans, of being overthrown in the House of Commons. The Tory backbenches were united with the Labour leadership in demanding action. The left-wing Labour leader, Michael Foot's House of Commons speech on the issue was particularly bellicose, displaying all the visceral offence of violated nationalism. Margaret Thatcher's very future depended on her retaking the Falklands, and that in turn depended on US support.

The American UN ambassador Jeanne Kirkpatrick headed up a faction in Washington which saw the US relationship with the Argentines as more important than its alliance with Britain (at the time the Americans were hoping for Argentinean support in Central America). But, after some wavering and a vigorous pro-British campaign led by Vice President George Bush, US support for Britain was finally forthcoming. The US base in the Atlantic at Ascension Island was a crucial supply base and listening post for the British, and the US supplied Britain with critical intelligence. Once Washington had come to the conclusion that at the height of the Cold War it could not possibly see a NATO ally beaten, the Reagan administration then swung into action behind the British, even going so far as preparing a US aircraft carrier – with US marking painted out – to replace the

British carrier in the south Atlantic should it be sunk or incapacitated. Yet it was only after Washington, in the form of Secretary of State General Haig, had announced publicly that the US would support Britain and provide 'material support' for Britain that the Thatcher government could breathe easily.

The Falklands war was a case study in the realities of the 'special relationship'. The US finally backed Britain, but its support was by no means automatic or immediate, and took place only after a heated debate in Washington. It was clear that when US interest dictated otherwise, US policy, even under Ronald Reagan, had no second thoughts about sacrificing the British – sometimes even without consultation. Reagan's decision to invade the tiny Caribbean island of Grenada in October 1983 was a case in point. Grenada was a member of the Commonwealth and the Queen was its head of state; so when the Americans invaded the island they violated the sovereignty of a Commonwealth country. And the Queen, in full Gilbert and Sullivan mode, was not amused. More importantly, nor was Margaret Thatcher. However, the fact that the US under Reagan (with his 'special relationship' with Thatcher) could so act, said volumes. Labour's Denis Healey called Margaret Thatcher Ronald Reagan's 'obedient poodle'.[6]

And the British were obedient again when in 1986 Ronald Reagan decided to bomb Libya in what was described as a counter-terrorist action. Even though Margaret Thatcher had doubts about the wisdom of the action, the British Prime Minister agreed to allow the operation to be carried out from British soil (whilst the French refused Reagan over-flying rights). She defended her decision in classic Cold War terms: 'the USA has thousands of forces in Europe to defend the liberty of Europe…it was inconceivable to me that we should refuse US aircraft and pilots the opportunity to defend their people'.[7]

Trident, Cruise, Star Wars

One reason for it being 'inconceivable' – that Britain should refuse the US – was the underlying strategic nuclear defence relationship between Washington and London. One of Margaret Thatcher's earliest decisions was to resolve a question literally passed to her by the outgoing Callaghan government: that of how to upgrade, if at all, Britain's nuclear forces – the Polaris-Chevaline missile – with a new delivery system. She chose, in a fateful decision, to employ the US Trident C4 missiles (updated by the US without consultation to D5 the following year), and in so doing tied the next generation British deterrent firmly to a US missile system which would be supplied and serviced from King's Bay, Georgia. In the process she rejected the alternative idea of an Anglo-French deterrent which the Heath government had been working to secure.

In the great scheme of things, however, the character of the British nuclear deterrent was far less significant than the issue of heightened east-west nuclear confrontation that was coming to a head in the early 1980s. NATO, in response to what western leaders saw as a definitive change in Soviet missile deployment aimed at western Europe – the arrival of the SS20 rockets targeted at western Europe – decided in December 1979 to counter with a major new US intermediate missile deployment. West Germany took the initiative in requesting these new missiles and the US agreed to locate 108 Pershing II and 464 ground launched cruise missiles in western Europe, principally in West Germany and Britain.

These 'euro-missiles' caused major protests throughout western Europe and became a test of the resolve of western European leaders to face down Soviet pressure and reinforce NATO under American leadership. The US missiles were finally deployed throughout western Europe and in Britain. For Thatcher this missile crisis – and the need as she saw it to deploy them to deter the Soviet Union – was yet another powerful reminder of the utter centrality of America, and the American strategic guarantee, in the defence of Britain.

It was the threat of removing this 'nuclear guarantee' that produced the only serious dispute between Reagan's Washington and Thatcher during her time in office. It took place in the run up to, and during, the Reykjavik summit between Reagan and Gorbachev which was held in October 1986. Some time before the summit Ronald Reagan had outlined his 'star wars' proposal – in which the US would switch from an offensive nuclear threat as a means of deterring Soviet power to a defensive shield that would shoot down incoming missiles, thus rendering the American nuclear arsenal, and with it the American nuclear guarantee to Europe, redundant. It amounted to a dramatic proposal for ending the nuclear age, and for Britain it would mean that the balance of power between east and west in Europe would be dependent upon conventional forces only – thus ensuring that the Red Army, and the Soviet Union, would become the primary military power on the European continent – a complete revolution in the existing geo-political power relationships. Reagan's proposal caused consternation throughout Europe.

For Thatcher, a vision of America with no nuclear weapons, and thus no longer the guarantor, upended her whole world. She was so disturbed by the prospect that she went as far as publicly opposing Reagan. It amounted to a potential split in the west on strategic policy. In the end, though, agreement at Reykjavik could not be secured, and there remained big questions over the viability of the project. And when the Soviet Union dissolved it ceased to be such a burning issue.

The Free World, Free Markets

For Margaret Thatcher, her total support for American policy around the globe was not a submission to America and its interests. Rather, it was part of the natural order of things during the Cold War. For her, as for many British politicians across the spectrum, Britain during the Cold War was only one part of a bigger ideological cause – the 'free world' and the idea of democracy for which it stood. She once said that 'America's cause is, and always will be, our cause'.[8] In Thatcher's world-view the American President, in this case Ronald Reagan, would be the automatic, unchallenged leader of this cause, and the British Prime Minister his Chief of Staff. And they would be serving a single, ideological, vision.

When Reagan came to Britain in June 1982, following Thatcher's success in the Falklands, he gave a major address to Parliament. The speech was vintage Reagan, a highly ideological and optimistic speech about the great cause of 'freedom and democracy' and the need to pursue it worldwide. The reception showed the divisions in the Tory Party at the time between the ideologues with their sweeping universalist ideas and the more cautious, more interest-based, realists. Whilst Thatcher, obviously moved, nodded vigorously in agreement, Reagan's approach obviously jarred with some of the 'wetter' Tories – Francis Pym and William Whitelaw in particular. They were less than enthused by the 'free world' rhetoric, but, like good, loyal, subordinate allies, they sat straining to be similarly moved.

For Thatcher, as for many Americans (both Republicans and Democrats) the 'free world' meant 'free markets'. For her, the two ideas were indissoluble. The west stood for clear economic principles, such as free enterprise and limited government, and those who did not agree – social democrats and socialists of various hues – were weakening the west in the Cold War struggle. Thatcher shared with most American political leaders a fundamentalist approach to the market. It was an approach that both sought to marketise as much as possible, remove as many restrictions to the market as possible, and, crucially, saw the market as having a political function – as extending human freedom and individual sovereignty. Thatcher was an extreme individualist in the mould of the American writer Ayn Rand, with a view of the world that led Thatcher, in her most famous of all pronouncements, to argue that 'there is no such thing as society. There are individual men and women, and there are families'.[9]

Thatcher had honed her belief in individualism and the 'free-enterprise system' at the feet of the classical liberalism of Enoch Powell, Keith Joseph and the Institute for Economic Affairs (the IEA) during the 1960s and early 1970s. They had introduced her to the Austrian thinkers Ludwig von Mises and Friedrich von Hayek, and, in the contemporary debate, to the Chicago School monetarist Milton Friedman. The IEA had been set up by the millionaire entrepreneur Anthony Fisher and from its inception was led by Ralph Harris and Arthur Seldon. In the 1970s Harris and Seldon hosted hundreds of IEA lunches, held in their small, cramped offices off Smith Square in Westminster – events which, literally, changed the thinking of a generation. And Seldon's house parties in his rambling home in Sevenoaks – always drawing a mixture of bright politicians, journalists and academics – were vibrant affairs, and had about them the atmosphere of a coming new orthodoxy. Seldon was able to write about the great adventure in his well-received book *Capitalism*, published in 1990.[10]

Harris and Seldon were ideology in action. They were utterly committed, clear and compelling arguers and thinkers; and, as with all good iconoclasts and successful campaigners, they had a credible target in their sights – the failures of the British economy in the 1970s and the consensus that supported it. Harris and Seldon put these failures squarely at the door of the social democratic policies and structures of Keynesian and welfare economics (whereas unbalanced trade union power and geo-strategic questions such as oil price rises were not particularly highlighted).[11] They played this theme for all it was worth. And as the very high levels of inflation and unemployment of the 1970s eroded confidence in the established consensus, opinion-formers were prepared to listen to a radical alternative.

These market fundamentalist gurus had a big influence not just on Margaret Thatcher's economic philosophy, but also on Thatcherism's US geo-political orientation. For Harris and Seldon, the US was their intellectual home, for the other great capitalist economies on the continent were seen as too 'statist' and 'quasi-socialist', stubbornly stuck in the social democratic consensus that they were trying to break in Britain. For the IEA gurus, US society, and not just its economy, was worth copying, and social reform in Britain should centre on overhauling and privatising the British welfare state, including health and education to give more freedom and choice to the individual.

There was something of the appearance of an old-fashioned English nationalist in Ralph Harris. A working class lad from Tottenham in North London, he affected a Colonel Blimp persona with his RAF bearing, his pipe and warm beer, and his affable, ironic, complaining about 'Johnny Foreigner'. It was therefore something of a natural progression when Harris became a leading light in the anti-Common Market and anti-EU campaign groups, particularly the Bruges Group. A bitter opponent of European federalism, he saw it as associated with socialism. Arthur Seldon, on the other hand, was less hostile to the Common Market. He was no Tory, always describing himself as 'Whiggish', and was suspicious of the nationalist impulses lurking within anti-European breasts. Seldon possessed none of the traditionalist prejudices about Europe. He saw Europe through free market eyes – as a huge internal market which Britain needed to be a part of; and he would constantly remind Eurosceptics that Britain could, should it want to, retain its 'precious sovereignty' but only at the expense of increasing poverty at home.

Yet, all in all, despite these home grown ideological influences, Margaret Thatcher came to power in Britain on a prospectus essentially made in Chicago. Her philosophy and her governments were not a one-off or a uniquely British affair. For they represented a part of a much wider transatlantic movement that in the 1970s campaigned and in the 1980s and 1990s ultimately succeeded in altering the economies and societies of much of the western world.

In essence, Thatcherism was the British version of an American-led conservative insurgency. The intellectual origins of this insurgency can arguably be traced way back to the early revolt in the United States against the 'big government' programmes of LBJ's 1960s 'Great Society' (that themselves had built upon FDR's 'New

Deal' in the 1930s). This revolt surfaced first of all at the Republican convention in 1964 when the radical conservative candidature of Barry Goldwater defeated the Republican liberal establishment, and set the Republican Party on a course which took it to the right both economically and socially – and, ultimately, led to a 'southern strategy' in which the old Democratic Party hold on the American south was defeated. At a party for conservative Republicans in 1985, just after Reagan's second victory, a member of his administration in the Department of Defence, Bruce Weinrod, pointed out to me all of those who had come into politics in the 1964 campaign in order to support Goldwater's run for the White House. He pointed to more than half.

In the late 1960s in Chicago, Milton Friedman was giving this Goldwater revolt of the free market fundamentalists some very heavy intellectual fire power. But the ideas offensive only got seriously underway as US 'Great Society' social democracy – which, in essence, was continued by Nixon into the early 1970s – faltered in the mid 1970s under the impact of oil price rises. Under Reagan after 1981 the 'Great Society' programmes (excepting the defence budget) were contained and a new orthodoxy of market economics and market fundamentalism took its place. In power and interest group terms what had happened was a serious accretion in the power of corporations and a weakening in the countervailing power of both the state and trade unions. When communism fell in the 1990s with consequentially huge increases in global markets and the global labour market the power of the private corporate sector was further enhanced. And market-based solutions came to be renamed as 'neo-liberalism' – and spread out around the world, establishing its ascendancy through growing globalisation.

This contemporary 'neo-liberal consensus' is a worldwide phenomenon, but remains in essence American-led. The growth of markets around the world quite naturally – without design – promotes the 'American model' of economics and in its wake even the American model of society – the American way of doing things. And Britain's Thatcherite revolution of the 1980s and 90s was part of this wider change, and should be seen in this global context.

As the Thatcher revolution took hold, doing things the American way became the gold standard for Britain's political class, but also, crucially for the country's most powerful opinion-forming interest group – the owners of the changing British media. The 'Murdoch

Press' – *The Sunday Times, The Sun* and the Sky TV network – and the Conrad Black empire were emerging as a major ideological powerhouse behind neo-liberal and geo-politically pro-American ideas and values. The BBC and other media were by comparison to the Murdoch and Black media much less committed, less sure of themselves, and less possessed of a sense of ultimate triumph. In consequence, they provided no serious counterbalance. And thus progressively during the late 1980s and 1990s the neo-liberals helped inform and condition thinking in the country, and established what amounted to a new British consensus. It was a view of politics and life that saw the world in much the same way as would Americans in America – very much through an American lens. This Thatcherite American revolution – as much as Tony Blair's own political will – became the basis for Britain's later support for post-9/11 American global policy and the invasion of Iraq.

Thatcher's Boys and the 'Anglo-Sphere'

Most British market fundamentalists were, almost by definition, attracted to the American economic model. They also, for the same reasons, tended to deride the European economies and, through them, the European project itself. Perhaps the most well-connected anti-European Thatcherite of his generation was the journalist John O'Sullivan. I first met O'Sullivan at the London University debating society in the early 1960s and he has remained a friend ever since. A journalist on *The Daily Telegraph* during the 1970s, he was a bitter critic of Edward Heath's government, so much so that, though a Conservative, he voted against his party in the February 1974 general election. He became an early supporter of the rising Margaret Thatcher and then, later, served in the No.10 policy unit and became her speechwriter and close advisor. He, later still, helped her with her biography. O'Sullivan always was, and remains, a free market true believer, and in the 1970s and 1980s he perfectly embodied the core neo-liberal support for America and opposition to the European Community and Union. For O'Sullivan, as for many Thatcherites, the EEC, as it then was, was Keynesian, corporatist and socialist – a depiction reinforced when Thatcher and the Commission fell out in the 1980s and further highlighted when Commission President, French socialist Jacques Delors, visited the TUC and began his none-too disguised campaign against Margaret Thatcher.

O'Sullivan's market fundamentalism, though winning in his native land, ultimately un-hooked him from a life in England, and, in the late 1980s, it launched him, quite naturally, into the home of neo-liberalism, the United States, and into the Washington conservative think tank the Heritage Foundation. He later became the Editor of the American conservative journal *The National Review* (following the editorship of conservative journalistic icon, William F. Buckley) and then the Editor of the Washington quarterly *The National Interest* (founded by the neo-conservative, Irving Kristol). He has subsequently settled in the US, and married an American from Alabama.

I once asked John O'Sullivan, when we were both in New York in the early 1990s, about Thatcher's deep-seated and visceral opposition to European integration. Were there any other reasons, apart from the obvious ideological ones? The answer was surprising, and fascinating. It could be found in the photographs – in the contrast between the team pictures of the European leaders at EU summits and the one-on-one Thatcher-Reagan White House photos. 'You see' said O'Sullivan, 'she's simply not at home in Europe – too many leaders. Gets lost amongst them. When she's in the States, though, she's one to one with the US President, and she shines'. As with Margaret Thatcher, so with media-conscious Tony Blair.

Another market fundamentalist who saw America as the 'model', if not quite the 'saviour', was the Tory MP John Redwood. Redwood, an ardent Thatcherite, was like O'Sullivan an ideologue. And, again like O'Sullivan, his free market ideology translated into a love affair with the US market economy and into a systematic opposition to the 'corporatism' of the EU. In his 2001 book, appropriately titled *Stars and Strife: the Coming Conflicts between the USA and the European Union*, he broke what had mounted to a taboo and openly talked of a future in which Britain became the 51st state of the Union. Without actually advocating such a course, he argued that 'we could try to become the 51st state of the American Union' and suggested that 'there would be no language barrier, and less of a legal, cultural and political barrier than submerging ourselves in Europe'. And he asserted that the 51st state option was one which Harold Wilson toyed with in the 1960s.[12]

John O'Sullivan and John Redwood were the advanced guard of a broader grouping – mainly of neo-liberal financial journalists and Eurosceptic Tories – who wanted closer formal and institutional relations between Britain and the United States. Worried about European influence, but aware that the '51st state option' was an impossible dream, they sought other ways to bind Britain irrevocably to the US. In the late 1990s ideas started emerging about Britain joining the North Atlantic Free Trade Area (NAFTA, the free trade area between Canada, the US and Mexico), and British Eurosceptics arranged a trip to London for some US Congressmen (including Senator Phil Gramm of Texas) to investigate the possibility. British membership of NAFTA was, though, a short-lived idea; for it soon emerged that Britain would have to leave the EU in order to take part in NAFTA – and many Eurosceptics, although they might welcome the idea, saw leaving the EU as both unpopular and a truly Herculean task.

Yet some conservatives refused to let the idea completely die out; and from time to time it was refined and re-floated in the guise of a broader free trade agreement involving the whole EU and NAFTA – a kind of grand transatlantic trading bloc. (The idea – in very general terms – was even given a welcome by European Commission President Jose Manuel Barroso in 2006.) At the same time some Thatcherites, seeking to break Britain off from Europe, started toying with a new concept called the 'Anglo-sphere'.

This 'Anglo-sphere' had no formal organisational basis, but was an attempt to describe, and to build on, what was seen as the common heritage and interests of the English-speaking world – the United States, Britain and Australia primarily – and, crucially, to distinguish it from the rest of the EU-dominated west. For a time, Thatcherite British opinion-formers, like historians Niall Ferguson and Andrew Roberts, joined O'Sullivan in using the term and attempting to get the idea off the ground. But it was this very 'Anglo-Sphere' – the US, Britain and Australia – that in 2003 went to war in Iraq; and, following the failure of this mission, the term fell into virtual disuse. For some time the term 'Anglo-Saxon countries' or the 'Anglo-Saxon economies' had been used to describe the USA and Britain; but it was something of a misnomer as the USA was certainly no longer ethnically 'Anglo-Saxon'.

Not all ardent Thatcherites were devotees of the free market and visceral pro-Americans. The journalist, the late Frank Johnson, a friend and colleague of O'Sullivan's in the leader page editorial team at *The Daily Telegraph* in the 1970s, was more laid back about both the market and America. He supported Margaret Thatcher (or 'the lady' – as he often called her) not through the prism of economic ideology but because he saw her as attempting to reverse the decline of the country – primarily through tackling Britain's 'trade union problem'. Because he was more interested in European history, and less ideological and analytical than O'Sullivan and Redwood, he was less attracted to the US and less opposed to Brussels. Indeed, like many traditional Tories he saw – even if he did not like – the case that joining fully in the European Union could place Britain at the heart of a new big power bloc in the world. Disdainful of the routine politicians at the top of British politics he was a great admirer of big historic figures, not least General De Gaulle.

Labour's Americans

Thatcher's American revolution garnered support way beyond the market fundamentalists in the Tory Party. Some Labour social democrats were amongst her most vociferous supporters – both publicly and privately. They saw aspects of the Thatcher revolution as providing an opening for their own brand of politics. In her early years as opposition leader and Prime Minister she often proclaimed that she favoured a more meritocratic Britain; she certainly believed in upward social mobility; and she was opposed by the two groups that many social democrats of the time hated the most, and blamed for Britain's problems – aristocratic Tories and left-wing socialists. Also, many of Thatcher's secret (and not so secret) supporters within Labour's ranks were schooled in the conflicts within the Labour movement of the 1970s, and they saw Britain's politicised trade unions as a serious threat – and saw Margaret Thatcher as the only politician in Britain willing to confront them.

Brian Walden, the Labour MP for Birmingham Ladywood, and later television interviewer, was one such. In the 1970s he had became progressively isolated within his party. He had started off in politics in the 1960s as a Gaitskellite, indeed as one of Gaitskell's parliamentary inner-circle. And during the 1970s, as he watched his party move dramatically to the left, he made few compromises with the advancing forces. He was very pro-American (he supported the US in the war in Vietnam) and pro-NATO. He detested Harold Wilson's political appeasing of the Labour left, and would regularly unleash, from the backbenches, his considerable invective against the Prime Minister – and against what he saw as the 'phoney middle class moralism' of many on the left. Walden was his own man, and not much of a team player. And in a move that increased his political isolation, he stayed out of what he considered to be the incestuous and somewhat prissy middle class grouping that in the late 1960s was gathering around Labour's right-wing leader-apparent Roy Jenkins.

Walden was, arguably, the most effective old-style parliamentary orator of his generation; the kind of speaker the Chamber of the House would fill up to hear. He was not in any sense a Tory. He was, rather, a Birmingham radical. And a populist radical at that – and he admired, and shared a pronounced Midlands accent with, Enoch Powell. He did not possess the discipline to be a party leader; but he had the flair, eloquence, and the sense of history that made a great parliamentarian of the old type. He was not a party man; and this independence (and daring) of spirit gave him the space and freedom to support Margaret Thatcher's revolution, which he did with gusto. His contribution to Thatcher's domination of the 1980s was no small thing: in 1980, in a final act of ingenious sabotage against the Labour left, he voted, together with Neville Sandelson and three other right-wing Labour MPs, for left-winger Michael Foot for Labour Leader – specifically in order to elect a leader who would make the Labour Party unelectable. He succeeded. And he later went off into a highly successful career as an LWT television presenter and interviewer.

David Owen was another Labour supporter of the Thatcherite revolution. Like Brian Walden he was in no way a socialist; and he saw the trade unions as 'over-mighty' and needing to be cut down to size. Also like Walden he was a natural Atlanticist, and was never, like the Jenkinsites, a fervent European (he was later to head up a Eurosceptic grouping and, should a referendum on Europe have taken place in 2005, he was positioning himself to become a leader of the 'no' campaign). Married to an American, Owen was always outside the traditional class system – neither an aristocrat or aristocrat-manque, nor a trade unionist. He brought a refreshing American-style of professionalism and telegenic charm to British politics. He was a modern, media politician in a way that the more staid Roy Jenkins could never aspire to be. Of all the four SDP leaders who set up the party he was the most pro-Thatcher. Unlike Roy Jenkins, who opposed the Falklands war, he supported it, indeed proclaimed his support regularly in television appearances. He also supported the Thatcherite trade union reforms of the late 1980s. He was also the most instinctively pro-American of the SDP top leadership, and this American leaning, together with his global economic interests, probably accounted for his developing anti-Europeanism in the 1990s.

David Carlton was yet another Labour politico more at home in America than Britain. A Labour candidate and historian (best known for his critical biography of Anthony Eden), Carlton was deeply involved behind the scenes in the politics of Labour in the 1960s and 70s. A long-time friend from our days as doctoral students at LSE, Carlton's immersion in contemporary diplomatic history convinced him that Britain's political leaders were hopelessly misreading Britain's true power position the world. He was attracted to America because, as he described it, the USA was a 'serious country' – a sobriquet Britain had forfeited by its bungling of the Suez adventure. Carlton represented a school of left-of-centre Cold Warriors who detested communism, thought it expansionary, and embraced America as the bulwark and bastion of the west, the homeland of the system. At the height of the left-right struggle in the Labour Party, when the left was riding high, Carlton and I were in Overseas Development minister Reg Prentice's office in Victoria and we raised a glass to the map of the USA on the wall. Prentice's toast said it all. 'Where would we be without them?' we intoned.

Reagan's Washington

In Reagan's Washington in the 1980s Margaret Thatcher was idolised. She had initially – as the first woman Prime Minister of a major western country – become well-known in America as an interesting, almost non-political celebrity. But as time passed and her alliance with Ronald Reagan became closer and closer, her anti-*détente* sentiments and her credentials as an 'iron lady' and Cold Warrior made her a conservative heroine. And after her victory over Arthur Scargill and the miners in 1985 she, at least in conservative circles, became an icon – a world-class leader who had 'turned around' a socialist country and put it on the road to recovery. Reagan himself in one of his valedictory speeches made the point that of the two revolutions – Thatcher's and his – hers was the bigger victory because she had had a greater mountain to climb.

Yet this American conservative adoration of Thatcher did not always extend to a positive view of Britain. Although Washington's liberals tended to be very Anglophile, most American conservatives and neo-conservatives were not. They ranged from neutral about Britain to suspicious. Most American traditional conservatives – or, as they were often called, 'paleo-conservatives' – were American nationalists who possessed few sentimental illusions about the 'old country'. For them Britain was an ally but was also a foreign country with a separate national interest. Conservative Irish-Americans – like Nixon speechwriter and Presidential candidate, Pat Buchanan – saw Britain in an imperialist role in Northern Ireland and as an occupying power. Conservative Catholic Americans – like Heritage foundation President Ed Feulner or even the Anglo-mannered *National Review* Editor William F. Buckley – saw Britain in the 1980s as half-socialist and unreliable. Above all, 'movement' conservatives were essentially realistic: few of them laboured under any sentimental illusions about 'Anglo-American cousinhood' (and many of them were not Anglo-Americans anyway); and for them, Britain was viewed in a wholly calculating geo-political manner – simply as a strategic asset in the great power game.

An interesting feature of conservative America in the Reagan-Thatcher years was that many of the conservative 'movement' types were from relatively modest backgrounds. For many of them the defining political moment of their youth had been – as mentioned earlier – the 1964 Presidential campaign of Senator Barry Goldwater and his fight against the liberal establishment led by Republican New York millionaire Nelson Rockefeller. In what was to become a major conservative theme many decades later – in Karl Rove's campaigning for George W. Bush – they saw and painted liberals as rich and hypocritical, and above all unpatriotic. 'Ordinary god-fearing Americans' were the patriots and were counter-poised to the eastern sea-board elite who were in thrall to foreign, primarily European, ideas and values. This mindset was the fodder for American nationalism and for Bush's unilateralism – and it had no particular truck with 'the special relationship': for the Brits were foreigners like everyone else.

Neo-conservative supporters of Reagan, on the other hand, unlike their 'paleo-conservative' cousins – were much more ideological. They saw the Cold War world as a great battle of ideologies as well as interests. During the Cold War, neo-conservatives would talk about 'freedom' and 'democracy' incessantly, and rarely about American interests. In fact the most pronounced characteristic of the neo-conservatives I came across in Washington during this time was their genuine interest in political ideas – and their long-term impact. This contrasted strongly with the mainstream conservative Republicans, the 'country club Republicans', who tended to be more practical, and more interested in business and money-making.

In Washington during the late 1970s and early 1980s two Democratic US Senators, Daniel Patrick Moynihan of New York and Henry 'Scoop' Jackson, were the political trailblazers of neo-conservatism. Both were from the left but were also deeply anti-communist. They were the original 'Cold War liberals' who were domestically still left-of-centre but saw the Cold War as an overriding issue. Many other neo-conservatives were former socialists and Marxists, some of whom had a strong trade union background and a civil rights history. During the 1970s these liberals and leftists broke with the mainstream American liberal left over the issue of *détente*. They saw the Soviet Union as using the cover of *détente* to build up its military strength and extend its influence around the world. Many 'neo-cons' signed up for an anti-*détente* political pressure group called 'The Committee on the Present Danger'.

By the late 1970s and early 1980s these 'neo-cons' were beginning to do more than support a strong defence. They were moving across the political spectrum to support the broader agenda of conservative Republicans like Ronald Reagan. In the autumn of 1977 Elliot Abrams and Charles Horner, two congressional staffers from Senator Moynihan's office, came round to my flat in Riggs Place, Washington, for a chat. We had much in common politically as we found ourselves renegades in parties moving to the left. They were so disillusioned that they wanted to leave the Democrats but had not yet made the move. They were worried that the Republicans would not welcome them. When I asked why, Horner said 'they kept us out of the country clubs, didn't they'. (Horner was a Jewish-American and was referring to the anti-semitic informal rules of the country clubs before the 1960s). I remember saying brightly, trying to cheer them up, 'try Ronald Reagan out in California'.

Some neo-cons were even going as far in their rightward move as to ditch their support for 'social liberalism'; and some even began to align themselves with the religious right on such questions as homosexuality and abortion.[13] In the move over, a number of Democrats and liberals joined the Washington conservative think tanks, including the writer Midge Decter who joined the board of the Heritage Foundation and congressional staffer and defence analyst Richard Perle, who joined the American Enterprise Institute.

In the 1980s the intellectual godfathers of this neo-conservative movement were Irving Kristol (who founded the journal *The National Interest*) and Norman Podhoretz (who was Editor of *Commentary* magazine published by the American Jewish Committee). Irving Kristol was the intellectually more agile of the two, possessing a lighter touch. Norman Podhoretz was the warrior. He became a powerful presence in American Cold War politics in the 1970s and 80s. A tough, uncompromising editor he put *Commentary* right at the centre of events – at least for a time. He had been a central figure in the great infighting amongst the New York intelligentsia in the 1960s and early 70s, and even on social occasions always seemed as though he had just emerged from an intellectual warzone. He was somewhat heavy-handed in his thinking, but there was always a clarity and straightforwardness that allowed him to make his arguments hit home. He would get to the point. He had some European friends, particularly the English journalist Huw Weldon, but I always sensed that he had little time for Europeans, including the Brits. He was probably the first to come up with the 'Euro-wimp' designation.

Amongst the younger generation of neo-conservatives in Washington at this time were those who were to go on to conceive, advocate, and support George Bush in the invasion of Iraq in 2003. They were Richard Perle (assistant to Senator 'Scoop' Jackson, then Reagan's Assistant Secretary of State for Defence and in 2003 member of the Defence Policy Board); Elliot Abrams (formerly a member of the Young Peoples Socialist League, then assistant to Senator Daniel Patrick Moynihan, later Assistant Secretary of State and in 2003 George Bush's White House Middle East Advisor); Michael Ledeen (an expert on Italian left-wing politics at the Georgetown Centre For Strategic and International Studies, CSIS, and in 2003 a senior fellow at the AEI); Kenneth Adelman (an advisor to Jeanne Kirkpatrick and member of 'The Committee on the Present Danger', and author of the 'Cakewalk in Iraq' article in the *Washington Post* on 2nd February 2002); Charles Krauthammer (in the 1970s a supporter of liberal Democrats Walter Mondale and Jimmy Carter, who in 2003 went on to become a leading print and Fox

News journalist in Washington); Paul Wolfowitz (another aide to Democratic Senator Henry 'Scoop' Jackson, he became, as Deputy Defence Secretary, the chief neo-con prosecutor of the Iraq war) and Bill Kristol (Irving Kristol's son, often described as a neo-con, but with a more orthodox conservative background – having entered Washington politics as assistant to Vice-President Dan Quayle).

During the Cold War, for these neo-cons the global contest with the Soviet Union was everything. They saw the Soviet Union as an 'evil empire', as highly aggressive and expansionary – and as anti-Israel. Richard Perle was the intellectual leader of this fight. He came to prominence in Washington in the 1970s when, then working for Senator Jackson, he was one of the brains behind the Jackson-Vanik amendment to the 1974 Trade Act which denied normal trading relations to countries that restricted emigration. One of Perle's main concerns was to help Soviet Jews to emigrate to Israel, and this amendment achieved that purpose. It was a great victory for Perle and he later went on to join the Reagan administration as an Assistant Secretary of Defence. His unrelenting anti-Soviet views together with his knowledge of defence systems and nuclear issues gave him the nickname – amongst friends as well as enemies – 'the prince of darkness'. Perle's success in Washington was partly due to his charm. He was soft-spoken and courteous, and combined tough, uncompromising opinions with an understated reasonableness. But behind the scenes he was a fixer and fighter. He divided the political world into Cold Warriors – whom he would describe as 'solid citizens' – and 'weak sisters'.

In the neo-con world it was the Europeans who were the classic example of Perle's 'weak sisters'. The Germans and the French had been behind the whole process of *détente* following Germany's '*Ostpolitik*' (opening to the east) in the Willy Brandt era, and had carried it forward ever since – particularly in the Soviet-European pipeline deal clinched against American wishes in the early 1980s. French policy towards NATO and Russia, and European policy on the Middle East, were other examples of European unreliability. All in all, the Europeans were seen as being 'soft on communism' – a 'softness' primarily caused by a combination of 'decadent' conservative elites who had natural inclination to appease Soviet power, and the socialist and communist, and 'euro-communist' impulses on the European left. The neo-con worldview from Washington was clear:

151

without American power in the world the Europeans would fall into the Soviet orbit. Europe was a 'contested zone' between east and west, and the Europeans could be divided up into pro- and anti-Americans. Though Margaret Thatcher was, in Perle's world, 'a solid citizen', less 'solid citizens' were French President François Mitterrand, Labour Leader Neil Kinnock, Commission President Jacques Delors, and most Swedes.

For many Americans during the Cold War the Europeans were considered allies who were somewhat irritating – because they were seen as not fully pulling their weight in NATO – but there was little animus. Amongst neo-cons, on the other hand, there was a decidedly hostile attitude. They saw Europe as not fully democratic (in the way they considered America to be) and Europe's elites as snobbish, overly world weary and still hankering after lost empires. They considered many European opinion-formers to be actively anti-American and they were amongst the few Americans who fully understood – and did not appreciate – the 'Greece to Rome' mindsets of many European leaders, including British Foreign Office types. Suspicion of Europeans could run quite deep. On one occasion in 1980 at an American-European academic conference I noticed that Neil Kozodoy, Deputy Editor of *Commentary* magazine, as he entered a room full of Europeans, most of them American sympathisers, had adopted a defensive, almost hunted look as though he was entering hostile territory in, say, Moscow.

One reason for this wariness and hostility was that most neo-cons were Jewish and many of them saw Europe and Europeans as anti-Israeli, even anti-semitic. European differences with Washington over the Arab-Israeli dispute (which had been first highlighted by the June 1980 Venice Declaration of the European Community) were often interpreted in Washington as being caused by an underlying European anti-semitism. This gnawing issue once came into high relief during a transatlantic academic conference in 1979 when former British Foreign Secretary George Brown gave the keynote speech. It was a standard pro-NATO address, and the Americans warmed to his anti-communism and to his powerful peroration on democracy and democratic values. But afterwards in the bar he took, as was his wont, to criticise the policies of Israel, almost in a standard British Foreign Office manner. But as he drank more he began to make the argument that Israel 'was a racist state'. The Jewish-Americans present took great exception to this and a row ensued, and some of the Americans threatened to walk out of the conference a day early. The event was only saved by George Brown not staying for the rest of the conference.

For the neo-cons Margaret Thatcher was the great exception. Alongside Ronald Reagan himself, she became a neo-con hero – and there were very, very few world leaders in that rarefied category. Her domestic policies were largely irrelevant to the neo-cons; it was her anti-Soviet and anti-communist rhetoric that got her their attention. In the first years of Jimmy Carter's Presidency the strategy of *détente*, started by Henry Kissinger following the US loss in Vietnam, was taken to a new level; and there was a sudden and perceptible loss of confidence in the west (in July 1979 President Carter even talked of 'a malaise'). And Britain's opposition leader Margaret Thatcher was seen as one of the few western leaders who was in favour of a tough anti-Soviet policy.

In the late 1970s most Washington and New York neo-cons were still Democrats. Elliot Abrams was one of them. Abrams, a modest, rather charming man with a sharp mind was Democratic Senator Daniel Moynihan's Chief of Staff, but on a visit to London in the mid 1970s he was speaking of Margaret Thatcher in reverential terms – as someone who stood out. He was keen to meet her so as to widen her American contacts beyond the relatively narrow circle of American country club conservatives. I managed to introduce him to Richard Ryder, Margaret Thatcher's assistant, at Ryder's London home in Earls Court, and Ryder then arranged his meeting with Thatcher. Also present that morning in Earl's Court was the late Noel Picarda, and the four of us had a lively anti-*détente*, 'Kissinger bashing', session.

Thatcher's Anti-Europe Crusade

Margaret Thatcher's views on Europe were hardly any different from those of the American neo-conservatives – indeed they could have come directly from the neo-conservative playbook in Washington. Almost a decade after she left office, Margaret Thatcher, reflecting back, made one of the most sweeping and shocking remarks ever made by a British Prime Minister. 'In my lifetime' she said '*all* our problems have come from mainland Europe and all the solutions have come from the English-speaking nations of the world'.[14] This extraordinary depiction of a whole continent was, though, a viewpoint held widely amongst English Tories (and some English liberals) who saw the continent as a dark place with a dark, undemocratic history, and saw its post-war development as bureaucratic and socialist – still reflecting this tradition. And along with this worldview went another Thatcher nostrum, shared widely by Americans, that anything that was good in post-war Europe was essentially a creation of America – who, from D-Day onwards, had liberated the continent, a liberation for which the continentals should be duly grateful.

Yet, Thatcher's hostility to Europe was hidden in her early years as Tory Leader. She had, in fact, made her political name during the Heath administration as mildly pro-European. And during the 1975 referendum she had taken a relatively high-profile role in the 'yes' campaign. She later took a leading role in shaping and implementing the single market reforms that were enshrined in the Single European Act of 1987. And she signed the Single European Act on behalf of Britain on the 28th February 1986.

She was, though, always suspicious of any development that would take Europe beyond the single market. And when it became clear that Chancellor Kohl, President Mitterrand and Commission President Jacques Delors, were moving towards the idea that the next phase of integration would involve a single European currency – with the political control of the currency in the hands of a federal central bank – she reacted strongly. In a speech in Bruges on the 20th September 1988 Thatcher talked of the need to resist a 'European superstate', and effectively unleashed a strain of British anti-Europeanism – later dubbed 'Euroscepticism' – that was later to influence the politics of the country. The British Prime Minister told journalists in October 1988 that 'I neither want, nor expect to see, such a bank in my lifetime...Nor, if I'm twanging a harp, for quite a long time afterwards'.[15] She also argued that 'we have not successfully rolled back the frontiers of the state in Britain, only to see them reimposed at a European level'. For her, it was all a case of opposing socialism, in Thatcher's words, by the 'Back Delors'. The 'Delors' being referred to here was Commission President Jacques Delors who had taken the offensive and come to Britain, to Blackpool, to speak to the TUC in Thatcher's own backyard about the 'social dimension to the single market reforms' and – in what reportedly really angered Margaret Thatcher – had received a standing ovation from the trade unionists and shouts of '*frère Jacques*'.

Yet, despite Thatcher's crusade, European integration, with bold and ambitious plans for the launching of a European currency, the Euro, proceeded apace. The Delors report came out in May 1989 and then the Inter Governmental Conference began in December 1989. And then in the middle of all this world communism came crashing down. The Berlin wall was breached on the 9th November 1989, and with German reunification suddenly in prospect, a new twist was added to the European debate.

Margaret Thatcher began, openly, to worry about what a strong, united Germany would mean for Europe and for Britain's position in it. And, yet again, D-Day thinking took over in Downing Street. The British Prime Minister's response to the exaltation in Germany about the reuniting of a people divided was that 'we must not forget that we have had two World Wars'. It was, again, a matter of looking backwards to Europe's liberation not forwards to a future Europe. Those close to Thatcher made the same point. Her cabinet colleague, Nicholas Ridley, in an interview in *The Spectator* attacked monetary union and the French – they were behaving as 'Germany's poodles' – and on the idea of handing more sovereignty to the Commission he opined that 'you might as well give it to Adolf Hitler, frankly'.[16] Diplomatic sensitivity was also on display when Thatcher hosted a seminar at Chequers on 'the German problem' and when she, joined this time by French President François Mitterrand, snubbed the Germans by refusing to attend their unity celebrations.

Thatcher's final denouement with Europe was to come in late 1990 when, outmanoeuvred by the European leaders at the European Council in Rome on the starting date for the second phase of monetary union, she went to the House of Commons and, in her famous 'No, No, No' speech refused to accept the majority European view about the date. It was this implicit refusal to sign up to the upcoming Maastricht Treaty that led the remaining pro-Europeans in the cabinet to finally move, decisively, against her. Her cabinet colleague Geoffrey Howe resigned from the government and from the backbenches publicly attacked her for her lack of team work on the European issue; and Michael Heseltine then stood against her in the ballot for Tory Leader and Prime Minister. Thatcher narrowly won the first ballot, but lost her cabinet's support ahead of the second; she resigned her premiership on the 22nd November 1990.

Thatcher had effectively been removed from office by a revolt of the pro-European faction in her cabinet. Her successor John Major quickly signalled that he would support the coming European treaty and would place Britain 'at the heart of Europe'; and the road to the Euro-zone was opened when the Maastricht Treaty was signed in February 1992 with British 'opt-outs' negotiated by John Major.

Yet, Margaret Thatcher's fall was not the end of the story. For, ever since the Bruges speech in 1988 her premiership had introduced into mainstream British politics a virulent anti-Europeanism that had previously been contained in the margins of political life. Enoch Powell's 1970s anti-EEC campaign was 'Little England' nationalist, Thatcher's 1980s crusade was the product of a belief in Pax-Americana; but both painted Europe in the same colours – as a dark threat to 'English' sovereignty and to the English way of life. And once articulated from Downing Street, and reinforced by sections of the popular tabloid media, it entered the political bloodstream, and has been present in large doses ever since.

Thatcher's Legacy: A Super-Rich Playground

This rise in Euroscepticism was, though, but a part of a more fundamental legacy of Thatcherism – the revolution in British society. Margaret Thatcher famously said that there is 'no such thing as society'. By this she meant that only individuals, and not collectives, counted – and it was this market-based individualism (expressed by consumerism) that changed the very character of British social life – and in a markedly American direction. And, as the full social effects of the Thatcher revolution continue to make their mark in the early years of the twenty-first century, then new social vested interests arise which further reinforce and embed the changes.

It was a clear aim of the Thatcher revolution to develop a strong, vibrant British middle class, and, although she would never say so publicly, she sought a middle class-dominated society in Britain that resembled that of the United States. Couched in rhetoric about 'standing on one's own two feet' she saw the suburban middle class society of the US – the independent, private-sector employed, family-oriented, largely Christian-inspired – as the ideal. She encouraged a process, already underway before she came into power, in which Britain's old social profile was eroded and replaced. The old structure was a hierarchical pear-shaped system with an aristocracy at the top, a small middle class and a huge industrial proletariat. In its place the new Thatcherite profile was one in which the largest and dominant group became an individualistic, consumerist, middle class. Like American conservatives, she was prepared to accept as the downside of this 'vibrant new middle class' society the emergence of a substantial underclass made up of the largely urban and 'ethnic' poor – although Thatcher's neo-liberals argued that their theoretical long-term objective was to erode this underclass by economic growth fuelled by low taxes, low welfare and 'trickle down' economics.

Privatisation was the key to Thatcherite social change. The idea was that a middle class would be built around a greater private sector. Council house sales became the flagship policy of privatisation but, beyond this popular measure, ownership in Britain was transformed. Public spending continued at a high level but huge amounts of tax-payers' money increasingly went to the private and corporate sector through outsourcing. The idea was that the middle class revolution would be affected by a 'virtuous cycle' as more and more people – who owned their own homes, demanded lower taxes and lower public expenditure (except when it would hamper private outsourcing) and pressured for less welfare – would remake society in their own image. The Thatcherite dream was that everyone would be middle class.

Yet, by the late 1990s the revolution's legacy was that the middle class was fragmenting. By the turn of the new century Britain certainly possessed a large middle class – in the sense that more people who used to consider themselves 'working class' now saw themselves as 'middle'. And it was decidedly a 'middle class' consumer society – indeed consumption was driving the economy. However, the downside was the growth of 'middle class' insecurity – an insecurity driven by lack of job security and a growing dependence by families and individuals on average-to-low wages on a private debt mountain of Himalayan proportions. On top of a widespread gnawing insecurity this insecure 'middle class' is also now breaking up. What Americans call 'the middle class squeeze' is causing both upward and downward social mobility. And although a portion of the middle class is becoming even more comfortable, some even rising into the super-rich category, more middle class people are downwardly mobile. And an American-style underclass is now becoming a permanent and growing feature of British life.

Thatcher's 'American model' of society has a very high tolerance of inequality, and a nonchalance about gigantic personal incomes and fortunes and the growing massive gap between rich and poor. Britain's leading supporters of the American model have been very clear about this question. Margaret Thatcher herself had no problem with inequality. She quite explicitly saw a distinction between meritocracy (which she was for) and income and wealth equality (which she was against). And Tony Blair in a famous interview in 2001 with Jeremy Paxman bluntly refused, after being pressed three times by Paxman, to deplore the widening gulf between rich and poor. For them opportunity was the key, not equality. The only time they would give house room to the word 'equality' was when it was part of three words – 'equality of opportunity'.[17]

The two and a half decades of the Thatcher consensus have seen inequality rise to such a point that in December 2005 even the Conservative Party's policy chief Oliver Letwin could contradict Labour's Prime Minister and argue that 'of course inequality matters. Of course it should be an aim to narrow the gap between rich and poor'.[18] Towards the end of the Blair era some of Labour's social democratic thinkers were also arguing that inequality had gone too far and were showing a renewed interest in equality as a goal. Labour's Roy Hattersley, a long-time critic of growing inequality under Blair argued that Blair's 'meritocracy is no substitute for equality', and, interestingly, noticed that in 2005 'equality is back on the agenda' amongst adherents of New Labour. In *The New Egalitarianism*, edited by Anthony Giddens and Patrick Diamond, an array of New Labour intellectuals argued that New Labour's broader objectives could not be realised in a society with growing inequalities of income and wealth. The MP Ed Miliband suggested that 'a focus only on equality of opportunity cannot be enough for progressive social democrats in the early twenty-first century'.[19]

Gushing Up, Not Trickling Down

Not only did Margaret Thatcher (and Tony Blair) have no objection to growing inequality, she was also unfussed about inherited wealth. Originally there was reason to believe that Margaret Thatcher's idea of spreading popular capitalism and elevating the individualist puritan ethic of work might just lead to some kind of erosion of Britain's still powerful aristocracy. In her rhetoric, the grammar school girl who made it on her own often poured scorn on the paternalism of the aristocrats in her party and she coined the derisive term 'wet' to describe them. Her Tory predecessor, Edward Heath, had abolished hereditary peerages, and, for a time it seemed possible that her middle class 'revolution' might just – as middle class revolutions should – lead to a serious reform of the institutions of feudalism: the House of Lords and monarchy. But it was not to be. In fact, in a somewhat bizarre move she actually reinstated hereditary peerages – and in 1983 gave one to William Whitelaw – although this may have been a purely political move to reward Whitelaw who, although a natural 'wet' nonetheless, during some of her intense conflicts with the 'wets', remained loyal to her. For Thatcher, Americanisation, with its republican virtues and institutions, was to stop short at the ancient privileges of Britain.

Far from weakening aristocratic wealth and privileges, Thatcher's 'American' middle class 'revolution' entrenched Britain's unearned social sector. When Thatcher took over, many of Britain's existing super-rich simply got richer through the lower tax regime on business and inheritance. Popular capitalism certainly allowed for the making of 'new money' but 'old money' also did extremely well out of the revolution. In Britain 'old money' (much of it tied up in land) was always mixed up with modern finance in the City of London, and thus did very well out of the 'revolution's' de-regulation of the financial district. In fact, one of the principal legacies of the Thatcher/Blair era was the creation of gigantic fortunes – as the already rich became super-rich and the already super-rich became mega-rich. Many of these fortunes could easily be placed outside the reach of the country's tax authorities, and those whose capital remained within the country benefited from the *comparatively* low tax regime.

A particular New Labour contribution to super-rich Britain was to open Britain's borders even wider to the global super-rich, and beyond them, the mega-rich, who during the Blair years have flocked into the country. A spectacular example of these new foreign money people were the Russian 'oligarchs', the hustlers to whom Boris Yeltsin literally handed gargantuan fortunes when he privatised Russia's state oil wealth. Roman Abramovitch, Eugene Shvidler, Valentin Yumashev, the aluminium magnet Oleg Deripaska, Victor

Vekselberg and Mikhail Chernoi – all were welcome. As was Boris Berezovsky who had been granted asylum in the country even though he was wanted for extradition by the Russian authorities.[20] Even *The Spectator* magazine blanched at all this, and Dominic Midgley argued that 'in London, the word "oligarch" produces a very different reaction, inspiring an enterprising collection of opportunists – aristocratic bankers, upper-crust lawyers – to reach for the telephone (to seek to act for them)'.[21]

In the US, in an earlier generation, Teddy Roosevelt crusaded against the 'malefactors of great wealth'. And today there is some opposition to creating a society of inherited fortunes – not least from amongst some of America's richest men. Warren Buffett, for instance, opposed President George W. Bush's proposal to drastically lower inheritance taxes – 'I love it when I'm around the country club', he argued, 'and I hear people talking about the debilitating effects of a welfare society. At the same time, they leave their kids a lifetime and beyond of food stamps. Instead of having a welfare officer, they have a trust officer. And instead of food stamps, they have stocks and bonds...'. Repealing the estate tax 'would be the equivalent of choosing the 2020 Olympic team by picking the eldest sons of the gold-medal winners of the 2000 Olympics'.[22]

Yet, Buffett is a relatively lone voice. For the contemporary American economic model virtually defines itself by allowing and celebrating super and mega-rich fortunes – even should these fortunes be inherited rather than earned the 'old-fashioned way'. The Thatcher consensus in Britain – notwithstanding its talk of work, thrift, and entrepreneurship – essentially agreed, and there has been little or no political opposition to the creation of a super-rich class that has secured its money largely through inheritance. John Major saw 'wealth cascading down the generations' as a good sign. And in the third term of the New Labour administration the inheritance regime was increasingly lavish: no-one paid any inheritance tax at all until the estate topped £325,000 – that was 94% of estates. The economist Julian Le Grand has found that total marketable personal wealth (not including pensions) stood at £2,594bn whilst the yield from inheritance tax stood at just £2bn. He reported that 'wealth passes almost untaxed between generations through lifetime gifts, through exempt items like agricultural land and forestry, and through devices like discretionary trusts'.[23] It was this inheritance bonanza that led to a country in which, by the turn of the century – two decades after the beginning of the Thatcherite popular capitalist 'revolution' – the top 1% owns 63% of the country's liquid assets while the bottom half owns just 1%. As Guardian journalist Polly Toynbee could argue: 'When you spell out the trajectory of future wealth gushing up to the top, almost everyone is alarmed…most think there must be some cap on inequality. Yet you don't hear the [New Labour] government argue the case'.[24]

This growing class of the super-rich is not politically neutral. Super-rich people have great power and influence and this has implications for policy, even foreign policy. There are exceptions, but, by and large, super-rich people tend to both demand and support low tax regimes, and thus tend to prefer the American model to that of the EU and continental Europe – with its high taxes and costs, its regulated labour markets and its welfare states.[25] In the pre-Thatcher era the super-rich were balanced out by working people organised in trade unions and by voting in elections. Today, though, the growing regiment of the insecure and the downwardly mobile do not redress the balance, at least initially. Downward mobility often leads to political apathy and exclusion. An increasing underclass can often mean increasing abstention.

The upshot was that the 1980s and 90s Thatcherite 'revolution' – as it was prosecuted by the three administrations of Thatcher, Major and Blair – may well have talked up meritocracy and social mobility, but, in fact, it created its very opposite: a new, rigid, class system based on inherited wealth. It was a society that was busily ditching the value of work and, instead, rewarding birth. It was a trend that became inevitable once the American capitalist model had been fully embraced.

10. 'Simply the Best: Britain is Back'

'It's Great To Be Great Again'
Tory election Poster, 1983

'We're in a very big world...We're a pretty ordinary little nation and yet we don't realise it.'
The Archbishop of Canterbury, 1994

Morale Restored: the Argentines and the Miners

Each generation in politics tells themselves a story about their country. And for the generation of Britons at the turn of the millennium – the Thatcher generation – the story was one of renewed success. The narrative was clear: the country had hit rock bottom in the 1970s as industrial strife culminated in the 'winter of discontent', but now – at the turn of the millennium – 'Britain was Back'.

And, for most people, like her or not, Margaret Thatcher and Thatcherism had played a significant part in all this. Whatever Thatcher's premiership actually accomplished, it served one, certain, role: it vastly improved the morale of the British. By the mid 1990s most of the political class and most commentators, both at home and abroad, were agreed that the Thatcher revolution, warts and all, had 'saved the

163

country' – and made it, if not great again, then at least a restored power in the world. There was an alternative story. No less a figure than the Archbishop of Canterbury had articulated it in the mid 1990s. 'We're in a very big world' he said 'and we're now very lonely...we have lost nearly all our navy and air force and so on...We're a pretty ordinary little nation and yet we don't realise it'.[1] He was right. Few did realise it.

The Falklands conflict of the late spring of 1982 was seen as a key event in this restoration of morale. For many Britons both at the time and when looking back on the events, the conflict in the south Atlantic represented a clear victory, one made sweeter after decades of national failure and decline. For a generation brought up on the failure at Suez, the slide down the league tables of the 1960s, and the decline into civil strife in the 1970s, the Falklands war was the first 'win' – one wag at the time suggested it was the first by the British alone since 'El Alamein' in 1942. Many people across the political spectrum developed an exaggerated reaction. Professor Ritchie Ovendale saw the Falklands conflict as proving that 'Suez was not the last imperial war' whilst also arguing that 1956 Suez, 'did not relegate Britain to minor power status'.[2] This evocation of continuing British power, indeed of an 'imperial' kind, may have been a minority taste amongst academics, but it resonated widely amongst the public.

US help to Britain during the Falklands conflict provided a perfect template for future British geo-strategy. In short, Britain and the British Prime Minister could still perform as a global player sure in the knowledge that US power stood behind her or him, underpinning the country's global pretensions. Twenty one years later Tony Blair, during the American war on Iraq, was working within this template.

The palpable sense of reviving national morale following the Falklands war was reflected in the processions and celebrations in London which, although controversial, established Margaret Thatcher as a national leader the likes of which the country had not seen since Winston Churchill. But there was also a sense that, morale aside, her true mission, economic recovery, would not be completed whilst Britain's powerful trade unions retained a veto over national policy. For, according to her inner circle, there was simply no way that a neo-liberal reform programme – particularly mass privatisation – could be introduced whilst trade union leaders (some of them quasi-Marxists, some, like Arthur Scargill, outright revolutionaries) could still wield political power.

In the minds of these Thatcherites (and many others) the trade union leaders and their followers through the labour movement had brought down the Heath government, had also destroyed the 'social contract' with Wilson and Callaghan, and stood poised to use their industrial muscle to limit, indeed derail, the Thatcher-Joseph economic programme.

But, following her election victory in 1983, Margaret Thatcher was able to oust her 'wet' colleagues (many of whom still sought to avoid a conflict with the unions) from the cabinet – and prepare the ground for a final showdown. And on the left, with Labour beaten in the election, many rallied behind the Miners' Union and its leader Arthur Scargill whose extra-parliamentary power had been displayed in earlier industrial conflicts and could yet stop Thatcher in her tracks. Thatcher, on the other hand, had prepared for the strike. When Scargill called the strike in the early summer of 1984 the outcome was not easily predictable. Many in the Westminster political system hedged their bets by not taking sides – including the young MP Tony Blair. During that fateful summer the violent pitched battles between police and trade unionists – one at Orgreave colliery on the 29th May involved some 5,000 pickets – was as near to a 'civil war' as an advanced industrial nation could come. Margaret Thatcher herself painted the conflict in lurid colours referring to an 'enemy within' and comparing the miners to the Argentineans. 'We had to fight an enemy without in the Falklands' she said, and 'we have always to be aware of the enemy within, which is more difficult to fight'. *Time* magazine reported to the Americans that it was a fight for the 'soul of Britain'.[3]

If Scargill had prevailed British politics would have taken a decisive shift to the left. Thatcher's revolutionary programme would have been abandoned before it had started; the 'wets' would have taken over the Tory Party and cabinet; the Labour left would have been in the ascendant in the Labour Party; and, more importantly, the militant trade union leaders (the right-wing unions had stayed out of the battle) would have become Britain's power brokers. No government would be able to introduce an economic and social policy without their approval. It would have meant one of two directions for the country: the more unlikely one was a benign outcome in which, after a while, the social democratic consensus which Thatcher sought to break was re-established. Or, alternatively, a Scargill victory would have created a dynamic in which a serious shift to the Bennite left became unstoppable – and with it the implementation of socialist economic policy (with an 'irreversible shift of power to working people and their families') and a siege economy.

This new socialist direction would have had major implications for foreign policy. Labour in 1983, under the leadership of Michael Foot, was already in favour of withdrawing from the Common Market and seriously weakening Britain's ties with NATO. Should the left – that is, Scargill and the left-wing unions and the Labour left – have won the civil war of 1984, then Britain's foreign alignment and geo-political position would have changed dramatically. It would have meant a decisive win for 'Little England' as a 'socialist Britain' said no both to Europe (by withdrawing from the Common Market) and America (by, in effect, detaching itself from NATO). Should the Labour left's economic programme have been implemented then it would have inevitably involved, no matter how dressed up, the introduction of a nationalist 'siege economy'. Such a siege economy, with the country on the way out of the Common Market and NATO, would have led to a continuing, and even deeper, crisis in the country.

1984 may have seen the defeat of one potential revolution, but it also saw the opening of the path to another. For, with the great road-bloc of countervailing trade union power removed Thatcher could go full pelt down her own revolutionary road.

The stakes were that high. However, the subsequent generation of political leaders and pundits has tended to downplay or ignore the importance, indeed perhaps even the existential importance, of this British civil war of 1984. The losers have little say in forming post-conflict opinions. And the winners were divided. Some Thatcherites trumpeted it as a milestone on the road to national recovery. Others, too embarrassed about how near the country came to Latin-American style instability, have drawn a veil over proceedings – in Basil Fawlty-like 'don't mention the [civil] war' denial.

But Thatcher needed a clear majority in parliament to properly prosecute her 'revolution'. This she achieved through her victories in the 1983 and 1987 general elections – particularly the 1983 one. But these electoral victories – and thus the whole 'revolution' – were carried through on only 42% of the vote, 42.4% in 1983 and 42.3% in 1987. Without the organic split in the Labour Party caused by the creation of the SDP-Liberal Alliance, Margaret Thatcher would never have secured the landslide majority in parliament necessary to carry through the radical changes at the heart of her revolution.

In sum, the creation of the SDP, although it failed to 'break the mould' of two party politics, did succeed in 'breaking the mould' of the post-war consensus – and was an indispensable part of the Thatcherite 'revolution'. The argument that by splitting the left the SDP leaders were playing with fire, and would simply hand over power to Thatcher, was always a contentious and touchy subject amongst the pro-European social democrats who did the deed. Roy Jenkins and Shirley Williams both remained bitterly hostile to Thatcher and Thatcherism as it developed in the 1980s; and it remains one of the great ironies that these pro-Europeans opened the way for Thatcher's great American adventure. But it was bound to be. For the clear fact was that these pro-European SDP leaders, when the chips were down and hard choices needed to be made, were more opposed to a Benn/Scargill future – of a socialist 'Little England' – than they were to Thatcher and US dominance.

Our Great Economy (c/o The American Model)

By the end of the 1990s there was another factor at play in this recovery in national morale: the idea that the British economy was no longer the 'sick man of Europe' – indeed, that it was healthy and vigorous, 'a leader' again in Europe. It was a theme that was helped forward by the problems confronting the erstwhile 'leader', Germany, during its difficult early years of reunification (when West Germany added, overnight, almost eighteen million people from the desultory, unproductive eastern states). And, as unemployment on the continent rose during the recession, and remained relatively high, the British, whose Thatcherite 'hire and fire' system allowed the creation of large numbers of low paid jobs, began to look better by comparison. British economic growth rates also began to look healthier than on the continent where orthodox Bundesbank, and then Euro-zone, policies were refusing to go for growth as a priority. And as the rise of China introduced low inflation into the global economy, Britain was able to sustain growth levels by low interest rates which allowed massively increasing private debt levels that kept consumption, and growth, up.

A particular American 'take' on the Thatcher era – one that became lodged in the collective mind of the transatlantic community of commentators – had it that Britain's first woman Prime Minister had played nothing less than an historic transforming role. She had, as the jargon had it, 'turned around' a sclerotic 'socialist' economy and restored the pride of the country. And, for many Americans, as for domestic British conservatives, it was uniquely the introduction of 'free market', neo-liberal, supply-side economics, that was seen as the positive agent of such change. In this powerful narrative, other factors that could also explain the 'turn-around' were far less prominent. The breathing space created by the huge North Sea oil bonanza that Margaret Thatcher inherited in 1979 – and the clear political and economic defeat of the militant trades unions that she engineered – were far less prominent.

Consequences

Over time, this view of the 1980s as a decade of national renewal based upon market economics became received wisdom. The belief that 'Britain was Back', and was restored as a global leader, had consequences. For an earlier generation global pretensions had led directly to the tragedy of the 1956 Suez invasion (and the humiliating withdrawal) and to the missed opportunity of 1957 (when Britain took no part in setting the rules for the Common Market and was later forced to join on inadequate terms). And for the new generation these renewed illusions also had consequences. For during the 1990s they led to a new round in the long, awkward relationship with Europe, and to a series of decisions that would keep the country out of the Euro-zone, on the European sidelines, and during the Blair years propel it into the sidekick relationship with the USA.

The first of these fateful decisions took place in the final months of Thatcher's time in Downing Street. For some time British politics had been dominated by the country's relationship with the European currency system – the ERM (the European Exchange-Rate Mechanism, the forerunner to the Euro). And a pro-ERM group in the cabinet finally got their way and persuaded Margaret Thatcher to sign up to Britain joining.

On 8th October 1990, the British government decided to enter the ERM. It did so with great fanfare, but without the courtesy of consulting its partners either about the entry itself or about the rate of exchange, which was set at a damagingly high rate of over 3DM to the Pound. This unilateral decision was accepted by the European partners but not with enthusiasm. It was widely seen as high-hand-ed. Jacques Delors made the less than ecstatic comment: 'I am happy about the decision of the British government, but I remain vigilant'.[4] Britain was later to pay for this unilateral act when on 'Black Wednesday' in 1992, it received little or no support from its conti-nental partners as it tried to stabilise Sterling and the country was forced to withdraw from its unsustainable position in the ERM. The humiliation of 'Black Wednesday' was on a par with that of Suez – and it unleashed a decade-long hostility to Europe (as we shall see in the next Chapter).

Simply The Best: A Superior, Exceptional People

For many of Britain's leaders in the 1990s – both Conservative and Labour – Britain did not really need Europe. The Thatcher revolution had made the country strong enough and important enough to resume a global role. After the traumas of the 1970s 'Britain was back'. And it was simply the best.

In December 1994 the then British Prime Minister, no less, could argue in a speech to Conservative women – which one columnist said was difficult to believe unless 'you heard it with your own ears' – that 'The United Kingdom – the greatest cradle of culture and academic and scientific and political achievement in modern times – that's not some trifle to be lightly set at risk...it is the highest cause this party knows – and we will defend it with every fibre of our being'.[5] John Major was echoing Margaret Thatcher herself who had made restoring British 'greatness' a key theme of her premiership. And even his own Foreign Secretary, Douglas Hurd, a man from the non-flag-waving wing of the party, was reported as accepting, indeed virtually recommending, the self-important idea of the country as 'punching above its weight' in world affairs. He could argue in 1993 to assembled luminaries at Chatham House in London that 'NATO is one of the principal props which have allowed Britain to punch above its weight'.[6]

This new overblown prideful mentality did not come out of thin air. It drew upon a vein of thinking and belief that had, in fact, never been expunged. For no matter the loss of empire and comparative economic decline, the morale boost of the Falklands war and the modest 1980s and 90s economic resurgence was all that Britain's leaders needed to justify yet another burst of braggadocio nationalism.

And they could draw on the long history of a belief in greatness, and upon long-held ideas and images that still resonated.

William Shakespeare could write about this 'sceptred isle set in a silver sea' that was 'the envy of less fortunate lands'. In the sixteenth century when England seemed to win most every battle they entered against a much larger military force (at Crecy they were outnumbered by three to one, at Poitiers by five to one) then 'perhaps for the first time, though certainly not for the last, the English began to suspect that God was an Englishman'. And Bishop Aylmer declared him to be so as early as 1558.[7] Oliver Cromwell believed, with most parliamentarians, that the English were a 'chosen people'. And in the nineteenth century Charles Dickens' Mr. Podsnap spoke for many when he opined that 'this island was blest, sir...to the direct exclusion of such other countries as – as there may happen to be'.[8]

Writing as late as the mid 1980s the historian Geoffrey Elton could talk of two English convictions having lasting currency: 'that every other realm groaned under despots and that everywhere else the peasantry had to live on mere vegetables, while in England Kings governed with the active consent of their subjects and people ate good red meat'.[9]

The conceit of exceptionalism was never a particularly partisan issue – for not only Tory nationalists, but also the country's late twentieth century radical, liberal and socialist thinkers mined its rich seams. The idea of England as the *special* home of liberty and freedom, and English history as the *unique* struggle against arbitrary rule, attracted many on the liberal left. As Elton suggested many of them believed that even the 'universal' rights of man were really English rights – 'the rights not of Man but of English men and women'.[10] The leading British socialist of the post-Second World War era, Michael Foot, whose heroes were Lord Byron and William Wordsworth (as well as Tom Paine and William Hazlitt), tended to buy into this idea of England as special. Foot, who made his political name as a firebrand socialist journalist working for the arch-imperialist press baron Lord Beaverbrook possessed more than a touch of 'Little Englander' nationalism. And towards the end of his long political career he formed a kind of bipartisan 'Little Englander' intellectual alliance with Enoch Powell in defence of parliamentary power. But in manfully trying to rescue English history from its Tory concentration on the 'Kings and Queens approach' he would often over-romanticise the parliamentary tradition. In 2006, Foot, on the home page of his website, 'Michael Foot at 90', displays a quote from Byron that started: 'England. With all thy faults I love thee still'.

This idea of a superior, exceptional, country served to foster the continuing thread of belief – held widely throughout the country, by left, right and centre – that the English were, are, and always will be a separate people, forever an island. The physical separation of an island people from the continent was always a powerful factor separating the Germanic tribes in England from those in the rest of northern Europe. And the physical island, and the English Channel, played a large role in forging identity ever since. In the latter half of the twentieth century the revolution in travel, particularly jet air-craft, and then, more powerfully still, the Channel Tunnel, eroded this sense of separation. But for the post-war and post-Cold War generations that now travel to the continent, or live there, the experience of war, and memories of the images of the Dunkirk evacuation, still resonate, and, for the moment, still outweigh the newer sense of Europe.

But more than the idea of an 'island race', it was the English language that has remained the greatest cause of separation – partic-ularly from the near neighbours on the continent. Indeed, the story of the development of the English language – and its battle with French and Latin after the Norman Conquest – is a key which may well even begin to unlock the mystery of English identity. In the late fourteenth century English was adopted as the official language of government by Henry V and then the great story-teller-poet of the English language, Geoffrey Chaucer, made his own contribution to the growing sense of Englishness.

The communications revolution in printing and publishing (led by William Caxton) which took hold in the fifteenth century, established the hegemony of English amongst the English and within England; and Caxton chose English (in fact London-English – the brand of English prevalent in London – there being several versions of English) as his published language. When his chronicle plays appeared, English was transformed from a primitive form of commu-nication into the language of a new learning, a process helped for-ward too by the publication and wide dissemination in 1604 of the King James Bible – published in English! And, some one hundred and fifty years later, by the time of the publication of Dr. Johnson's seminal English Dictionary (1755), the English language was fast becoming not only a major language but the primary cultural agency for the spread of English manners and ideas – of Englishness itself. Of course, this emergence of an increasingly popular and standardised English was crucial to popular consciousness of being English. Yet, even whilst this standardised English was destroying French and Latin in Britain it remained seriously fragmented by dialect, a diversity which, intriguingly, has lasted well into the television age of the late twentieth century.

All nationalism is about separateness, and this particular history of separateness – of an 'island people' being separated from others by geography, by the sea, and by language – remains very strong in contemporary English writing, analysis and polemics, resonating right up to the present day. Churchill himself talked of 'the island race' and evocatively of 'the island story' and issued the famed declaration that 'if I ever have to choose between the continent and the open sea I will choose the open sea'. In the 1970s the country's most prolific author and one of its leading nationalists and Eurosceptics, Paul Johnson, wrote about 'The Offshore Islanders' in a book of the same title.[11]

Enduring Hubris

Yet a fascinating question remains: why did such a strong strain of British nationalism – what amounted to a comparatively ripe form of the genre – endure well into the late twentieth century, and now into the twenty-first? One explanation lies in the formative years of the Thatcher generation of political leaders. After all, Margaret Thatcher herself, born in October 1925, was a teenager during the Second World War and an ambitious young politician in the 1950s. This was a time still dominated by empire. The English ruling classes only gave up on their empire after the war and continued to be beguiled by the enterprise long after the sun had set upon it. And, in consequence, the national culture of Englishness was to exhibit a decidedly imperial character well into the late twentieth century. Margaret Thatcher might well have been amongst the schoolchildren of the late 1930s who were being told 'we're all subjects and partakers in the great design, the British empire...[a] job assigned to it by God'.[12] And in the mid 1950s, secondary school children throughout the country were still assembling for something called 'Empire Day' to be told that they were the inheritors of a world power.

And long after the formal demise of empire, the imperial sensibility still lingered – and fed the idea of a 'world role'. Aphorisms of empire – 'Britain is a trading nation or it is nothing', 'Trade Follows the Flag' – continued to dominate political debate. Winston Churchill, an avowed supporter of empire, even during his post-war premiership, put a stop to Labour's process of decolonisation, and further colonial independence had to wait until Harold Macmillan became Prime Minister. Although Churchill was the last imperialist Prime Minister, Anthony Eden acted like one, and his invasion of Egypt in 1956 possessed all the hallmarks of the imperial mentality. And, as late as 1962 the Labour opposition leader, Hugh Gaitskell, was evoking not only 'a thousand years of history' but memories of the military support from the dominions at 'Vimy Ridge' and 'Gallipoli' in the First World War as part of his anti-Common Market campaign.[13]

With the empire still resonating, the new Queen and her court – both inside and outside of Parliament – continued to play a role that fostered the imperial illusion. And the immediate post-imperial generation of British political leaders – Edward Heath, Harold Wilson and James Callaghan all still took an oath of allegiance to the Queen. Later post-imperial Prime Ministers all grew up under the influence of the post-war global ethos and agenda set at the Queen's coronation and by the 'new Elizabethan age'. At the time of the coronation Margaret Thatcher was 28 and John Major was an impressionable 10 years of age.

This image of Britain as a global power was so ingrained that even the humiliation of Suez in 1956 had only a marginal effect on thinking. Lord Franks reflected a general view of the Westminster official class when, following Suez, he asserted grandly that 'Britain is going to continue to be what she has always been, a Great Power'.[14] And there was something in this prediction: for politically Britain still counted in the world as one of the 'magic circle' of western nations – she had a seat at the United Nations, a privilege denied to Germany, Japan and China, and, for a while, was one of 'the big three'. Even as late as the late 1950s Harold Macmillan could, just about, get away with being considered a world leader, and through the Commonwealth of Nations the UK political elite (and particularly the Queen) could still present themselves as leaders of a meaningful multi-national alliance of states.

Even the emergence of the USA as a world power that was replacing Britain had a paradoxical rub-off effect upon this continuing imperial mentality, particularly amongst the somewhat defensive English upper classes. The English elite could legitimately claim pride of authorship of the institutions of the powerful new superpower. And English, not French or German or Spanish, was its language. In the immediate post-war period, during American world supremacy, the levers of power and culture in the USA were still largely controlled by anglophile white Anglo-Saxon Protestants. Britain could piggy-back and pretend she was a partner in the growing American empire. Even as the country took the decision to pull out of 'East of Suez' British Prime Minister Harold Wilson could still say, in one of the most deluded and bombastic statements of the whole post-war era: 'Britain's frontiers are on the Himalayas'. Coming from such a personally modest man, this extraordinary and bombastic perspective shows the depth of belief within the broader political class.

One explanation for this hold of the imperial mindset on the late twentieth-century British leadership class was, of course, the sustaining effects of the two world wars. Defeat in war could have expunged the imperial memory. But Britain went through no such catharsis. In the twentieth century, Britain's grievous losses in the two wars – both in human and material resources – was, in fact, a defeat. But no sense of defeat took hold. Ernest Bevin, the first British Foreign Secretary to take office in the utterly crucial period following this devastating war, was a case in point. His sympathic biographer Alan Bullock put it clearly: 'he continued to identify Britain's national interests with the maintenance of the world role which the UK no longer had the resources to sustain'. Bullock also suggests that Bevin believed that this 'declining power was not permanent, but could be reversed'.[15]

In fact, rather than a sense of defeat, the two wars inculcated a culture of victory, indeed triumph – and triumphalism. The fires of patriotism, and nationalism, were re-stoked as 'victory' in the Second World War reinforced the sensibility not only of a separate, but also of a virtuous, English and British identity. It was this identity of separateness and superiority that, late in the twentieth century, was to be reinvigorated by the Thatcher revolution – and this renewal of national, and nationalist, sentiment severely limited the ability of the

Prime Ministers who followed Margaret Thatcher – John Major and Tony Blair – to pursue their desires to engage with Europe.

Thatcher's immediate successor, John Major, came to power in Britain in late 1990 as the Cold War and the bi-polar American-Soviet global order was ending. It was a time that was to see a huge leap forward in plans for European integration – culminating in the historic construction of the Euro-zone. But Britain, as in the lead up to Messina and the Treaty of Rome in 1956, was to stay on the sidelines.

11. John Major and the Beleaguered Europeans

'For us in Britain Europe is part of our lives.'
John Major, 1992

'The same Conservative Party which sacked Lady Thatcher is falling over itself to say No, No, No to Europe as vigorously as she once did.'
Charles Powell, 1997

The End of the Cold War

The Soviet Union formally came to an end on Christmas Day, 1991, thus bringing to an end the Cold War. A new world order was being born in which the bi-polar world would be replaced. The USA would become the lone superpower, but the size of her population (roughly 4% of the world total) and economy (roughly a quarter of the total) meant that talk of American 'hegemony' over the world was somewhat far-fetched. More likely was the birth of a multi-polar world. And in such a world, with the Soviet threat to Europe a thing of the past, it was clear that Europe would no longer be dependent on the US. And as European leaders unveiled their final plans for the Euro-zone – in the very same month that the Soviet Union dissolved – it seemed that, through this bold geo-strategic step, the blueprint of Europe as a united, equal, and independent global player was actually being implemented.

However, for British foreign policy the end of the Cold War brought special problems. For the previous forty Cold War years Britain's official class had seen dependence on the USA as unavoidable. Britain needed Washington's post-war loans and Marshall aid, and then the US nuclear guarantee. Britain's leaders gritted their teeth and, after Suez in 1956, fully accepted their new dependent status. During the long years of the Cold War, they had carved something of a niche out for themselves. As the USA's best friend in Europe, in a Europe reliant through NATO on American leadership, Britain even played something of a key strategic role. London was top European sidekick to the leader of the western system. As long, that is, as the Cold War continued.

Once the Soviet Union disappeared from the geo-political scene then for Europeans – to coin a phrase – 'the world would never be the same again'. Once the bipolar structures were eroded then there were only two serious alternatives on offer for the Europeans – either continued American hegemony or, alternatively, some form of greater European unity would emerge to replace the American role. Looking at the world in the early 1990s, many commentators were clear that – with the EU's 300 million people, a similar sized economy to the US, and now with firm plans for a currency that would compete with the dollar – the American hegemony option was simply unsustainable.

There was a palpable sense throughout the western side of the continent that Europe was on the move – that full unity would be difficult, but that it was now only a matter of time. In the first two years of the 1990s Germany was re-united, Sweden, Cyprus and Malta, and even Switzerland had applied to join, agreements were signed with the newly-freed eastern European countries, the Euro-zone plan was born and the Maastricht treaty signed. It seemed that Europe was emerging into a global power and that John F. Kennedy's long sought-after 'twin pillars of the west' were, indeed, under construction.

John Major's Tragic Standoff
John Major took over from Margaret Thatcher in November 1990. In what was virtually his first political move as Prime Minister, Major

was to issue a memorable statement from Ten Downing Street that signaled his wish for nothing less than an historic change in the country's foreign alignment. He declared – in what looked at the time like a huge snub to Margaret Thatcher and a reversion to the Edward Heath years – his desire to see the country 'at the heart of Europe'. Major was a sympathiser with the aims of European monetary union, and, earlier, had taken Britain into the precursor of the Euro, the Exchange Rate Mechanism, much against the better wishes of his own Prime Minister. Also, whilst a seemingly loyal supporter of Margaret Thatcher he had never been party to her visceral anti-continental – and pro-American – sympathies, and he came to the premiership following what amounted to a pro-European coup from within the cabinet.

For a time it seemed as though John Major might well tilt Britain's foreign alignment away from Washington and towards Europe. Major was not one of nature's Atlanticists: and apart from a minor interlude at the Foreign Office, he had not been very involved in defence and security matters, and therefore did not embrace the culture of Washington-led NATO. Also, his relations with the United States became strained when President Bill Clinton took over the White House following the Presidential election in November 1992. Clinton, who did not get on with Tories, believed that Major had improperly interfered in the American election campaign in 1992 in order to aid his opponent, George H. W. Bush.

The test of whether John Major was truly in the business of re-orienting British foreign policy towards Europe was to come within weeks of his taking over in Downing Street. In December 1990 the European leaders, including Major, moved to set up an Intergovernmental Conference (an IGC) to plan for the Euro – and also, so they said, for 'political union'. The conference was scheduled to last for a year; and, for Britain, and Major, it was to be a fateful year. Fervent pro-Europeans believed that in the IGC negotiations Britain should 'go for it', help shape the outcome, and become a founding member of the planned Euro-zone, introducing the new currency with the others in the late 1990s. Once it was clear that Britain was actually planning to be a founder member of Euroland it would bring to an end the two decades of Britain's awkward and often hostile relationship with the neighbours.

In guiding the furious European debate in the Tory Party Major was, though, dealt a difficult hand. He was by no means a free man.

The 'palace coup' that had brought him to Downing Street continued to sour relationships with the still very strong Thatcherite grouping in the party; following her ouster, Margaret Thatcher herself was to remain an active 'Eurosceptic' exerting considerable political influence in the background of Tory politics for the next fifteen years. Major was aware that these Thatcher supporters on the backbenches could always effectively veto any attempt by him to join the Euro at launch date. Even the Maastricht Treaty – in which Britain stayed outside the Euro-zone only agreeing to 'opt-in' at a later date – was bitterly opposed by the Tory 'Eurosceptic' rebels (led by a future Tory Party leader, Ian Duncan-Smith).

And in the middle of these Euro negotiations Major was faced with a major geo-political crisis which would dominate his first weeks in office and affect the rest of his premiership. Out of a clear blue sky Saddam Hussein had invaded Kuwait, and on 17th January 1991 a US-led coalition started 'Operation Desert Storm' to evict the Iraqis from the small sheikdom. With Europe beginning to reassess its new position in a world without superpower rivalry, the conduct of the Gulf War was a great demonstration of American military prowess, and reminded the European allies of their dependence on US power to protect their oil supplies. President George H. W. Bush was proclaiming that a 'new world order' was coming into being. And following his success in the gulf it certainly seemed that American global leadership would be an indispensable aspect of the new world order. This belief that America would remain the 'indispensable power', as Secretary of State Madeleine Albright would later so describe the USA, took the shine off Europe's new global ambitions, at least for a time.

More damaging still for European credibility in the new era was the collapse of the Yugoslav federation and the subsequent Balkans conflict. During 1991 the German government was becoming the major power in the area, and Chancellor Helmut Kohl took the fateful step of encouraging Croatian independence. And the German Chancellor may well have lit the touch paper which ultimately exploded and broke up the federation. Indeed, the Bavarian Interior Minister could say that 'Helmut Kohl has succeeded where neither Emperor Guillaume nor Hitler could'.[1]

But Washington did not want Germany or the EU to become a pre-eminent power in the region, and the Clinton administration influenced the Izetbegovic government into refusing to sign the peace agreements arranged by the European leaders in 1993. Instead, Washington sought NATO control of the area. And when the federation then fell apart in ethnic conflict, and the EU was unable to deal with this problem 'in its own backyard', the US entered the Balkans fray and took the lead role in the Kosovo conflict and the NATO air war over Serbia, which ended in June 1999. This Balkans episode was a great defeat for Europe. The major European powers were divided on what to do and who to support. And the geo-strategic lesson was clear: that Europe could not act to deal with a crisis even on its own continent, and still needed to call in 'Uncle Sam' and 'the new world' to 'redress the balance of the old'.

This Balkans crisis also became a dry run for the neo-conservatives in Washington. Although out of power, there was quite a debate amongst Republicans. The 'realist' old guard led by Jim Baker (later to Chair the Iraq Study Group which reported in 2007) wanted to keep the USA out of the Balkans. He famously put it that 'we have no dog in this fight'. However many neo-conservatives saw it differently, seeing the Balkans crisis as an opportunity to weaken Europe, put US power on display, and develop a unilateralist approach sidelining the United Nations. Leading neo-con Richard Perle has reportedly argued that the US-led air war against Serbia was a useful precedent – 'the first precedent' – for the US to act unilaterally in overriding a UN Security Council resolution, a precedent which was followed in the later invasion of Iraq in 2003.[2]

In Britain during the 1990s the lessons of the first Gulf War and the Balkan crises were clear: Europe was not, any time soon, going to supplant the USA as a global power, and Britain had no urgent need to review 'the special relationship' and draw closer to the EU. Yet, these geo-political lessons aside, it was to be a 'domestic' economic event that decisively turned the British against European integration for another decade or so. In September 1992, the Major administration was suddenly rocked by what amounted to a national humiliation – which quickly turned into a source of British hostility towards the continent, and particularly the Germans.

Only months after its election victory on the 16th September 1992, on what became known as 'Black Wednesday', Britain was forced to leave the Exchange Rate Mechanism of the European currency system, the forerunner of the Euro-zone. At first, this dramatic event was portrayed by much of the press as a defeat on the level of Suez in 1956. But, within days, the Chancellor of the Exchequer, Thatcherite 'dry' Norman Lamont would, Dunkirk-like, successfully turn this defeat into a win. He declared that instead of moping, he was 'singing in my bath'. And he began to argue that the country, now outside the currency system and floating its currency, was, at last, 'free' to develop its economy without the constrictions imposed by the continental monetary system.

As the days passed, the true story of the currency crisis became public with the revelation that the Germans, in the form of the Bundesbank, had refused to intervene to support the Pound thus letting sterling fall out of the system. British opinion-formers, with some justification, then publicly blamed the Germans, and British-German relations cooled dramatically. The Germans pleaded that, so soon after re-unification, they could not afford to bail Britain out; the British responded that, under the rules of the currency mechanism, they had an obligation. The problem for Britain was that it had a less than co-operative record on the European currency question. In 1990 it had entered the ERM unilaterally without consultation and when the 'Black Wednesday' crisis blew up John Major had already decided – at Maastricht – that Britain would not become a full member of the Euro-zone at launch-date, and only join at a possible later date. Had Britain been playing a full part in the projected Euro-zone then the Germans, when put on the spot, would have found it difficult not to support Sterling. They could hardly contemplate letting a projected inner-core Euro-zone member go under.

The fact was that both the British and the Germans had fallen foul of the exigencies of the new situation in Europe following the end of the Cold War – particularly the initial economic and financial difficulties caused by German reunification. But the British remained sore, and Major's government struck out on a more detached direction – with its 'wait and see' policy towards the Euro. British *amour propre* was not soothed when some days after the Pound had fallen out of the ERM German Chancellor Helmut Kohl in the Bundestag made a none-too-veiled threat: he declared, obviously referring to the British, that 'no one in Europe – and I repeat, no one – should labour under the illusion that it is in a position to go it alone'.[3]

For nationalists and Eurosceptics 'Black Wednesday' may have been a short-term national humiliation, but it soon came to be seen as 'White Wednesday'. For, in one fell swoop, Britain was out of the

ERM, and the continentals, particularly the Germans, were the culprits. Following the fiasco John Major and the Europeanists were never again able during the Conservatives' time in office to put Britain 'at the heart of Europe'. September 1992 was to become a turning point in the long British European debate.

Major's government never recovered from 'Black Wednesday'. The Conservative Party's support in the opinion polls slumped dramatically, intriguingly flat-lining for the rest of the parliament and not even recovering by much during the 1997 general election. And Major's attempt to push through parliament the ratification of the Maastricht Treaty led to a bruising fight within the Conservative Party – the bitterness from its fallout leaving deep scars. 'Black Wednesday', the Maastricht Treaty ratification, and the loss of popular support, all conspired to create a serious party crisis in which an anti-Euro faction of Conservative MPs formed a 'party within a party' and for a time lost the Tory whip. This grouping, which included MP John Redwood, was to form the heart and soul of the contemporary British Eurosceptic movement.

These Tory Eurosceptics – they were, in reality, much more 'anti' than they were 'sceptical' – carried on a successful parliamentary guerilla warfare against the Major government with the ultimate aim of getting it to abandon its residual commitment to future Eurozone entry. They sought, by initially rejecting Euro entry, to turn the Tory Party against the whole European Union integration process – with the ultimate aim of either turning Europe into a free trade area or, should that not be possible, leaving the Union altogether. A decade later this small, and somewhat eccentric, grouping had succeeded beyond their wildest expectations. In two elections, 2001 and 2005, Britain's Tory Party had opposed Euro entry and had by so doing forced Labour to abandon its own earlier attempts to enter the currency zone. By New Year's Day, 2007 – even though *The Financial Times* could report the historic news that the Euro was in sight of competing with the Dollar as the world's reserve currency – the British *Zeitgeist* had turned, seemingly decisively, against Europe.[4]

The Tory Europeans
Ever since Margaret Thatcher turned against the European project in her Bruges speech in 1987, the pro-Europeans were always in the

minority in the Conservative Party. But, even so, they also always held serious cards. One such was the fact that these pro-Europeans – including such Tory luminaries as Michael Heseltine, Kenneth Clarke, Geoffrey Howe, Chris Patten, Douglas Hurd and Leon Brittan – all held senior positions in the Thatcher and Major cabinets.

Yet as the 1990s progressed this generation of pro-European Tories increasingly seemed somewhat time-warped. Formed in the Heath era, they had all been, as young politicians, active in the successful battle over the Common Market in the years leading up to the referendum of 1975, and they had gone on in government to support the Single European Act of 1987. In the early 1970s they had the benefit of a party consensus behind entering the EEC, they had most of the press on their side, they had a failing economy at home and successful economies in Europe and they could present the leading anti-Europeans as extremists (what Bob Worcester, Chairman of MORI Polls had called the 'men with staring eyes syndrome').[5]

By the 1990s, however, the pro-European Tories seemed totally nonplussed as they found the political ground shifting from under them: the pro-European consensus had disappeared, the press was mostly hostile, the European economies were believed to be faltering, and Euroscepticism was no longer the preserve of eccentrics. During Major's premiership they were unable to secure British membership of the Euro-zone and they saw their party turn away from Europe. In the ten years following the end of the Tory government they lost battle after battle as a succession of Tory leaders took the party in an overtly anti-EU direction. They waited for Tony Blair to give a lead first on the Euro issue and later on the constitution; and when he did not they refused to take the lead themselves. They simply lost their way, and in the process the European cause in Britain was set back a generation: with the further consequence that the 'special relationship' with the USA was given a new lease of life, and was still flourishing well into the new century.

During the Thatcher and Major governments the two leading pro-European figures, Michael Heseltine and Kenneth Clarke, both held very senior positions. Michael Heseltine became Deputy Prime Minister in the Major government and the leading pro-European in the Tory Party. He had the added aura of being the only man to stand up to Thatcher during her reign when he resigned from her cabinet over the Westlands helicopter crisis. He had secured a surprisingly high vote against her in the first ballot for Tory leader in 1990, and had effectively destroyed her premiership.

Heseltine was, of course, hated by the Thatcherite Eurosceptics, but even so, was recognised as a potential Tory PM with great mass popular appeal. His hour came when in July 1995 John Major, frustrated by his anti-European Tory opponents, sought, in a surprise move, a vote of confidence from his MPs in order to settle the leadership issue once and for all. Instead of entering the fray himself Heseltine decided to support Major. Should he have stood against Major, Heseltine may well have won the contest and, from the premiership in Downing Street, would have been in a strong position to muster a consensus for placing Britain on the glide-path to joining the Euro when it was eventually launched in 1999. It was a huge missed opportunity – both for Heseltine and also for his great cause of Europe.

During the 1990s and beyond Michael Heseltine shared the leadership of the pro-European Tories with Kenneth Clarke who became Chancellor of the Exchequer in May 1993. From the moment he took over in 11 Downing Street, Clarke used his position in Major's cabinet to almost single-handedly block the ascendant Tory Eurosceptics from getting what they wanted – a clear policy commitment against Britain joining the Euro. And following the defeat of the Conservatives in 1997, with Tony Blair toying with a quick referendum on the Euro, Clarke offered Blair his own support in any referendum campaign the new Prime Minister might want to call.

Such a cross-party pro-Euro campaign at such a time, with Blair as a new and popular PM asking for a 'yes' vote, would likely have succeeded. Indeed Clarke was to consistently offer Blair his support throughout the next eight years – both on the Euro issue and on the projected constitutional treaty. But Clarke, though a crucial voice in any national referendum campaign, was losing ground in the Tory Party itself as it swung increasingly in a Eurosceptic and then anti-European direction. Clarke was to lose out to three Tory competitors in successive leadership elections (to William Hague in 1997, to Ian Duncan-Smith in 2001, and to David Cameron in 2005). But, like Heseltine before him, he too missed an opportunity. It came following the Tory defeat in the 2001 general election. In that election Eurosceptic Tory leader William Hague had based his whole campaign on his anti-Euro views being an election winner and had gone round the country holding up a pound coin and pledging to 'save the Pound'. Consequently, his defeat was also a big defeat also for the Eurosceptics.

The Liberal Democrats had done well in the election, gathering an unprecedented post-war crop of seats, and were in a mood to broaden their base in a deal with Clarke should he raise the European issue and set up his own backbench group of pro-Euro Tory MPs (in a kind of reverse repeat of the Redwood grouping during Major's government). Two Tory Members of the European Parliament, John Stevens and Brendan Donnelly, had taken the courageous step of breaking with their party and setting up a pro-Euro Tory Party list of candidates for the European elections in the summer of 1999 – and by 2001 they were a readymade political apparatus for Clarke to join. Yet Clarke refused Stevens' insistent blandishments, arguing that he would continue the fight within the Tory Party.

After the general election of 2001, with Blair becoming unpopular and Duncan-Smith not catching on with the public, a Clarke-Kennedy tie-up and ticket could have had a good chance of holding the balance in the election of 2005. It could have been expected to do somewhat better than did the Liberal Democrats alone, and might well have denied Tony Blair his overall majority or even reduce the Tories, led by Michael Howard, to third party status. In the event, Clarke stayed loyal to his party and served under its new leader, David Cameron.

In the great European debates of the post-Thatcher era, Michael Heseltine and Kenneth Clarke fought hard for their corner, but, unlike the Labour pro-Europeans in the early 1980s, they ultimately balked at going the final yard and splitting their party. Heseltine's timidity was a product of his continuing sensitivity about his assassin's role in ending Thatcher's premiership; and Clarke hung on because he believed right up to the last minute – that minute ending when Cameron defeated him for the Tory leadership – that he could at some future point lead the Conservative Party.

During their tenure at the top these pro-European Tories did succeed in blocking moves within the Tory Party to take Britain out of the EU altogether. But, ultimately, they watched their great cause of Europe lose ground after ground, and saw the British people turn increasingly against Britain joining the Euro. Ultimately, they did not take a stand. They put their party before their country.

There was, though, a deeper problem affecting Britain's whole European movement in these years. Thatcher's powerful offensive against European integration had over the years taken its toll on the confidence of the pro-European camp, and a sense of defensiveness prevailed. The pro-Europeans seemed unable to offer a vision to match the European vision of an earlier generation who had sold the European cause as indispensable for peace in Europe. It amounted to an unwillingness to engage the argument on a fundamental level – to argue the case publicly that was being proffered privately: that the new post-Cold War geo-politics opened the road for a change in the country's foreign alignment, that Europe was the future and that Britain no longer needed to be dependent upon the United States.

Ever since Margaret Thatcher made the 'f word' ('f' for 'federal' Europe) and the idea of a superstate unacceptable in the late 1980s, the British pro-European establishment remained suspicious of anyone campaigning for political union in Europe, let alone for federalist ideas. In pro-European political circles in Westminster federalists, like John Pinder and Ernest Wistricht, and their colleagues in The Federal Trust and the Federal Union, were respected but hardly taken seriously. Instead, Britain's pro-Europeans preferred the 'softly-softly' approach to campaigning, hoping to bounce Britain into the Euro-zone whilst no-one was looking. Or alternatively trying to sell Europe to the British on technical, tourist grounds of making currency exchange easier – the so-called 'Thomas Cook' argument for Europe. And in the process, the key Eurosceptic arguments were not met head on: as the successful Eurosceptic themes of 'British Law versus Euro Bureaucracy' and 'Democracy versus Brussels Unaccountability' were rarely rebutted.

And even when, after 9/11, security became the primary issue, pro-Europeans rarely argued that Britain's security could only be properly secured through Europe-wide common security policies – and that Britain needed the strength of European unity in a 'dangerous world'. And, again, even after the invasion of Iraq in 2003 the pro-Europeans still refused to turn anti-US sentiment into pro-European policy – even when an argument that Britain had been 'dragged into war by America' would have resonated, the pro-European establishment remained timorous. Liberal Democrat Charles Kennedy dipped his toe in this water during the 2005 general election, but there was no sustained campaign against British war support for America amongst the pro-Europeans. No political leader was prepared to use opposition to the war to make out a broader geo-strategic case for de-linking Britain from the US and joining our main European allies in opposing the American war and its expected tragic ending.

In fact, the whole pro-European movement in the Major/Blair era avoided a direct intellectual and political confrontation with its opponents. Part of the reason for this reticence was that such a clear confrontation would inevitably raise the awkward question of Britain's 'special relationship' with the USA. The fact was that most of Britain's pro-European political leaders, partly because of age, were, in reality, tied in to the Westminster political establishment. And this establishment, having signed on lock stock and barrel, and as an act of faith to a strong American relationship in NATO in the Cold War years, now found it very difficult – even in the new circumstances of the post-Cold War era – to walk away from this previous commitment. Even those Westminster establishment politicians – in the Liberal Democratic Party or in New Labour – who ardently opposed the unilateralist, regime-change global policy of the United States and Britain's support for America in 2003 in the war in Iraq, found it difficult to launch any serious systematic critique of 'the special relationship' and American policy. Such an approach would automatically place the protagonist outside the Westminster consensus.

So, because too serious an engagement in any serious debate about Britain's future would raise the American question, the strategy of the Westminster pro-Europeans in these years was not to directly engage the ascendant Eurosceptics on the big issues. Rather it was to leave the pro-European campaign (both on the Euro and the constitution) to the Prime Minister, who was constantly hinting that he would lead a referendum fight at the right time. The sad truth for the pro-Europeans was that for a full decade they waited for Tony Blair, but the Prime Minister never showed up.

Tony Blair Bottles It

Blair, when on form, was a far better advocate for Europe than the Tory pro-Europeans. When he bothered to campaign for Europe he adopted a more modern, relevant approach than the establishment Tories. He sometimes gave glimpses of what his leadership of a referendum campaign might actually look like should a vote ever be scheduled. It would have been led by Downing Street and Tony Blair personally and backed by a full New Labour PR operation – with simple, easy arguments put in a straightforward manner to appeal to middle England, and with the 'no campaign' opponents being painted as either extremists or stuck in the past.

Indeed, almost all pro-Europeans were keen for Tony Blair to enter into the ring as their champion. Blair had positioned New Labour as a pro-Euro party from the moment he became Labour Leader in 1994. And immediately upon becoming Prime Minister he changed Major's 'wait and see' policy on the Euro to one in which the country would 'prepare and decide'. For the whole period of his premiership Euro entry remained a publicly proclaimed aim of his government. Even during the height of his geo-political disputes with President Chirac and Chancellor Schröder over European relations with America, he would always argue for it as a goal and would always be prepared to state that 'Europe was our destiny'. And when the proposed European constitution took precedence over the Euro as an issue, he supported joining up and even proclaimed that he would lead the fight for a 'yes' vote in the coming referendum.

But, although the seeming champion of European integration, he would never actually appear in the ring – and for a simple reason: because he could not guarantee to himself that a pro-European referendum could ever be won. A decisive moment in the history of contemporary Britain's foreign policy took place in the late spring of 1997 when Blair placed a pledge in his manifesto to hold a referendum on Euro entry should Labour decide to join.[6] This fateful decision to hold a referendum was to frustrate pro-Europeans for the rest of Blair's time in Downing Street – for once having granted a referendum, he could hardly withdraw the idea, but nor could he risk holding a vote, for fear of losing. And at no time between 1997 and 2007, either in the Euro or the constitution debate, could Blair guarantee a 'yes' vote. Ironically, this original decision in 1997 had been a political manoeuvre considered essential in order to rob John Major of wrapping himself in the union flag in the then coming election; but, as it turned out, Blair's election victory in 1997 was never under threat.

Tony Blair came very near to calling a referendum just after the 1997 general election, and again just after the 2001 general election. But on both occasions he thought better of it. By insisting on a referendum back in 1997 he had tied his hands. And with every passing year since Blair came into office public opinion inched ever further against entry. In order to win a referendum Blair was convinced that he would not only have to overcome widespread mild Euroscepticism amongst the public, but also a ferocious campaign from the increasingly confident anti-European tabloids, which in any campaign would be covered in full xenophobic war-paint.

12. Tabloid Xenophobia

'No-one ever lost any money underestimating the intelligence of the public.'
H.L. Mencken, September 1926

'I know Tony Blair. Blair is one of Thatcher's children. I think he knows it.'
Irwin Steltzer, Rupert Murdoch's Advisor.

'The Sun Backs Labour'
March 1997

Blair, Washington and Europe

Tony Blair came into office pledging a European future for the country. His promise of a referendum on Britain joining the Euro-zone was not initially seen as a ploy to push the issue 'into the long grass', but rather as an earnest expression of genuine intentions. Yet, once he had decided he would not hold an immediate referendum, and the polls continued to show a high level of public opposition, Euro-zone entry went onto the back-burner, never truly to revive. It was soon quite clear that Blair's premiership was not going to usher in any radical change in

Britain's foreign policy alignment. There would be no further British integration in Europe nor any downgrading of 'the special relationship'.

Only days after Blair had arrived in Downing Street the new, young and eager British Prime Minister hosted a visit to Britain by none other than the President of the United States, William Jefferson Clinton. Blair had probably already decided that Britain was not going to join the Euro-zone any time soon and that the transatlantic status quo would therefore be preserved. And he announced at the joint press conference with Clinton that he and the President agreed that 'Britain does not need to choose between being strong in Europe or being close to the United States of America'.[1]

Blair had forged a strong relationship with Clinton and the American Democrats soon after becoming leader of the Labour Party in 1994. He had worked on the 'Third Way' proposals which had originated across the Atlantic in Clinton's Democratic Leadership Council and he authored a Fabian pamphlet 'The Third Way: New Politics For the New Century' which was published in 1998. 'The Third Way' formed a bond between the two men and Clinton became Blair's role model. Blair admired Clinton's 'triangulation' electoral strategy but also Clinton's political persona – the laid back charm and the engaging lightness of touch with few rough edges or discordant ideas. In Blair's premiership style there was also a clearly discernible attempt to mimic the public relations approach of the Clinton Presidency: from the regular 'presidential' Downing Street press conferences (equipped with 'presidential' podium and red carpet) to – an idea that didn't fly – an aircraft called 'Blair One'.

Blair's close relations with Clinton became even closer when Clinton, after some hesitation, decided to enter the European arena with military force during the Kosovo crisis in 1999. Tony Blair had taken the lead in the political planning of NATO's Kosovo intervention and the air war over Serbia and in getting the US involved. For Blair, the successful outcome in Kosovo and Serbia had proven the value of both American involvement in Europe and the policy of intervention. Indeed the Prime Minister went to Chicago in late April 1999 to deliver a landmark speech about the merits of 'liberal interventionism'. Kosovo had served to considerably strengthen Blair's Atlanticist and NATO instincts (and somewhat weaken his pro-European ardour).

By the very late 1990s, at the same time as Blair's relationship with Washington was growing ever closer, it was becoming clear that

Britain's economy had been reviving during the last years of the Major premiership, and that when Major handed over to Blair in May 1997 he gifted him what amounted to a relatively strong economy. And, slowly but surely, a new narrative began to be constructed by the New Labour public relations team. It was a theme that built on the earlier ideas of 'national recovery' developed during the Thatcher/Major era before the humiliating events of September 1992; and it was purpose-built for New Labour's pitch in the next election. The message was simple: not only was Britain's economy thriving, but so successful was Britain that it could set an example to Europe, even to the world.

In what was to become a central theme of the Blair era, Tony Blair and his team, in speeches and briefings, began to suggest that the continent needed to learn from us – from the 'Anglo-Saxon' economies – and not the other way round. He and other Labour ministers spoke regularly of Britain 'leading in Europe' and would regularly point the way forward to the laggardly continentals. The assumed superiority of 'Anglo-Saxon' economics over continental 'Rheinish' capitalism was also the constant refrain coming out of Bill Clinton's Washington, most specifically out of the office of Treasury Secretary Rubin.

Blair continued to favour Britain joining the Euro-zone *when the terms were right*, but his new approach – the idea that the British needed to teach the continentals about the merits of 'Anglo-Saxon economics' – was bound to annoy some of the continental leaders. It would also subtly undermine the pro-European campaign at home. Blair argued to his 'Britain in Europe' supporters that the message of 'Britain leading and guiding Europe' would help gather support amongst the British for the European project. Yet, with Britain doing 'so well' and the continent 'so badly' the question became: why bother joining a failing outfit?

This new hubristic and 'teachy' New Labour nationalism was to meld in rather well with the 'ideology' of Britain's new power elite in the tabloid media. For some time, just like New Labour, the tabloids had been able to combine two contradictory messages: on the one hand an overt 'British is Best' nationalism with, on the other, geo-political subordination to foreigners in Washington and Wall Street. There were no press campaigns by the 'patriotic' press against the 'special relationship'; no systematic questioning of the unequal closeness of the American and British leaderships; and no Washington bogeymen to equal the Brussels Eurocrats. Indeed, this great contradiction was exemplified by the lives of the leading media moguls themselves. For, intriguingly, whilst their papers pumped out patriotic messages – 'proud to be British', 'sovereignty under threat from foreigners' – these same media moguls were living and working for much of their lives in foreign lands, in New York (Rupert Murdoch), in Toronto (Conrad Black), and in Paris (Lord Rothermere). And the leading voice of British patriotism, Rupert Murdoch, was an American citizen.

Although the main press moguls supported Blair's close relationship with the USA (with particular intensity during the 2003 invasion of Iraq) Blair would be on the receiving end of tabloid invective whenever it looked as though he might be preparing a pro-European initiative – whether on the Euro-zone or the constitutional treaty. In the summer of 1998 following a European summit in Cardiff, the BBC reported that Blair was all set to join the Euro-zone immediately following the next general election. *The Sun* immediately responded with a headline describing Blair as 'The Most Dangerous Man in Britain', an intervention that was treated in other media outlets like a major political event. There followed much speculation about whether Blair would secure the support of *The Sun* at the next election. In the event, Blair was to make no pledge about Euro-zone entry, and *The Sun* duly supported him in the election of 2001.

In early 2004 Blair began to talk positively about the new European constitution that was emerging out of the Constitutional Convention chaired by ex-French President Giscard D'Estaing. His position was that Britain should ratify the constitution through a parliamentary vote. In almost an exact replay of earlier big European decisions, Blair, threatened by Murdoch, had backed down. *The Guardian*'s political correspondent, Nicholas Watt reported that 'to the delight of the Tories and Rupert Murdoch, who recently threatened to withdraw support if Downing Street refused to change tack, the Prime Minister will declare that the "weather has changed"'.[2] Having opposed a referendum, Blair now supported holding one. One pro-European Tory insider said that 'agreeing to a referendum was like handing the decision over to Rupert Murdoch'. *The Sun* supported Blair in his third general election quest a year later.

Moguls: Business, Europe and America

Blair was more aware than most that media corporations, and the moguls who ran them, were the new political power elite. He had watched as they came to the fore as brokers of political power during the Thatcher and Major years. Indeed, the struggles of the media moguls were a key part of the story of the Thatcher revolution – a revolution which Blair supported and deepened. During the epic struggle between the Thatcher government and the left-wing trade unions the moguls became key actors in the drama. For Murdoch needed the defeat of the unions – in his case the powerful print unions in Fleet Street – as much as did Thatcher. And, by the late 1980s, Thatcher's victory was Murdoch's victory – and vice versa. The defeat of the print unions at Murdoch's plant at Wapping ushered in more than a new technology of print production and enhanced power for media owners. It was a building block in Thatcher's wider political success, a success that allowed the later political go-ahead to be given for Murdoch's plans for cross-media ownership.

The political needs of the media moguls – a business-friendly environment sustained by business-friendly parties – was bound to lead to an affinity with America, the home and heartland of business, and support for 'the American model' of low taxes and flexible labour markets. And, conversely, business-friendly politics was bound to lead to a natural suspicion of the EU, and the EEC before it, because of Europe's 'social model' of limitations on business through higher taxes and more regulated markets. During Blair's premiership the most politically influential newspaper owners were the trio of Murdoch, Black and Rothermere (father and son). Murdoch's *Sun* had a circulation of 3.84 million in 1997 when Blair became Prime Minister, and his *News of the World* had a circulation 4.37 million. Conrad Black owned the *Daily Telegraph* and *Sunday Telegraph* (*Daily Telegraph* circulation was 1.13 million) and the Tory opinion-forming magazine *The Spectator*. And the Rothermere family's *Daily Mail*, increasingly influential amongst women, sold 2.15 million.[3] But it was not just the sheer size of the circulation of these papers that gave their owners great political power. More important was the fear – the fear amongst politicians of getting on the wrong side of the populist technique of sustained day after day, drip, drip propaganda and news slanting based upon targeting specific issues.

195

All the moguls had strong connections with the United States. Rupert Murdoch lived there, became a US citizen and had large interests in both US newspapers and television. Conrad Black was born in North America and possessed major interests in Canada as well as the US. And Jonathan Harmsworth – who took over as Chairman of Associated Newspapers from his father, Lord Rothermere, in 1998 – had a classic 'Anglo-American' transatlantic education: Gordonstoun public school and Duke University, North Carolina.

However, 'selling America' too openly to the British people – particularly the need to Americanise the post-1945 welfare state – was always a difficult task. The American socio-economic model – with its private health system – may well have attracted the business class but it had a very limited appeal to 'Middle England'. Margaret Thatcher well understood this: hence her pledge whilst Prime Minister that 'the health service is safe in my hands'. She, and her political and business supporters, also understood that the domestic electoral support for her ambitious neo-liberal 'revolution' did not come out of any desire for a grand ideological pro-American 'free market' change of economic course. Rather the opposite: it came from a domestic, *British*, patriotic desire for the restoration of national confidence and success after the debilitating 1970s – and for a strong democratic leader to carry it through.

Thatcher, as well as the businessmen who owned the tabloids, understood that good old-fashioned flag-waving patriotism was the key to winning hearts and minds, and therefore to electoral success. Tabloid nationalism had been born out of this key understanding. And in the late 1980s, and onwards, sensing that a renewed pride in the nation was a winning line, owners and editors played the patriotic card more and more boldly – and, under the pressure of growing competition for readers, the political posturing of this conservative press mutated from a generalised national pride into a rampant, crude xenophobia.

'Page Three Girls' and Xenophobia

A populist media climate and culture lends itself to the emergence of xenophobia – or extreme, simplistic, aggressive, nationalism. And a populist approach has been a feature of the British media ever since the birth of mass newspapers. Yet, during the 1980s and 1990s British tabloid populist journalism took populism to a whole new level. Even a cursory review of the tabloids of the 1950s and 1960s will show a level of news reporting and commentary that, although popular, was by today's tabloid standards of simplicity and coarseness both sophisticated and informed.

A milestone in this degeneration was Rupert Murdoch's decision to introduce topless photographs on 'page three' when he re-launched *The Sun* newspaper in 1969 with the first topless photo-graph appearing in 1970. It was a sign that tabloids would enter new territory in the circulation wars – and it succeeded. H. L. Menken famously said 'No one ever lost any money underestimating the intel-ligence of the public'. It was a point that Britain's tabloids took to heart as they systematically engaged in a seemingly unstoppable process of 'dumbing down' both culturally and politically. Coarseness and xenophobia seemed a winning formula. In 2000 *The Daily Express* changed its ownership and in the process, according to Roy Greenslade 'bowed the knee to pornography, misogyny and vul-garity'.[4] And the valiant attempt in 2002 to take the *Daily Mirror* upmarket failed in 2005.

For a while though, even as tabloids began to change, the degen-eration had little influence on wider journalism – what the British still like to call 'the quality' press. But, during the early 1990s, as an even more competitive climate began to bite, tabloid mass populism ceased to be confined, and, instead, began to set the standards – lower and lower standards – for the wider media.

By the turn of the new century political coverage and content in *all* the newspapers and on *all* television channels was being reduced from being policy and information-led to personality and life-style centred. News and commentary was becoming an acknowledged branch of the entertainment industry. Throughout the British media images replaced history, catchphrases replaced thought-out opinion, and journalism replaced genuine expertise.

Indeed the journalists became the experts – and journalists, rather than politicians and academics, became leading opinion-for-mers. And in the process the commercial interests, which owned the media and employed the journalists, came to possess a larger sway over public opinion than at any time in the recent past. Serious political discourse – particularly geo-political discourse – in Britain, as in North America, retreated back into universities and think tanks.

It was this new character of the British media – with its blend of news, entertainment and sensationalism – that allowed patriotic pride to turn into popular nationalism and xenophobia. And it was the 1982 conflict with the Argentina over the Falklands islands that both ushered in, and then later legitimised, this new tabloid popular nationalism. 'Gotcha' was the crude and insensitive headline in *The Sun* newspaper after a British submarine had killed hundreds of Argentinean sailors in May 1982. 'Gotcha' was an early salvo in a new type of raw, tasteless, and triumphalist nationalism not even seen during the Second World War. It was clearly designed to appeal to the often inarticulate pent-up feelings of national decline and impotence held by millions of people in post-war Britain. And it was a success in that, although bitterly criticised, *The Sun* had correctly identified prevailing majority national sentiment and found no need to backtrack, let alone apologise.

'Gotcha' was later followed by other 'patriotic' headlines: in November 1990 by 'Up Yours Delors', a rebuke to the European Commission President; by 'Up Your Senors' (after England defeated Argentina in the 2002 World Cup); by 'Chirac Est Un Ver' or 'Chirac Is a Worm' (handed out free in a French edition of *The Sun* in France following France's decision not to enter the 2003 Iraq war); and by 'One Down Three To Go' (on the death of 27-year-old Brazilian Jean Charles de Menezes, shot as a suspected terrorist in a London Tube station on 23rd July 2005, and later revealed to be an innocent bystander).

'Gotcha' was much more than a sign of coarsening standards. It was a highly political act – as it set the tone for a tabloid nationalism that was later to successfully garner public support for the regular use of force abroad – in the Gulf War, in the Serbian air campaign, and in 2003 in Iraq. The formula for success was clear: tabloid circulation would rise as the humdrum lives of millions of Britons would be enlivened and excited by war and violence in which British dominance was established over foreigners. As long as the bombs and the violence were safely distant, and there was no conscription at home, or indeed much sacrifice, support for war and conflict abroad, and British power, would sell.

Such vicarious valour (sometimes dubbed 'couch potato courage') is a feature of modern xenophobia that makes it quite different from earlier, twentieth-century national sentiment – which went hand in hand with mass volunteering (in the First World War) and conscription (in the Second World War and, in the US, in the Vietnam conflict). And it was this new kind of nationalism that, in the 1990s and into the new century, was both reflected in and stimulated by the British populist media. And it travelled well – particularly across the Atlantic. This kind of 'macho' nationalism – in which patriotic sentiment would be whipped up by political and media figures who often had no track record in military service, or indeed, as in George W. Bush's case, had avoided it – later became a key aspect of Murdoch's media in the USA and a 'product' promoted by Roger Ailes' leadership of the Fox News Channel following 9/11.

Foreigner Bashing

1990s British tabloid populist nationalism had two main themes: a positive message and image of 'British greatness' and 'goodness' and the creation of a generally negative image of foreign life and foreignness. Also, a culture of 'enemies' and 'threats' was created, a development made much easier following 9/11. And the tabloids sought to give colour and meaning to the fear and sense of threat through a systematic campaign of demonisation of selected foreign leaders. This demonising was not a part of a principled democratic campaign against authoritarianism and dictatorship in the world. Rather, it was a highly selective propaganda tool used to create a mood for war – as it did successfully in 1982 with Argentine General Galtieri, in 1999 with Serbian President Slobodan Milosevic, and in 2002-3 with Iraqi President Saddam Hussein.

The climate of fear in Britain following 9/11 was exacerbated both by the tabloids and Britain's political leadership, which saw benefits in a more compliant public. And public opinion was manipulated – as in the case of the run-up to the Iraq invasion of 2003 – when fear of mass casualties in Britain (of a WMD attack on the country with '45 minutes' notice) was a claim recycled by many tabloids. This use of fear to marshal support for political objectives was a formula that had worked well in the Britain of the late 1980s and 1990s – and, after 9/11, it was also used to great effect by George W. Bush's strategist Karl Rove.

Part of this tabloid xenophobe package involved a policy of foreigner bashing. And, within that, there was a particular anti-continental angle. A tabloid assault on France was opened by

Margaret Thatcher herself when her relations with European leaders deteriorated during the 1980s. French President François Mitterrand was a particular problem for her. Politically agile, with a sophisticated mind and serious geo-political ability, he became a good target as the slippery foreigner. For Thatcher, though, a special place in the rogue's gallery was reserved for another Frenchman, President of the European Commission, Jacques Delors. Delors was everything Thatcher both detested and feared. He was an unelected international bureaucrat, a socialist with a taste for intellectuality, and a Frenchman.

Delors threw down the gauntlet to Thatcher when he accepted the British TUC's invitation to speak at their annual conference in Blackpool in 1987, and, in her own country, in her own backyard, he taunted the Prime Minister by talking up the 'social dimension' of EU policy. The result was a sharp response. Thatcher herself proclaimed that she had not presided over ending socialism in Britain just to see it introduced by 'the back Delors' (and the inevitable *Sun* headline, revelling in its now licensed vulgarity, would reply 'Up Yours Delors').[5]

The tabloid attack on Delors brought into high relief British post-war attitudes towards France and the French. The British political class has always possessed its fair share of Francophiles – Winston Churchill was one such. The war leader even offered to merge the two nations as in the summer of 1940 – although, with the Germans approaching Paris, the exigencies of the time probably explain this extraordinary and extravagant gesture. And since the war, literally millions of British people have voted with their feet and set up home in France.

The standard post-war British attitude towards France – good food, stylish, weak government, easily-overrun in 1940, overly-sophisticated, and intellectually pretentious – was not laudatory, but it was hardly hostile. It was only when the troubles between the Thatcher administration and the French hotted up in the 1980s that the tabloids, and Thatcher herself, unleashed an anti-French prejudice that went surprisingly deep within parts of Britain.

France and the French figure prominently in the building of English nationalism, and France has been the chief 'other', the outside force, by which Englishness could be measured, encouraged, and honed. It is always difficult to measure the lasting effect of past conflicts on the thinking of present generations; but in raising France as a bogeyman there was certainly something there to mine. In the eighteenth century the country was faced with a series of invasion scares and insurrections orchestrated from France by the ousted Stuart dynasty. They tried an invasion of Scotland in 1708, and in 1715 there was a serious uprising throughout Scotland and parts of northern England in favour of James Edward Stuart who some thirty years later was still at it, launching an invasion which came close to capturing the capital. Later, the events of 1789, and the long wars against both revolutionary and Napoleonic France established France as a revolutionary threat to Britain's established classes – and unleashed a patriotic propaganda offensive against France.

Residual anti-Catholic sentiment was also at work in anti-French attitudes. Ever since Henry VIII the idea of a Protestant England set against a Catholic continent was a subtle, though powerful, image in the forging of national identity. In the contemporary debates about Europe, suspicions were sometimes voiced, very privately, about whether the sympathies of pro-European politicians, like Shirley Williams, were fuelled by Catholicism. Hugo Young described Mrs Thatcher as having a sense that Roman Catholicism was 'alien', a sense he suggests may have 'begun in childhood when she, the daughter of a fiercely Methodist house, lived opposite a Roman Catholic church and a "Roman Catholic manse", as she once described it'.[6]

Tabloid nationalism also targeted Germany. Stereotyping the Germans grew easily out of the post-war allied British and American bombardment of war movies which flooded the country – and the media's somewhat gruesome fascination with the Nazi regime and Adolf Hitler. At the political level, though, for much of the post-war era West Germany was seen as a prosperous and stable democracy, a key ally in NATO. But this began to change in Britain following German reunification in 1990 when Margaret Thatcher – and she was joined in this by French President Mitterrand – worried publicly about the emergence of a powerful new Germany in the heart of Europe.

Both Thatcher and Mitterrand rebuffed the Germans by refusing to attend their unification celebrations in 1990 (President George Bush Snr., a keen supporter of reunification, did attend). Thatcher went further and, in an unprecedented diplomatic snub, held a tasteless seminar at the Prime Minister's country retreat at Chequers in which academics, diplomats and journalists met to discuss 'the German problem'. The British Prime Minister's attitude was fodder for the tabloid nationalists as it gave official blessing to media caricaturing of Germans and Germany which until then had been relegated to the sports pages during England-German rivalry on the football pitch.

George Urban, an influential writer and journalist who supported Margaret Thatcher, was to reveal the full extent of her anti-German sentiments. In December 1989 he was invited, with other members of the board of the Centre for Policy Studies to a lunch with the Prime Minister. He reported the event. '"You know George" she said coming quite close to me "there are things that people of your generation and mine ought never to forget. We've been through the war and we know perfectly well what the Germans are like, and what dictators can do, and how national character doesn't basically change..."' and so on. Urban suggested that 'if the British Prime Minister feels these things to be true, then we are heading for an unregenerated Europe, and most of our work over the last thirty or forty years, from [Jean] Monnet to the present day, will have been wasted. I only hope my fears are unfounded'. Later, George Urban confided in me that as far as her attitude to foreigners was concerned he thought she had 'a madness'. It was a 'madness' that I had witnessed in others on the political right – both of her generation, and younger.[7]

On top of anti-French and anti-German campaigning, the late 1980s saw the beginning of what was to become a long-running anti-Brussels campaign, one that would last for the next twenty years, and, at the time of writing, was still in full flood. There were two key aspects of this sustained attack. First, there was the supposed EEC threat to the 'British way of life': a tabloid-constructed cosy 'Little Englander' life of warm beer, British sausages and the monarchy. It was a way of life, it was argued, that was threatened by 'soulless bureaucrats' in Brussels who were driven by a power-crazed need to standardise. And a seductive patriotic/nationalist message, one made more powerful by the regular insensitivity of the Brussels Commission, was developed.

Indeed, so appealing was the Eurosceptic campaign that a leading pro-European, Foreign Secretary Douglas Hurd, was forced to agree that the Commission should not involve itself in the 'nooks and crannies' of national life. Hurd, an Eton-educated liberal Tory, had served in Thatcher's government and was too timid to point out that it was Thatcher's own great project – the level playing field of the single market – that could only be properly implemented by an 'intrusive' harmonisation of standards.

The continentals were also portrayed as a threat to British democracy. Margaret Thatcher herself had constructed the powerful narrative: 'Britain', so it went, 'stood uniquely for liberty; and in the war we had stood alone; and then we had liberated Europe, for which all Europeans should be grateful'. It was a mindset, derived from a war that could not be 'let go', that had travelled well beyond the Westminster elite and into the British hinterland. It could be seen in the braggadocio slogan 'We Won the War!' chanted by English football hooligans in many a continental city in the 1980s and 1990s – themes tailor-made for tabloid nationalists.

The constant tabloid repetition of key words like 'unelected bureaucrats' or 'Eurocrats' increasingly disarmed the pro-Europeans in Britain. The very word 'Brussels' became a term of abuse. Tabloid nationalism had successfully identified a central weakness of the nascent European polity – the fact that could hardly be contested, that one of the EU's primary institutions, the Commission, was, in essence, unaccountable and undemocratic. However, the tabloid nationalists of the era had little positive to say about the democratically elected European Parliament; nor did they, apart from generalised abuse of politicians as a genre, offer much of a critique of the democratic deficiencies of the Westminster/Whitehall set-up; nor, in their defence of the 'British way of life', did they place any of the blame on the architect of the single market, Margaret Thatcher, or the free market ideology that had driven it.

'America Is Just Not Foreign'
Tabloid nationalism was specifically directed at Europe. Few tabloids of the era criticised – in any systematic sense – the 'special relationship' with the USA. Nationalists in the popular media would argue about the need for Britain to be 'self-governing' and to be 'independent' and saw the threat to such 'independence' coming from Europe though not the USA; also, they would assert British interests as being separate from Europe, but not from those of the USA; and they would suggest that the threat to British democracy and Westminster 'sovereignty' came exclusively from the 'bureaucrats in Brussels' whilst Wall Street and Washington, certainly in terms of any impact they might have on 'British sovereignty', remained relatively immune to

criticism. When challenged about this lack of even-handedness a leading conservative editor said to me 'I get the point, but to British journalists, America is just not foreign'.[8]

In the tabloids of the time, however, uncritical support for American foreign policy went strangely hand in hand with petty anti-Americanism. The British media generally gave inordinate publicity to most anything American, particularly the eccentric and the extreme. Critical stories about American life and 'the American way of life' suffused most every newspaper and many television news programmes – even the conservative tabloid media. During the Iraq war many tabloids, whilst supporting American policy, would also take critical shots at the American right – the 'guns, gays and god' syndrome in American life. Intriguingly however, these critical pieces rarely translated into calls for a change in Britain's subservient foreign policy. Rather, they represented a turn of the century tabloid version of the 'Greece to Rome' conceits of earlier years.

This mixture of blind support, an underlying superiority and resentment, and a blank refusal to confront and deal with Britain's relationship to American power, was the true mark of how far the post-war British had slid into an unhealthy colonial master and servant relationship.

By the time of the Iraq war in 2003, however, the 'special relationship' had, for the first time since the Vietnam crisis in the late 1960s, become highly controversial amongst the wider British public. So much so that Downing Street felt it needed defending. Even Tony Blair argued that the relationship with America should not be a one-way street. Talking of policies favoured by Britain he argued, on the eve of the Iraq war, that 'we should *in return* [for Britain's support] expect these issues to be confronted...proportionately, sensibly, and in a way that delivers a better prospect of long-term peace, security and justice'.[9] Even so, the tabloid nationalist press rarely objected when British policy objectives – say in the Middle East or in the Kyoto treaty controversy – were not taken up by Washington.

Norman Tebbit

The tabloid nationalist campaign of the late 1980s onwards had no more authentic voice than the British Tory politician Norman Tebbit. Tebbit came to prominence in the Thatcher administrations as Employment Secretary and as Tory Party Chairman in the 1987 election. He was an archetypal Thatcherite. A fervent anti-socialist, he saw 'big government' as an enemy of aspiring working class families. And he saw the free market as opening up the economy and therefore society. He was the quintessential 'Essex man' and in extolling upward mobility he was also talking about his own story, as he later recalled in his biography *Upwardly Mobile*.[10]

He was also the leading Tory social conservative of his generation, whose mix of immigration, law and order and nationalism made him something of an inheritor of the mantle of Enoch Powell. Also, his cockney accent, like Powell's Midlands accent, set him apart from most Westminster Tories and gave him an appeal to the southern white working class. In 1987 I joined him, former Labour MPs Neville Sandelson and Brian Walden, and former Liberal Party leader Jo Grimond, in founding a debating society, *The Radical Society*. Tebbit's reputation at the time, led by the media, was that of a populist 'bully boy', a stoker of prejudices. He was that; but he was also, in reality, a sophisticated politician with a keen forensic debating talent. Essentially uninterested in foreign policy, he was a 'Little Englander' concerned above all to preserve traditional ways. Yet, like many conservatives he failed to appreciate how it was business interests, rather than the state, that were eroding these traditional ways. And, again like so many of the conservative Eurosceptics of his time, he saw these 'traditional ways' as threatened only by Europe, not by the forces of the market and the Americanisation of Britain.

Towards the end of his active political career, Norman Tebbit appeared in a weekly 'head to head' Sky TV show with the Labour MP for Grimsby, Austin Mitchell. Mitchell was a social democrat, a Gaitskellite by tradition, and he saw himself as a progressive – and he disagreed with Tebbit about most contemporary political issues. They agreed, however, about the need to resist EU influence on British life, Mitchell seeing it as a threat to British parliamentary democracy.

Austin Mitchell, like many Labour MPs of the time, was willing to criticise Britain's 'special relationship' with the US – but not as systematically and as fervently as he did the country's membership of the EU. In this respect Mitchell represented a serious strain of sentiment amongst Labour MPs in the Blair era. Many would be critical, privately often quite severely, of specifics of US foreign policy; but they would never take a public stand against the 'special relationship', or, indeed, against the centrality of NATO in the post-Cold War era. The Iraq war placed many Labour MPs in a serious quandary, some even were emotionally torn. Many vehemently opposed Britain's siding with America. But, in the final analysis, career concerns led many to support Blair. And, for the less career-minded, old habits ran deep. Sticking by America in a crisis was deeply embedded in the mental framework, the very DNA of established Westminster politics.

Manipulating The Wounded

The key to the Murdoch/Tebbit tabloid populist and nationalist appeal in Britain was similar, indeed almost identical, to the nationalist populism that President George W. Bush, his adviser Karl Rove, and the Murdoch-owned Fox New Channel employed following 9/11. The writer Anatol Lieven, in his fascinating and insightful work *America Right Or Wrong: An Anatomy of American Nationalism*, identified the well-springs of populist nationalism in America, and particularly amongst George Bush's base vote: white southerners. He suggests that the key to understanding the xenophobia of white American southerners, particularly white southern men, is to see them as a defeated people with a wounded sensibility – the kind of sensibility that responds to 'macho' strength and xenophobia.

Lieven argues that this mentality leads to an over-identification with the US as a powerful country which places them, for once, on a winning team: and what is more, as the American tabloid lingo would have it, a 'kick-ass team'.[11] In this American case the wounds go back to the continuing effect of the south's defeat in the civil war, and to more recent mid to late twentieth-century wounds inflicted by a sense that 'others' – blacks, new ethnic groups, and women – have made advances at their expense.

British tabloid nationalism also played on wounded feelings, in this case those of the British white working class male's sense of insecurity. By the end of the 1990s fewer and fewer British men over the age of 50 were in the kind of full-time work that previous generations enjoyed, and, like their American counterparts, they were feeling increasingly beleaguered. Social changes gave them a sense of declining status compared to 'others', particularly women and new ethnic groups. These British men also felt keenly – because many of them had lived through it – the decline of their country as a world power. It was, and is, an unsettling environment which creates amongst these people a sense that 'enough is enough'. And in response xeno-phobia – with its venting of suppressed racial and national preju-dices, and the promise of 'not being kicked around any more' – can easily take hold, becoming the perfect outlet: one willingly provided by the tabloid nationalists.

Murdoch's 'Enger...land': The Red Cross of St. George

Tabloid xenophobia – with its admixture of nostalgia for a lost great past, and a present-day visceral nationalism – had been a growing feature of British working class life during the late twentieth century, ever since it became clear that Britain was no longer a world power and was taking a back seat to the USA. But, at some point during the 1990s it transformed into a new, and even narrower, form of nation-consciousness: *English* xenophobia and nationalism.

English xenophobia was slowly building during the 1980s. But it only began to show itself fully in the 1990s when, suddenly and spontaneously during World and European Cup international football events thousands and thousands of English flags – the red cross of St. George on a white background – appeared throughout the country. They were flown from vans and from homes mainly in working class areas. The 1990 World Cup, 'Italia 90', saw huge television audiences and set the tone for the subsequent contests, and these sporting events provided tabloid nationalism with a rich seam of vicarious valour to mine.

The England team became a nationalist symbol, and support for it was rallied by the tabloids – particularly against old adversaries like Germany and France. Through televised football the Second World War could be replayed, this time as entertainment. And the fact of a sporting context, rather than a political one, could allow tabloid 'cre-ativity' – and bigotry – full reign, with opponents dubbed 'Krauts' and 'Frogs' and 'Argies'. And in and around the stadiums during these contests the trademark football chant 'Enger...land' had a raw, assertive, xenophobic edge to it.

Tabloid xenophobia in football was sold as innocent, competitive, sporting fun. But at the same time it created a wave of support for more serious ideas – principally, the emergence of the idea of England as a separate nation, separate that is from Scotland and Wales. As it happened the organisation of British football played right into the new nationalist 'Enger...land' theme. For some quirky historical reason Britain (or the UK) had no football team. Instead, the 'national' game had four 'national' sides – Scotland, Wales, Northern Ireland and England. And, thus, 'England' rather than 'Britain' became the symbol though which many Englishmen expressed their growing 'patriotism' and xenophobia. And with large amounts of money to be made out of the 'England' team – television coverage, mass marketing of team jerseys and insignia, player sponsorship of products – huge commercial and media interests further promoted the idea of 'Enger...land' and a separate England at that. As did 'English' celebrity footballers, like David Beckham, who were supplanting old 'British' celebrity institutions like the Queen.

But the massive commercialisation of English football was only one reason for the new English xenophobia, and not the primary one. More important was a growing but real sense throughout the country that the UK union was creaking, if not actually breaking up, and that there was a kind of inevitability about Scotland eventually going it alone and Northern Ireland severing its links with the mainland. For many English people it seemed that with the empire gone, the Celtic nations in their insistent search for greater devolution were in fact seeking to leave a sinking ship. Following devolution in 1997 there was no majority in either Scotland or Wales for breaking the union, but there was a continuing, indeed growing, sense of Scottish and Welsh consciousness (and nationalism) which resisted, and often resented, English influence.

Scottish national sentiment had been developing during Margaret Thatcher's administrations – when the 'English' Thatcher government in London was bringing in radical economic and social changes north of the border without a mandate from the people of Scotland (where the Conservatives remained in a decided minority). Also, although Margaret Thatcher's brand of patriotism sought to give all of the British their pride back, her 'revolution' had been a very English affair, led by a very 'English lady', and it had stirred English emotions, not resonating very much north of the border.

By the time of the 1997 general election the nationalist tide was again running strongly. Many within the London establishment became convinced that the only way in which it could be stemmed was by the setting up of a Scottish Parliament with some law-making powers. It was a measure of this sense of urgency that Tony Blair's very first parliamentary act was to establish a parliament north of the border.

Yet Westminster's concessions to Scotland produced a backlash in England. The politicians were seen in England as pandering to the Scots. For the tabloid-reading Englishman south of the border 'England', no longer 'Britain', was becoming the repository of patriotic, nationalist instincts and emotions. And there was a widespread sense that, for all the talk of renewal, England was not what it was, was on the retreat, and was on her own. If an Englishman had at the beginning of the century been dealt the 'top card in life', now, having risen the furthest, he was falling the hardest. For him, England's finest hour, 1940, was long gone, as was England's last football success – in 1966. Globally, he had already lost out – to Americans who had replaced him as the inhabitants of a superpower, to Europeans who were still the arbiters of style and taste, and even to the Chinese, the new rising power.

From this vantage-point, with the empire gone, and with Britain fragmenting into separate parts, England was becoming the last refuge of the nationalist 'scoundrel'.

Euroscepticism
This new English nationalism was not just the preserve of the tabloid classes. Throughout England, in 'the country', and the 'county', a quiet xenophobia had long existed. This refined, more mild, nationalism was the key ingredient of the 'Euroscepticism' which increasingly dominated establishment Westminster political life during the Major/Blair years. These 'Eurosceptics' expressed themselves more carefully, and more politically correctly, and they did so without much overt 'flag-waving'. The very term 'sceptic' suggested a measured, less aggressive approach than the tabloids. But, at root, they possessed the same instincts and values, and took the same positions, and signed on to the same policies, as the xenophobes in the tabloid media. Specifically, they opposed any change in Britain's foreign alignment – specifically entry into the Euro-zone; and they supported, even with much gnashing of teeth, the 'special relationship' with the USA.

By the turn of the century, this 'Euroscepticism' had become the near-dominant political instinct amongst the 'home counties' southern elites in top positions in the finance service sector in the City of London, in the professions and the 'up-market' media. And it filtered through to the parties. New Labour, which had started off the Blair era as Europhile, ended the era as a mildly Eurosceptic party. During the same period the Conservatives became more Europhobe than Eurosceptic, so much so that in 2006, their new leader David Cameron, although determined to project a progressive and green image at home, was forced to de-align his party in the European Parliament from Europe's mainstream centre-right parties and, instead, to seek an alliance with some eccentric Europhobe populist parties of the right.

These English 'Eurosceptics' shared one overwhelming characteristic with the tabloid xenophobes: a seriously provincial perspective. They inhabited a vantage-point that saw the Channel as a threat, insisted that Britain, or England, had little or nothing to learn from abroad, and still believed 'sovereignty' was attainable. In the age of globalisation most of the great changes in the world economy and in geo-politics had passed them by.

13. American Empire or European Home?

'We could try to become the 51st state of the American union.'
John Redwood MP, 2001

'Of course, Britain could survive outside the EU...We could possibly get access to the single market as Norway and Switzerland do.'
Tony Blair, speech in Ghent, Belgium, 2000

'What I think and fear is that Britain will draw back from the US without moving closer to Europe. In that sense London Bridge is falling down.'
Kendall Myers, US State Department, 2006

The New Nationalism: Unfit for the 21st Century
By the time Tony Blair announced the coming end of his premiership, in the autumn of 2006, the country was as enmeshed in the American empire as it had ever been. Indeed, with British troops still in Iraq, Britain had become Washington's chief European outpost. The country was geo-politically tied to Washington, economically under the sway of the neo-liberal American model, and culturally, through television and the tabloidised mass media, increasingly

Americanised. Yet, on the other hand, Britain was still a full member of the European Union, whose core countries, Germany, France, Italy and Spain, had distanced themselves from the US occupation of Iraq, and, through their membership of the increasingly strong Euro-zone, were slowly but surely establishing a separate unifying European world role. It was an awkward posture.

Also, unlike all the European neighbours, there was, in Britain, no settled and agreed national consensus about where the country's future lay. In what Timothy Garton-Ash has called 'Janus-Britain', British imaginings of the future differed radically.[1] A small coterie of pro-Europeans still argued that the country's 'destiny' lay in Europe. But ever since Margaret Thatcher's Bruges speech in 1987 a two-decade trend amongst opinion-formers had gone the other way; and the ascendant neo-liberals were envisaging a more globalised, or, as some would argue, 'American' future.

This 'geo-political' identity crisis was – is – a feature of something deeper. For, at the turn of the century, there was no certainty about how to answer a crucial question: what kind of people are the British? Are we an 'Anglo' nation whose language will forever tie us to Washington? And what are the geo-political implications of the growth of English nationalism? Will Scotland and Wales gravitate to a European future should England stay out? What are the implications of a multi-cultural society, and sizeable Islamic populations, for foreign policy? And what of vast, cosmopolitan London? Will London and its environs lead the way into Europe whilst much of the rest of England resists? And, will the British elite's love affair with the US neo-liberal economic model propel the country away from Europe's 'social model' and the Euro?

This identity crisis is one cause of the revival of extreme nationalism. And these nationalist instincts – renewed by xenophobic Englishness – run directly counter to the realities and values of the real world in which the English people actually live. For instance, in this real world seriously urgent problems are lapping at the shores – problems like carbon emissions, mass immigration, terrorism, and the social and economic effects of globalisation. Yet not one of these problems can be solved by national solutions. But national solutions, based upon 'national sovereignty' and an old and odd ideology of national separateness, is all that was on offer from Britain's established elites.

In November 2006 the British government announced, amid much fanfare, a *national* report on *global* climate change – the Stern Report. And when challenged about the impossibility of *national* solutions to this *global* problem, the response from Westminster was that Britain could best achieve its objectives not by integrating with other countries to solve joint problems, but rather by 'setting an example' and by giving 'a lead'.[2] As the Thatcher-Blair era drew to its close, the British political class were inhabiting a strange, twilight-like, provincial vacuum.

Avoiding The Choice
This hold of nationalist thinking – and nationalist illusions – is, of course, not just the product of the country's traditionalist culture. It is also the result of vested interests. Britain's national elites, whether in Westminster or in the national media, owe their positions and power by definition to the nation state. And they will not easily yield up this existing power to a supra-national system which may well be better at solving problems, but will interfere with precious 'sovereignty'. And for these British elites, a foot in both camps – in the US 'special relationship' on the one hand, yet membership of the EU, but not the Euro, on the other – preserves their flexibility, and their own power position. Many outside commentators see Britain's geo-political position as a high-wire act, one which gets higher as the Atlantic widens, and predict that it cannot go on for too long. Some, like French Presidential candidate Ségolène Royal in 2006, have publicly suggested that Britain should cease to be a 'vassal' of the United States and should 'make a choice' between the US and the EU.[3]

But Britain's political leadership has not seen the need to make such a choice. In fact, proclaiming the need to avoid such a choice has become one of the chief characteristics of its foreign policy. Prime Minister Blair has even argued publicly the case that 'to choose between America and Europe is a false choice'. He simply did not see the need to choose. 'I would be insane – yes, I would put it as strongly as that – for us to give up either relationship'.[4] The writer and analyst Charles Grant has argued that sometimes a choice does need to be made, and that 'when we had to choose, as we did over Iraq, I would have chosen Europe'.[5]

Sooner or later, the likelihood is that the integration dynamic will be renewed. And there will then come a time when a clear consensus in the EU will demand to move forward; and should Britain not agree to join in, then 'core Europe' may well go ahead without it. Such a crisis could arise over a new constitutional treaty or, also, over monetary relations (should, say, the Pound Sterling float down against the Euro and the Euro-zone members demand that Britain join the zone or re-negotiate their position in the single market).

To adjust to further serious European integration would, though, initially at any rate, be very difficult for Britain. Indeed many 'Eurosceptic' economists believe it would be traumatic. The 'Eurosceptic' fear is that Britain has gone too far down the neo-liberal road to turn back now. And the 'Eurosceptic' vision – or nightmare – is of a future EU outvoting Britain on a range of 'social Europe' issues from harmonising the labour market to standardising tax rates. In such circumstances – with Britain forced to adopt more labour-friendly policies – the country's whole low-cost, low-wage, 'hire and fire' labour strategy would be in tatters, leading to higher unemployment. Also, an agreed European tax policy (with higher levels across the board) would mean that the global super and mega rich now populating London and the South-East would leave for easier climes. And an even tighter EU trade protection policy, in which the EU imposed tariffs on a whole range of Chinese imported goods and services, would hurt key retail sectors of Britain's consumer-driven economy. Also, should the country join the Euro-zone, then locking Britain into the zone at too high a rate could seriously hurt British economic growth for years to come.

Should it ever face these EU 'impositions' it would be good news for social democrats; but a neo-liberal administration in London might well confront Brussels. It might, in league, say, with the Poles, either cause a crisis by refusing to implement the decisions or seek to repatriate powers back to Westminster. In the 2005 general election campaign the Conservative opposition under Michael Howard's leadership proposed repatriating some powers, but assumed that it could be done in a friendly and co-operative manner. However, such a friendly environment might not, in reality, be on offer, and the situation could get very fraught. In any event, Britain would then be on a trajectory which would take the country out of the EU altogether.

Leaving the EU: 'The Tiger' Option
It is this kind of future – of a neo-liberal Britain being forced to adapt to the European social model – that leads many 'Eurosceptics' to

advocate the radical path of Britain leaving the EU, hopefully by negotiation. By leaving the EU Britain would then be outside the world's largest single market; and Eurosceptics are naturally anxious to seek arrangements with the EU which will allow Britain continued access. Some hope that Britain could come up with an ingenious scheme to stay in the single market through rejoining EFTA (the European Free Trade Association) and through EFTA join Norway in the AEA (Associated Economic Area). Yet, the idea that after the controversy, rupture and pain of withdrawing from the EU, the Union would then grant Britain special continuing access to its single market remains highly fanciful. And even should Britain get the same deal as Norway it will then become a so-called 'Euro fax' country – subject to the rules of the single market – sent to them by fax – but having no say in drawing them up.[6]

A British withdrawal would thus likely be exactly what it says – a full withdrawal. It would amount to a 'go it alone' strategy – and face the country with the urgent need to make a living outside of the trade bloc. It will be a dramatic, bold, and risky, move. Yet, during the 1990s some British opinion-formers were becoming more and more confident in the viability of this 'go it alone' strategy.

It was a strategy in which 'Little England', facing the global economy alone, would prosper by remaining highly competitive and entrepreneurial. It would amount to a future role for the country that its supporters – like the novelist Frederick Forsyth – describe as creating 'an independent, global Britain'. Taking this road, 'Little England' would, in effect, become a 'Tiger Economy' – an option named after the 'Tiger economies' of South Asia, the small countries that prospered in the late 1980s and early 1990s through achieving a competitive edge in a rapidly globalising world.

But the big question remains: can Britain, on the other side of the world and off-shore of Europe, become such a 'Tiger'? Supporters of the option assume that once outside the EU and its single market, relations with the EU will, maybe after an initial hiccup, remain amicable. However, Britain would have left in order to seek a competitive advantage (lower costs and taxes) and in such a competitive environment the EU could easily erect trade barriers against British goods and services for many of the same reasons that are deployed against China. In a trade war, trying to live outside a trading bloc could become a very uncomfortable place.

215

Yet the key question about the viability of a 'Tiger' future for Britain is whether, outside of a trade bloc, the British economy will be strong enough to prosper. Britain's recent record on growth and unemployment and in some service sectors (mainly financial services) more than stands comparison with most of the other EU member states – even though it has been achieved during Britain's period in the single market, and in a relatively benign global trading environment which has allowed Britain to grow its consumer-driven and debt-led economy.

But growth rates aside, is Britain big enough, and diverse (or balanced) enough? For size and diversity (meaning a balanced economy) can matter. A superpower economy like the United States has the ability to absorb shocks and adapt to change mainly because of the flexibility that sheer size and balanced diversity gives an economy as it operates in the global system. Size also allows a huge economy like the US to both impose rules on others and also ignore these same rules should it not be in its interest. In a case in point, the US' huge external trade imbalances would drive a smaller economy, as it did the UK in 1976, into the hands of the creditors and bailiffs of the IMF. Also, huge economies can benefit from the 'safe haven' phenomenon – for the sheer size of the economy leads to big inflows of capital during crises. Twenty-first century Britain is simply not big enough – on its own – to secure these benefits, whereas both the US and the EU are!

How big then is the British economy two decades into the Thatcher era revolution? Britain's good growth rates have helped her grow from her ranking in the early 1980s when she was tying with Italy for third place in the EU. By 2006 the UK economy amounted to $2,201,473 million or 4.9% of the global GDP. It ranked fifth in the world (behind the US, Japan, Germany and Mainland China), and was roughly the same size as France and just ahead of Italy. And it was only one sixth the size of the total EU economy, and also of the total US economy.[7]

These figures tell the story of a Britain that during the 1980s and 1990s had stabilised its shaky situation. But, in truth, it did little more than that. For by the end of the 1990s British national income was almost exactly equal to that of France and only about 20% higher than that of Italy. (Figures show: UK 1403, France 1453, Germany 2103, and Italy 1162. These are exchange-rate sensitive and could easily change by 10-20%. They also show growth rates for UK

(1965-99) coming in behind France, Belgium, Italy and most of the EU 15 nations; figures for Germany are unavailable because of the eastern states addition.)[8]

Taking the longer view – that of the whole post-war period – Professor Bernard Alford, at the end of his exhaustive work on Britain's recent economic history, came to a clear conclusion: 'the thrust of our analysis' he wrote in 1996 'is that there are few signs that Britain has reversed the condition of relative economic decline that has been endemic to its development since the late nineteenth century'. He adds, though, that the status of nations is often a matter of perception, 'but that perception is so easily clouded by delusion'. In the decade since Alford's report, very little has changed that would alter his assessment.[9]

Yet, no matter its size, is the British economy strong enough? Is it able to withstand pressures from the global economy, from downturns and shocks? And here there is a problem – for Britain, no matter its good growth rates, remains a very vulnerable economy, much more so than many other advanced economies. One vulnerability is that the country remains highly dependent on the continuing robust health of the global economy. Britain's economic growth rates have largely been sustained by global growth which in turn has been sustained by the low inflation era caused by China's low costs. This virtuous low-inflation cycle has allowed Britain to pursue low interest rates and a massive increase in private debt levels (based on a housing boom). This whole economic structure is heavily trade dependent, more so than many of its competitors, and in any downturn would be hurt disproportionately.

The City of London
Alone in the global economy, a medium-sized economy like Britain's needs to be able to adjust to change – and in order to so adjust, the more balanced the economy the better. Yet, Britain's economy is far from balanced. As part of the late 80s and early 90s neo-liberal restructuring – when market forces eroded the uncompetitive industrial sector – Britain witnessed many decades of decline in manufacturing, and a quite dramatic switchover to services – primarily financial services. The City of London – always a large and profitable sector – became even larger and even more profitable. Britain's financial services industry has done extremely well in the post-Cold War

global economy. In 2003 Britain's trade surplus in financial services was reported to be 'more than double that of any other country'.[10]

In July 2004, researchers at the University of Sheffield portrayed the British economy in atlas form and revealed that Britain was becoming dominated by London (or, rather, the City of London), and that to the north and west there was 'an archipelago of the provinces – city islands that appear to be slowly sinking demographically, socially and economically'.[11] It was an analysis which led *Guardian* economist Larry Elliott to argue that the 'City wields more power than ever' and that 'Britain has become a huge hedge fund making big bets on the markets. One day the luck will run out'.[12] In his 2006 powerful study of Britain's elites, Hywel Williams reckoned that 'the City, in combination with New York now controls 90% of the world's wholesale financial activity'. And he recorded that at the end of 2003 310,000 people were employed in the City (and nearly 150,000 in financial services).[13]

Yet, two questions stand out: can 'the City' and its allied commerce continue to carry on its shoulders a country of 60 million people? And, what happens when China and India start seriously competing in financial services as well as in manufacturing? The mere posing of these questions may serve to show the vulnerability of a national economy which includes such a uniquely successful sector.

Whether 'the City' can or cannot continue to carry the country, its leading players will certainly remain highly influential, if not dominant, in determining British foreign policy and alignment – more so even than the media moguls. And within 'the City' elite there is considerable support for the 'Tiger option'. As financial services prospered in the Blair era, many in the square mile turned increasingly against Europe and the EU.

This dominant view saw London's financial services as a global player working in a global market – very much a 'Tiger', and perhaps even the world's most successful 'Tiger' in the global jungle. By comparison, tying 'the City' down in Europe – even should 'the City' become the EU's primary financial centre (similar to 'New York' in North America) – was seen as too restrictive a vision. In a December 2006 after dinner speech to London financiers, the EU's financial services action plan ('Mifid') was introduced by Charlie McCreevy the Internal Market Commissioner. Reportedly, McCreevy and his plan was given a less than enthusiastic reception – much less so than that accorded to the American comedienne Ruby Wax, who, bizarrely, but perhaps aptly, followed him. A *Financial Times* report by Gideon Rachman suggested that 'as the biggest financial centre in Europe ['the City'] would do well in a huge liberalised [European Union] market'.[14] However, the EU remains too regulated for City tastes; as does even Wall Street following the Sarbanes-Oxley Act passed in the aftermath of the Enron scandal (a tough US regulatory regime providing a huge – though probably temporary – boost for 'the City').

The successful and profitable world of British finance provides, though, another vulnerability to the British economy – that of the country's Himalayan dimension of private debt. A report commissioned by the Conservative Party in 2005 reported that 'personal debt levels of more than £1 trillion mean that about 15 million people are exposed to external shocks such as a sharp rise in the price of oil' and went on to call the debt issue a 'time bomb'. These debt levels have been fuelled by the 'wealth effect' felt by rising house prices.[15]

These vulnerabilities in the British economy – the reverse side of its successes – make Britain's 'Tiger option' a huge gamble. Britain is more exposed to global forces than any other major western country (including the US). And should the country leave the EU, then everything will depend upon a continuingly robust global economy – and one in which competition in the service sector from China and India remains weak.

Britain's 'successful' economy – no matter its vulnerable and exposed global position – will likely continue to convince a powerful faction of opinion-formers that the country can, with confidence, 'go it alone'. After all, the 'Tiger option' will continue to appeal to more than just the profit-makers; it will have an abiding resonance with the popular instincts of English exceptionalism – of a uniquely entrepreneurial people surviving and prospering alone on the global 'open seas'. This appeal combines short-term profits and nationalist romance – the two impulses that built the empire and will be difficult to combat.

The American Option: A Colony, Not a State
Should Britain leave the EU, and then should the 'Tiger option' fail, Britain will be 'alone on a boundless and bottomless sea', and could, as the nightmare adage goes, 'sink into the middle of the Atlantic'.[16]

The good ship Britannia could *try* to secure a safe haven by returning to the original port on the European continent, but as the ship's company would have left in some acrimony, this would seem an unlikely outcome. More likely, much more likely, is that the global political and economic tides will, sooner or later, carry the ship into the waters of the western Atlantic. Britain will, inevitably and ineluctably, drift into port in the American homeland.

In practical terms – with Britain outside of the EU and the European single market, but not prospering – then pressure may well grow for the country to join NAFTA (the North Atlantic Free Trade Agreement). Such an adhesion though would have to be on the terms already set by the NAFTA treaty. And although joining NAFTA could be sold by reference to historic sentiment – to the 'Anglo-sphere' or the 'English-Speaking Union' – the reality would be different. For Washington dominates the NAFTA trade bloc, and Britain would, by joining, further deepen its subordinate role. The prize of American statehood would continue to elude it; and it would in effect become a fully-fledged province of the American empire.

There is little or no chance that Britain could become a state of the union – the 51st state. The United States has no plans to extend the number of states. Indeed, the republic has a firm resolve not to. And if Britain joins NAFTA it will live within the American empire, but without statehood it will have no say over the governmental and economic institutions which will control its life. Britain will have no vote in the electoral college for President; no Senators in the US Senate; no representatives in the lower house of Congress; no justices on the US Supreme Court; and, perhaps most fateful of all, no representatives on the central bank, the US Federal Reserve. At the same time, now outside the EU, Britain would have given up its votes on the EU Council, Commission, Parliament and Court of Justice (including, should it have joined the Euro-zone, a seat on the European Central Bank).

In such circumstances, without statehood, influence in Washington would become all that mattered to the people of Britain. It would be politically all-important and all-consuming. The country's future would then lie in its lobbying function only, and it would be forced to compete with the powerful domestic American lobbying groups (such as the American Farmers' Lobby and, in foreign policy, the American Israel Public Affairs Committee). It would also have to contend with the greater influence in

Washington of the EU. The British embassy on Massachusetts Avenue in Washington D.C. would become a beehive of activity, an extension of the great lobbying avenue on K Street. But, for Britain, it would amount to a poignant reversal of the eighteenth-century relationship between the two countries before the American war of independence: as the great decisions which govern the lives of the British would be taken 3,000 miles away – in Washington – in institutions in which no Briton was represented. The country would become a non-voting province. It would amount to a modern form of 'taxation without representation' – the classic defining characteristic of a colony.

Should Britain ultimately choose a life in the American empire there will be no American Viceroy in London. And the British Prime Minister will continue to report to Parliament. But in the coming multi-polar world Washington, not Brussels, will become the effective capital of the peoples of the British isles. It will represent a strange twist.

Life in the American Empire

For Britain and the British, life in the American empire will not be the worst fate that could befall a western people in the coming century. The twenty-first century will likely not be another 'American century', but the American republic will remain a great, democratic and relatively prosperous power with global reach and influence second to none. And as a key player within this American system Britain will have a lot going for it, certainly compared to other outlying parts of the empire.

Even so, life in the American empire will come at a heavy price – particularly economically. American-led corporations will become more and more dominant, both directly and indirectly, in Britain's domestic market and in British economic life. The City of London will likely remain a global player, but the politicians in Washington will have much more leverage over the British regulatory regime and, under pressure from Wall Street, can be expected to use their increased influence to limit the City of London's competitive edge.

In what will seem like a natural progression, Britain's already dominant neo-liberal Thatcherite economic regime will tighten its hold even more. As in the US, pressure for lower taxes and lower public expenditure will lead to more and more private provision in areas like health-care. And the logic of greater private health provision may well mean that, eventually, as in the US, insurance companies will take over the bulk of the health insurance function from the government. The NHS would become a shell. And all the time pressure for a more and more market-based, deregulated economy would be applied through even greater US media ownership and output – in movies, television, communications and publishing.

But the most striking effect of life in the American empire may well be felt in social and community life. Britain can expect to witness an acceleration in the kind of social changes already underway – changes that have been going on in the US for some decades. We can expect a social profile in which a sizeable, but insecure, middle class continues to fragment, splintering into both the upwardly and downwardly mobile. At the top, it would see the development of a highly influential, almost dominant super-rich and mega-rich class which is global in character and unlinked in any real way to the domestic economy and society. And at the bottom it would produce a large and growing 'underclass' – based primarily in the cities, but also existing in pockets throughout the countryside – which would become so large that it would seriously threaten social cohesion.

Once Britain is outside the EU, and fully entwined in the American orbit, there will be few obstacles in the path to rapidly growing inequality. The system will promote low taxes for the rich and upper middle classes – but lower public expenditure will cause lower standards of welfare, including health and education. And an increasingly flexible 'hire and fire' labour market will ensure a large low wage sector so that Britain can 'compete' in the global economy. As long as global growth holds up growing inequality can be contained, and with it social stability; but in the event of a recession, social tensions could become acute.

The US has become used to inequality; and its governing consensus is unfazed by big disparities in income and wealth existing alongside a growing 'underclass'. The days of Teddy Roosevelt raging against the 'malefactors of great wealth' and the egalitarian impulses of FDR and LBJ are well and truly over. Today's American neo-liberal elite sees no threat to social stability from any amount of inequality – as long, that is, as unemployment remains fairly low. Unlike Europeans who worry about the social consequences of inequality, US administrations have tended to manage rather than 'solve' social problems. They have policed the underclass and have expanded, at considerable cost, the prison population. And ideology and religion also play a crucial social role. The growing numbers of American working poor – on low wages and few benefits – are still largely reconciled to the American system, particularly in the south and midwest, through a continuing strong belief in the ideology of individualism and fear of the state, and are distracted from seeking systemic change here and now by the power of religious faith.

The British, even after decades of Thatcherism, have little in the way of a popular and populist capitalist belief system. And since the collapse of Methodism in the north, the country has no mass religious base and no dense network of Protestant churches to act as a surrogate welfare state. Should inequality dramatically worsen then political and extremist opposition to the system could grow very quickly.

Joining a Declining Empire

Life in the American empire may well alter the country's economic and social life, but it will hardly change Britain's security policy. The country will simply become even more deeply enmeshed in the US military-industrial complex – with British firms tied even more closely into the Pentagon and its defence procurement system. Also, the Britain intelligence services will continue to have unrivalled access to the best intelligence – US intelligence – available.

There will, though, be a cost. For, in return, the country will be expected to provide an uncritical support system for US global ambitions and interventions. The British armed forces will become – in the term used in NATO planning – a 'tool-box' which the US can dip into to help it in whatever missions its own national interest deems necessary. On 12th January 2007 Tony Blair outlined this very vision in a speech on HMS Albion in the naval town of Plymouth. He argued that British foreign policy must be based upon a 'strong alliance with the United States' and 'a willingness to project strong, as well as soft power' around the world 'wherever that may be'. And he called for a long-term increase in British defence spending to fund this pro-American interventionist vision.[17]

Yet Britain may well, should it choose the 'American option', be backing the wrong horse. For, on some readings, the country would be throwing its lot in with a weakening, not an expanding, global power. The US for the foreseeable future will remain a 'superpower'; indeed, in the absence of a united EU, it will remain the primary 'superpower'. But, with only 28% of global GDP and 5% of the global population, the USA increasingly inhabits a geo-political world which is now multi-polar in character. The EU (with a higher GDP than the US), fast-growing China and India, and energy-rich Russia, are all, in the short-term, potential competitors as global superpowers. And in military strength and reach – an area in which the US can legitimately continue to claim dominance – the Iraq imbroglio may have shown the limits of such hard military power.

Also, the American economy is no longer what it used to be. Raw figures of US economic strength do not reveal how the foundations of the American economy are weakened and undermined by the twin deficits of trade and budget, the global imbalances – particularly between China and the US – and America's massive domestic debt structures. The fact is that Americans are living well beyond their means, and have been doing so for many years. And the world outside the US is complicit in this arrangement – for high US consumption continues to fuel world trade. It is a mutuality that will ensure that American consumers can probably continue to live beyond their means for some time to come.

Yet, such a dynamic of dependence does not an enduring superpower make. This mutual dependence has already placed the US in a weak position vis a vis another potential competitor superpower – for China now has a hold on the US through the huge global trade and financial imbalances. Of course, as long as China is entwined within the global economic system it needs the US as much as the US needs it, just as a banker needs its largest debtor. Yet, even so, China is not a western country and is still controlled by a centralised Communist Party, and may yet, potentially at any rate, take future decisions about its relationship with the USA based upon political, and geo-political rather than economic grounds. Should politics ever come to dominate the relationship, and a new Cold War ensue, then China would possess some very high cards indeed. For this reason the sheer size of current Chinese lending to the US, including the US Treasury, would in normal times be considered – by geo-strategists in Washington – as a national security failure.

On top of its weaknesses vis-a-vis China, American policy in the Middle East has also served to weaken the world position of the USA. The failure of the American occupation of Iraq has raised a major question over the validity in today's world of America's great advantage in world politics – its unchallenged lead in hard military power, particularly high-tech mobile military forces. Although peace-keeping and peacemaking forces will likely remain important for America (and for Europe), is the huge amount of America's treasure spent on the Pentagon budget worth it – when it cannot be used to quell such a weak military power as Iraq?

Already a declining America is causing a power vacuum around the world – into which new poles of power are emerging: the European Union, China, India and Russia being the most obvious; but potentially also regional groupings like ASEAN, MERCOSUR and the AU.[18] This new multi-polar world will inevitably, sooner or later, lead to a reassessment in Washington about the proper extent of its worldwide interests and reach. Such a review is bound to involve some measure of retrenchment.

This retrenchment may not be overly dramatic; but as the US turns from a 'lone superpower' to 'one amongst equals', the American role in Europe will be the first to be affected, and reduced. Already, before 9/11, US troops and bases were being wound down in 'core Europe'. And, as always with retreating powers, the retreat leaves a problem for its most loyal allies like Britain and Poland. The UK's 'special rela-tionship' constructed around and dependent upon, Cold War-style heavy US involvement in Europe, could become a casualty of a weak-ening American presence.

However, even though the US may draw down somewhat its secu-rity involvement in the Europe, its relations with the continent will remain a central concern. The American strategist and former National Security Advisor Zbigniew Brzezinski has outlined why the US has a continuing vested geo-political interest in Europe. No post-9/11 hawk, Brzezinski had severe misgivings about the Bush Two doctrine of pre-emption and regime change. Yet, like many in the Democratic foreign policy establishment he came to support the idea of American primacy in the world and to advocate an American glob-al policy that attempts to secure that primacy for the next century. Brzezinski tends to avoid the bombastic language of 'hegemony' and 'domination' used by neo-conservatives, but only because, like his fellow Democrat former President Bill Clinton, he believes American primacy can be secured through more subtle means.

In his book *The Grand Chessboard* Brzezinski argued that American primacy could only be secured by a forward strategy for

America, and that the key to such a forward strategy was US control of Eurasia.[19] Eurasia is the key. The father of contemporary geo-politics, Harold Mackinder, argued early in the last century that whoever 'rules the world-island [of Eurasia] commands the world'. The landmass of this 'world-island' of Eurasia stretches in the west from the Atlantic shores of Ireland and Portugal all the way across the Urals and Siberia through to China and the North Pacific Ocean and down around the shores of South East Asia and back to India. It is, unquestionably, the key strategic area in the twenty-first century. In size it is virtually equal to the Americas (about 50,000,000 square kilometres each); but it has three quarters of the world's population, almost 70% of the world's GNP and, crucially, about three quarters of the world's energy sources.

Washington's great unspoken fear, and Brzezinski's spoken fear, is that the USA may well be marginalised in Eurasia – or even ejected from the continent altogether. Should this indeed happen, then, by mid-century, the USA – restricted to hegemony over the western hemisphere and influence around the edges of Eurasia (say, in parts of South East Asia and Australia) – would no longer be the world's only superpower.

Great challenges to American primacy in Eurasia loom. China will prove the most formidable. Yet, such a challenge is still some time off. More immediate is the challenge now developing at the western end of Eurasia in Europe. Brzezinski himself worries that, as western Europe is 'America's geo-strategic bridgehead on the Eurasian continent', then 'any ejection of America by its western partners from its perch on the western periphery [of Eurasia] would automatically spell the end of America's participation in the game on the Eurasian chessboard'.[20]

In order to keep this geo-political toehold over the western end of Eurasia the ideal scenario for the US would be for Britain (as well as, say, Poland) to continue its membership of the EU but, within it, continue to act as an awkward partner and thus dilute and divide a potential superpower rival. But should this not be possible, then Britain outside the EU – as an American satellite nation off the coast – with perhaps another satellite, Poland, on the other side of the Euro-zone, would be a good second best.

Should Britain opt for this wrecking role it will, though, have consequences for its own European continent – many of them bad. Such a rejection of Europe by Britain will probably find allies in other quirky corners of the continent, particularly in eastern Europe, and even, perhaps, in Scandinavia. It would serve to create an inner and outer Europe, with outer Europe aligning with the US, and against inner Europe, on key issues. If such a split caught on, Europe could become permanently divided.

And such a 'balkanised' European continent would be in no shape to meet the coming twenty-first century challenges posed by the geo-politics of the coming multi-polar world. A weakened and divided – inner and outer core – Europe would make it all the more easy for the US in the west and China (perhaps with Russia) in the east to estab-lish separate spheres of influence, and divide and conquer the conti-nent. This 'balkanisation' of Europe, of course, would further seal Britain's fate as a colony of the American empire in Europe.

'Core Europe' Could Prosper
Alternatively, inner 'Core Europe' – shorn of Britain and Poland – could prosper. This 'core' would comprise the Euro-zone countries plus others who, over time, would join it. If the Euro-zone developed political institutions to govern it, it could then add foreign and secu-rity policy to its functions, and could become a fully-fledged federal state. It would comprise well over 250 million people and would be the world's second largest economy. It would be the hub of a wider Europe, and it would have the unity and decision-making efficiency to act as a new player on the world stage.[21]

Although 'Core Europe', built around the Euro-zone, would, ini-tially, be highly divisive, it could also act, over the longer term, to unify and federalise Europe. For 'Core Europe' could, just like the original Common Market founded by the Treaty of Rome, act as a magnet for those countries outside on its periphery. These outriders could later join, but this time they would be joining a truly united Europe.

Ready For Europe?
Is Britain, though, ready for Europe? Ready, that is, for a full and positive contribution as a member state of the EU, and, ultimately, as a member state of the Euro-zone? Much will depend, as it always does, on outside forces. Change could be forced on a British Prime Minister by real exigencies: for instance the Middle East situation

requiring a break with the US, or a sudden deterioration in the energy or security situation requiring a common European policy. And much will also depend on the comparative reputations in Britain of America and Europe. As the century progresses will the British feel they have more in common with secular Europe or quasi-religious USA? With the European 'social model' or with the 'free enterprise model'? And, just as importantly, who in British eyes – America or Europe – will be the twenty-first century success story in terms of power and prosperity?

But ultimately the answer will lie in the domestic scene, in how British politics develops in the post-Blair era. Blair's administration, it is now clear, was essentially a continuation of the Thatcher era – both domestically through its largely neo-liberal agenda and in foreign policy through its pursuit of a world role through the 'special relationship'.

The question remains: will the post-Thatcher/Blair generation be able to set out on a new course? Can they end the stubborn fixation with a world role and with overblown ambitions? A more modest and realistic approach to Britain's place in the world will allow the country to re-order its relations both with Europe and America. Europe will never accept British leadership, but the European partners will certainly welcome Britain playing its part as one of the leading countries. Should the British be able to accept a more realistic regional, 'European', vision for the country, then Britain will no longer need the 'special relationship'. After all it was the country's continuing unrealistic global pretences – the barking of the Churchillian bulldog – that led directly to the strategy of subservience to the USA – and to the whimpering of Blair's lapdog. And, finally freed from the 'special relationship' Britain, through Europe, can help create the European-American equal partnership that the times warrant.

Endnotes

Chapter 1

1 See: http://www.newamericancentury.org/
   statementofprinciples.htm
2 Full speech by Tony Blair at: http://www.pbs.org/newshour/bb/
   international/jan-june99/blair_doctrine4-23.html
3 Labour Party Conference Report, 2001.
4 *The Guardian*, 19th September 2005.
5 See: Downing Street press briefing on 12th March 2003 for Tony
   Blair's response to Rumsfeld's remarks.
6 Reported in *The Guardian*, 17th August 2006.
7 This was written in 1951. Quoted in Alex Danchev, *Oliver
   Franks: Founding Father*, Oxford, 1993. I have used the American
   spelling of counselor as in this quotation it is appropriate
8 Peter Riddell, *Hug Them Close: Blair, Clinton, Bush and the
   Special Relationship*, London, 2003. The words 'hug them close'
   were reportedly those used by a senior Blair advisor.
9 Report in *The Independent*, 18th September 2005.
10 Article by Tony Blair in *Newsweek*, Series 2006 available in
   Newsweek 2006 series on msnbc.msn.com
11 Hywel Williams, 'Britain's Ruling Elites Now Exercise Power
   With A Shameless Rapacity', *The Guardian*, 11th April 2006.

See also: Hywel Williams, *Britain's Power Elites: The Rebirth of a Ruling Class*, London, 2006.

12 Paul Krugman's most recent book is *The Great Unravelling: From Boom to Bust in Three Scandalous Years*, London 2004.

13 See chapter 6 for an analysis of Thatcherite economics and inequality.

14 See: Neil Chenoweth, *Virtual Murdoch: Reality Wars on the Information Highway*, London, 2001, p. 247.

15 British newspapers broke the story of Ruth Kelly's association with Opus Dei on 22nd December 2004. See *The Times* for that day.

16 A conversation recorded in Andrew Neil's memoirs, and referred to in 'Rupert Murdoch, Bending with the Wind', Tina Brown, *The Washington Post*, 15th September 2005.

17 Chenoweth, op. cit., p. 203.

18 Chenoweth, op. cit., p. 202.

19 Chenoweth, op. cit., p. 274.

20 Chenoweth, op. cit., p. 277.

21 *The Mail on Sunday*, 18th September 2005. Price's exact words were later disputed.

22 Reported in *The Guardian*, 1st July 2006.

23 Hywel Williams, 'Britain's Ruling Elites Now Exercise Power With a Shameless Rapacity', op. cit.

24 Jackie Ashley 'Quiet Rise of the King of Downing Street', *The Guardian*, 14th July 2004.

25 The MI6 chief, for instance, Richard Dearlove, was reported to have believed that the US 'fixed' the intelligence to create the need to go to war. Reported in *The Sunday Times*, 20th March 2005.

26 Christopher Meyer, *DC Confidential: The Controversial Memoirs of Britain's Ambassador to the US at the Time of 9/11 and the Iraq War*, London 2005.

27 Former British Ambassador to Washington, Chairman of the Press Complaints Committee, 12th November 2004 on the Today Programme, BBC Radio Four.

28 John Dickie, *Special No More: Anglo-American Relations: Rhetoric and Reality*, London, 1974.

29 Azmet Begg told the story – to a hushed Liberal Democrat conference – of his son. He wanted him tried in Britain rather than being held in Afghanistan and Guantanamo Bay outside the law. Lib Dem Annual Conference, 2003.

30 See: Tom Bower, *Gordon Brown*, London, 2004.
31 The constitution was signed by all the heads of government on the 29th October 2004 in Rome. It would need to be ratified by all 25 members of the EU to come into being.
32 Frost on Sunday, BBC TV, 20th June 2004.
33 Channel Four News interview with Jon Snow, 14th June 2005

Chapter 2
1 Correlli Barnett, *The Collapse of British Power*, London, 1972, p. 573
2 See: John Charmley, *Churchill: The End of Glory*, London, 1993, p. 649
3 Quotations from Nick Crafts, 'Managing Decline? 1870-1990', *History Today*, vol. 44 (5), June 1994, p. 38-9.
4 See: Barnett, op. cit., p. 82.
5 See: William Engdahl, *A Century Of War: Anglo-American Oil Politics and the New World Order*, London, 2004, chapter 5. Also see: Michael Klare, *Blood and Oil: How America's Thirst For Petrol Is Killing Us*, London, 2004, chapter 2.
6 J. R. Seeley, *The Expansion of England*, 1884.
7 For the most authoritative account of Neville Chamberlain's approach to British foreign policy see: Robert Self, *Neville Chamberlain: A Biography*, London, 2006. See chapter 8 for some of Chamberlain's ideas on imperial economics.
8 C. A. Vlieland, of the Malayan Civil Service, in a letter to Barnett, p. 28.
9 From George Laming's *In The Castle of My Skin*, cited in J and A Lively, *Democracy in Britain: A Reader*, Oxford, 1994.
10 Vlieland, in Barnett, op. cit.
11 Letter, August 1937 quoted in Self, op. cit., p. 276.
12 W. K. Hancock and M. M. Gowing, *British War Economy*, London, HMSO, 1953, p. 116
13 The Chancellor of the Exchequer in the Cabinet minutes, CAB 66/11 324, 21st August 1940
14 Barnett, op. cit., pp. 14-15
15 Barnett, op. cit., p. 593. Some of the figures about British military and technical dependence on America during the Second World War come from Barnett, chapter 6.
16 Speech in London, 10th November 1942.

17 My italics. *The War Speeches of Winston Churchill*, London, date not supplied, vol. 3, p. 512. Compiled by Charles Eade.

18 John Charmley, *Churchill: The End of Glory*, London, 1993, p. 649.

19 D. R. Thorpe, *Eden: The Life and Times of Anthony Eden, First Earl of Avon, 1897-1977*, London, 2003, p. 270.

20 A. J. P. Taylor, *English History, 1914-45*, Oxford History of England (vol. 15), London, 1975. For the mainstream view see: Martin Gilbert, *Churchill: A Life*, London, 1992 and Roy Jenkins, *Churchill*, London, 2002.

21 Data and quotation from Dickie, op. cit., pp. 35-36.

22 Barnett, op. cit., *The Lost Victory*, p. 41.

23 Dickie, op. cit., p. 38.

24 Cabinet Minutes, 6th November 1945.

25 Hugo Young, *This Blessed Plot: Britain and Europe from Churchill to Blair*, London, 1998, p. 27.

26 See: Andrew Roberts, *Holy Fox: Life of Lord Halifax*, London, 1997

27 Britain exploded her own nuclear bomb in 1952. See below for further analysis.

28 Ritchie Ovendale, 'The End of Empire' in Richard English and Michael Kenny (eds.), *Rethinking British Decline*, London, 2000, p. 275.

29 House of Commons debates, 12th-14th December 1950.

30 Ibid.

31 Reported in Thorpe, op. cit., p. 584.

32 Young, *This Blessed Plot*, op. cit., p. 15.

33 Ibid., p. 16.

34 Reportedly Bevin's remarks to M. Hickerson of the US State Department logged in United States Foreign Relations Documents. Quoted in Alan Bullock, *Ernest Bevin: A Biography*, London, 2002, p. 518.

35 Speech at Columbia University, November 1952.

Chapter 3

1 Speech in London, 10th November 1942.

2 Quote about Wilson from Pankaj Mishra, 'The Unquiet American' in *The New York Review of Books*, 12th January 2006

3 Bullock, op. cit., p. 111.

4 Quoted in Katherine Tidrick, *The Empire and English Character*, London, 1992, p. 227.

5 Barnett, op. cit., p. 120 and 176.

6 Tidrick, op. cit., p. 232.

7 Quoted in Bullock, op. cit., p. 352.

8 Ibid. The quotation was from Sir Michael Perrin and was unearthed by Professor Peter Hennessey in an article in *The Times*, 30th September 1982. Reported in Bullock, op. cit., p. 352

9 Bullock, op. cit., p. 353.

10 See: John Scott, *Who Rules Britain*, Cambridge, 1991, Tables in chapter 6.

11 Barnett, op. cit., p. 24.

12 Tidrick, op. cit., p. 43.

13 Quotation cited in Hugh Cunningham, 'The Conservative Party and Patriotism' in Robert Colls and Philip Dodd (eds), *Englishness*, Beckenham, 1986, p. 298.

14 Quoted in Ian Gilmour, *Inside Right: A Study in Conservatism*, London, 1977, p. 77.

15 Frank Reeves, *British Radical Discourse: A Study of British Political Discourse About Race and Race-related Matters*, Cambridge, 1983, p. 114.

16 Andrew Roberts, *Eminent Churchillians*, London, 1994, pp. 213-4.

17 Quoted in Alan S. Milward, *The European Rescue of the Nation-State*, London, 1992, p. 432.

18 First quotation from Lady Selina Hastings, in Phyllis Hatfield, *Pencil Me In: A Memoir of Stanley Olsen*, London, 1994, p. 94. Second quotation, ibid., p. 95.

19 Tidrick, op. cit., p. 3.

Chapter 4

1 From Thorpe, op. cit.

2 See: Thorpe, op. cit. For a more critical biography see: David Carlton, *Anthony Eden: A Biography*, London 1981.

3 Speech to NATO Council in Paris, December 1953.

4 Speech at Columbia University, 11th January 1952.

5 Thorpe, op. cit., p. 453.

6 Thorpe, op. cit., p. 382.

7 See: Thorpe, op. cit., p. 383.

8 Quoted in Simon Heffer, *Like The Roman: The Life of Enoch Powell*, London, 1998, pp. 122-3.

9 See: Carlton, op. cit., p. 460.

10 In an interview with Michael Charlton, in 'Last Step Sideways', in *Encounter*, September 1981.
11 See: Anthony Nutting, *No End of a Lesson: The Story of Suez*, London, 1962.

Chapter 5

1   Broadcast on Booktalk on BBC TV Parliament Channel, 14th January 2006.
2   Macmillan in conversation with John Colville (30th May 1952), in John Colville, *The Fringes of Power: Downing Street Diaries, 1939-55*, London, 1985.
3   Richard Lamb, *The Macmillan Years 1957-1963: The Emerging Truth*, London, 1995; see chapter 14 for the most detailed account of these negotiations over Skybolt and Polaris.
4   Reported in *The Sunday Telegraph*, 9th February 1964.
5   Peter Riddell, op. cit., p. 31.
6   From the Campaign For Democratic Socialism's bulletin, *Campaign*, 18th July 1962.
7   See: Stephen Haseler, *The Gaitskellites*, London 1969. And the authoritative biography: Phillip Williams, *Hugh Gaitskell*, London, 1979.
8   Martin Holmes, 'The Conservative Party and Europe' The Bruges Group, Paper No. 17. Access at http://brugesgroup.com/mediacentre/index.live?article=73

Chapter 6

1   Hugh Thomas (ed.) *The Establishment*, London, 1959 p. 20
2   Vaizey, p. 46, Balogh, pp. 83-129, Sandelson, pp. 129-171, Hollis, pp. 171-191, Fairlie, p. 208.
3   *The Cecil King Diaries, 1965-70*, London, 1972.
4   Barber's comment on 17th December 1973. Quoted in Andrew Gamble, *The Conservative Nation*, London, 1974, p. 219.
5   See: chapter 16, 'Conclusion' in English and Kenny, op. cit.
6   Barnett, op. cit., p. ix.
7   Barnett in English and Kenny, op. cit., p. 42.
8   Ibid., p 41.
9   Andrew Gamble, 'Theories and Explanations of British Decline', in English and Kenny, op. cit., chapter 1.
10 Andrew Gamble, *The Conservative Nation*, London, 1974.

Another of his books was *Britain in Decline*, London, 1981.

11 The academics Richard English and Michael Kenny produced a superb summary of these varying approaches in the final chapter of their own edited work referred to above. Other books and works cited are Martin Weiner, *English Culture and the Decline of the Industrial Spirit: 1850-1980*, Harmondsworth, 1981. Stuart Holland, *Strategy For Socialism: The Challenge of Labour's Programme*, London, 1975. James Bellini, *Rule Britannia: A Progress Report For Doomesday 1986*, London, 1981. Also, David Marquand, 'Reflections on British Decline', in English and Kenny, op. cit., pp. 117-120.

12 Both quotes from Peter Riddell, *The Thatcher Era and its Legacy*, Oxford, 1989, p. 7.

13 Ian Gilmour's memoirs of the period, *Dancing with Dogma: Britain Under Thatcherism*, London, 1993, told, in its title, of his frustrations with Thatcherism.

14 Idea set out in a letter to me in February 1978.

15 In Fay and Meehan 'British Decline and European Integration' in English and Kenny, op. cit.

16 Richard Body, *England For The English*, London, 2001, p. 118. Body, a fervent opponent of a federal Europe, and leading anti-EEC campaigner in the 1970s, sets out in this book a case for England existing as an independent country and global actor outside of both the UK and European unions; and he also outlines an oft times romantic political and social history of the English people based around what he argues is their unique contribution of individualism.

Chapter 7

1 My italics. Henry Kissinger, *The White House Years*, London, 1979, p. 964.

2 Reported in *The Times*, 4th December 1973.

3 Reported in John Campbell, *Edward Heath: A Biography*, London, 1993, p. 558.

4 Henry Kissinger, op. cit., p. 993.

5 Henry Kissinger, op. cit., p. 933.

6 William Keegan, *The Observer*, 17th December 2006.

7 My italics. Quoted in: Anthony Jay, *Oxford Dictionary of Political Quotations*, 2001.

8 For an insightful, insider account of these rivalries see: Giles
   Radice, *Friends and Rivals: Crosland, Jenkins and Healey*,
   London, 2003.

Chapter 8
1 See: Stephen George, *An Awkward Partner: Britain in the
   European Community*, Oxford, 1998.
2 Quote from Stephen Haseler, *The English Tribe*, London, 1996,
   p. 87. See: Arthur Marwick, *Culture in Britain Since 1945*,
   Oxford, 1991.
3 Analysis drawn from: Stephen Amidon, 'Overlong, Overdone
   and Over Here' in *The Sunday Times*, 8th May 1994.
4 Quoted in Marwick, op. cit., from Charlie Gillett, *The Sound of
   the City*, rev. ed., London, 1983.
5 Marwick, op. cit., p. 34.
6 Amidon, op. cit.
7 Marwick, op. cit., pp. 56-7.
8 See: Robert McCrum, William Cran and Robert MacNeil,
   The Story of English, New York, 1986, chapter 7. Also, for the
   influence of Yiddish on British English see: Leo Rosten, *The
   Joys of Yiddish*, London, 1971.
9 See: Robert F. Kuisel, *Seducing The French: The Dilemma of
   Americanisation*, New York, 1993.
10 Speech to The Radical Society, Atheneum Club, 1992.
11 See: Simon Heffer, op. cit. and Robert Shepherd, *Enoch Powell*,
   London, 1998.
12 John Mander, *Great Britain or Little England*, London, 1963
13 See: Haseler, *The Gaitskellites*, op. cit., p. 92.
14 From: Stephanie Lewis, *The Times* Shopping Section, 23rd April,
   1994.
15 See: Haseler, *The English Tribe*, op. cit., p. 57.
16 See: *Country Life*, 11th November, 1993.
17 'Yellow Socks and Coronets' and 'How a Gentleman Should
   Dress: A Duke Advises', by James Knox in *Country Life*, 19th
   August 1993.
18 'Whatever The Weather' by June Marsh, *Country Life*, 23rd June
   1994.
19 Ibid.
20 *Country Life*, 30th June 1994.

21 Phyllis Hatfield, *Pencil Me In: A Memoir of Stanley Olsen*, London, 1994, pp. 3-4.

22 Ibid., p. 52.

23 *Country Life*, 11th November 1993; 19th May, 7th July 1994.

24 David Edelstein, 'Leather on Rural Willow', *Country Life*, 12th May 1994.

25 Paul Addison, 'The Day the Dream Began to Die', *The Independent*, 6th June 1994.

26 Depiction of J. B. Priestley was by Paul Taylor 'Bennett and the Betrayal of Englishness', *The Independent*, 23rd May 1994.

27 Ibid.

28 From 'The Lion and the Unicorn: Socialism and the English Genius' in *The Collected Essays: Journalism and Letters of George Orwell*, vol. 2, London, 1968

29 Paul Johnson, *Wake Up Britain*, London, 1994.

30 Quoted from David Starkey, 'Freedom and Responsibility', *LSE Magazine*, Spring, 1994, p. 24. My italics. Such a starkly narrow assessment as that of Priestley begs large numbers of questions – some of them not wholly facetious. What about those English people who don't play cricket? Are they considered not really English at all? Is a writer who does not write like Betjeman – that 'most English of writers' – in fact under the influence of a 'foreign' canon? What about those who play cricket, but are obviously not English? Are they honorary English?

Chapter 9

1 My Italics. In Anthony Jay, *Dictionary of Political Quotations*, London, 2001.

2 All quotes from: Margaret Thatcher, *Statecraft: Strategies For A Changing World*, London, 2002, pp. 19-20.

3 *The Times*, 6th October 1999.

4 Reported in David Reynolds, *Britannia Overruled: British Policy and the World*, London, 1991, p. 276.

5 Quoted in Michael Smith, 'Britain and the United States: Beyond the Special Relationship', in Peter Byrd (ed) *British Foreign Policy Under Thatcher*, London, 1988. p. 9. Also see: Peter Jenkins, *Mrs. Thatcher's Revolution: The End of the Socialist Era*, London, 1987.

6 Quoted in Reynolds, op. cit., p. 289.

7 Reynolds, op. cit., p. 280.

8 Margaret Thatcher, *Statecraft: Strategies For A Changing World*, London, 2002, pp. 19-20.
9 Quotation in *Woman's Own*, 31st October 1987. See: Ayn Rand, *The Fountainhead*, New York, 1943 and *Atlas Shrugged*, New York, 1957.
10 Arthur Seldon, *Capitalism*, Oxford, 1990.
11 The monetarists and free market thinkers at the IEA tended not to see trade union power in the 1970s as the problem. 'Unlike governments, trade unions do not print money' they would argue. Enoch Powell once described British trade unions as 'clean as the driven snow'.
12 John Redwood, *Stars and Strife: the Coming Conflicts between the USA and the European Union*, London, 2001, p. 28
13 For instance, in the early 1980s the erstwhile 'Cold War liberal' Midge Decter began to attack homosexual lifestyles in the same manner, though not for all the same reasons, as the Christian evangelists.
14 My italics. *The Times*, 6th October 1999.
15 Reynolds, op. cit., p. 271.
16 *The Spectator*, 14th July 1990.
17 During the 1980s there were increases in the measure of inequality for all leading Western nations, with the intriguing exception of France. In the US the Gini index (which measures inequality) rose from 31 to 34 (compared with 27 to 31 for Britain, 25 to 27 for the Netherlands and 23 to 23.5 for Belgium). OECD figures also show that the US had the highest percentage of low-income persons of any of the OECD countries. And in the 1990s – as globalisation grew apace – an in-depth OECD study of inequality in the leading Western nations, published in 1995, showed that the US was leading the world in terms of inequality, with Canada second, Australia third, Britain fourth and New Zealand and France joint fifth. And in the new century inequality continues to worsen throughout the 'free market'-oriented, highly globalised economies like the USA and Britain. They remain at the top of the inequality league tables for western countries. Interestingly, most of the continental European nations – in particular Norway, the Netherlands, Belgium, Finland and Sweden and others of those shielded from the full impact of globalisation by a social market or social democratic tradition – come well

down the field. For further details see: Stephen Haseler, *The Super-Rich: The Unjust World of Global Capitalism*, London, 2000, chapter 3.

18 *The Daily Telegraph*, 6th December 2005.
19 All quotations from Roy Hattersley in 'NS Essay', *The New Statesman*, 6th February 2006.
20 Details from: Dominic Midgley, 'Oiling Up To the Oligarchs', *The Spectator*, 8th October 2005. This wrath on behalf of *The Spectator* was limited to Russian 'oligarchs'. The magazine rarely exposed Britain's own indigenous mega-rich to such scrutiny.
21 Ibid.
22 Buffett quoted in http://thinkprogress.org/2006/06/26/buffett-estate-tax/
23 Professor Le Grand quoted by Polly Toynbee, 'Cameron Has No Clue What Middle England Earns', *The Guardian*, 4th July 2006
24 Toynbee, op. cit. Figures from Toynbee, op. cit.
25 See my own work, Stephen Haseler, *The Super-Rich: The Unjust World of Global Capitalism*, op. cit., particularly chapters 1, 2 and 3 for further analysis and argument.

Chapter 10

1 Reported in *The Times*, 6th April 1994.
2 Ritchie Ovendale, 'The End of Empire', in English and Kenny, op. cit., p. 274.
3 Reported in *Time Magazine*, 30th July 1984.
4 Quoted on 8th October 1990 in 'BBC On This Today', BBC Radio Four.
5 Quoted in Joe Rogaly 'A Dangerous Battleground', *The Financial Times*, 6th December 1994. The comment is from Rogaly in the same article.
6 Quoted in BBC News, The Open University, 'Open Politics', 12th February 2007.
7 For aspects of this perceived relationship between the almighty and the English see: Christopher Hill, *God's Englishman: Oliver Cromwell and the English Revolution*, London, 1970.
8 Quoted in Jack Lively and Adam Lively (eds), *Democracy in Britain*, Oxford, 1994, p. 15.
9 Geoffrey Elton, *The English*, Oxford, 1992, p. 235.
10 Elton, op. cit., p. 70.

11 See: Paul Johnson, *The Offshore Islanders: England's People From Roman Occupation To The Present*, London, 1972.
12 See footnote 9, chapter 2.
13 Cited in Philip Williams, *Hugh Gaitskell: a Political Biography*, London 1979, p. 735.
14 Quoted in D. Gowland and A. Turner, *Reluctant Europeans: Britain and European Integration*, 1945-98, London, 1998, Introduction.
15 Bullock, op. cit., p. 111.

Chapter 11

1 Quoted in, among other sources, John Cherion, 'Balkan Scapegoat' in *Frontline* India's national magazine, vol. 23 issue 6 Mar-April 2006.
2 Ibid.
3 Speech on the 23rd September 1992. Quoted in Bernard Connolly, *The Rotten Heart of Europe: The Dirty War For Europe's Money*, London, 1995, p. 165. See this book for a stimulating and powerful Eurosceptic account of the politics of the currency crises of the 1990s.
4 See: *The Financial Times*, 28th December 2006. It reported that the value of Euro notes in circulation overtook those of the Dollar during 2006.
5 Bob Worcester's remarks during an account of the politics of the Euro given at a European Research Forum seminar on 'The British and the Euro' at London Metropolitan University, February 2001. Also see: Stephen Haseler and Jacques Reland (eds.), *Britain and Euroland*, The Federal Trust, 2000.
6 See Labour's election manifesto 1997.

Chapter 12

1 www.cnn.com/ALLPOLITICS/1997/05/29/clinton.blair
2 *The Guardian*, 19th April 2004.
3 Figures from The Audit Bureau of Circulation for 1997
4 Mencken quote from *Chicago Tribune*, 19th September 1926. Greenslade quote from Roy Greenslade, *Press Gang: How Newspapers Make Profits From Propaganda*, London, 2003, p. 59.
5 Delors was in provocative mode again in the aftermath of Thatcher's ouster from Downing Street. With Thatcher's anti-EU posture widely thought to be the reason for her dismissal, the

Commission President grandly opined that should Britain continue to be unhelpful in Europe he 'would not hesitate to provoke a crisis'. Reported in Connolly, op. cit., p. 106.

6 Hugo Young, *One Of Us*, London, 1989, p. 419.

7 See: http://web.univ-pau.fr/~parsons/antigerm.html

8 Frank Johnson, former editor of *The Spectator*, to the author, January 2005.

9 My italics. Speech to the FCO leadership conference, QE2 Conference Centre, 7th January 2003.

10 See: Norman Tebbit, *Upwardly Mobile*, London, 1991

11 Anatol Lieven, *America Right or Wrong: An Anatomy of American Nationalism*, London, 2005. See particularly chapter 3, 'The Embittered Heartland'.

Chapter 13

1 See: Timothy Garton Ash, *Free World: America, Europe and the Surprising Future of the West*, New York, 2004, for a stimulating and authoritative account of contemporary American-European relationships.

2 Interview with government spokesman on The Today programme on BBC Radio Four on the day of the Stern report launch, 30th October 2006.

3 *The Daily Telegraph*, 20th November 2006.

4 Speech to Lord Mayor's Banquet, 13th November 2006.

5 Charles Grant, 'Choosing Europe' *Prospect*, September 2004.

6 Other ideas to keep Britain in the single market include that of Tory MP and front-bencher, Bill Cash, who seeks to create a broadly-based Associated European Area in agreement with the EU. For the various 'Eurosceptic' options of a new relationship see: Mark Baimbridge, Brian Burkitt and Philip Whyman, *Britain and the European Union: Alternative Futures*, London, 2005.

7 These rankings depend on exchange-rate fluctuations so Britain, depending on the Pound/Euro rate, could easily slip from fifth to eighth. UN statistics.

8 All figures are from UN statistics set out in Baimbridge, op. cit., p. 89.

9 B. W. E. Alford, *Britain in the World Economy Since 1880*, London, 1996, p. 33.

10 See: Hywel Williams, *Britain's Power Elites: The Rebirth of a*

Ruling Class, London, 2006, p. 163.

11 Daniel Dorling and Bethan Thomas, *People and Places: A 2001 Census Atlas of the UK*, Bristol, 2004.

12 *The Guardian*, 5th July 2004.

13 Williams, op. cit., p. 163. See his chapter 4 on 'The Financial and Business Elites: Dividing the Spoils'.

14 Reported in, and quoted from, Gideon Rachman, 'How The Square Mile Fell Out of Love With Brussels', *Financial Times*, 12th December 2006.

15 Read the news report about the report on http://news.bbc.co.uk/1/hi/business/4366225.stm

16 The conservative political philosopher Michael Oakeshot described statecraft as being able to manoeuvre the state which was like a boat 'alone in a boundless and bottomless sea'.

17 Reported in *The Guardian*, 13th January 2007.

18 ASEAN: The Association of Southeast Asian Nations; MERCOSUR: The Latin American 'Southern Common Market'; and AU: The African Union.

19 Zbigniew Brzezinski, *The Grand Chessboard: American Primacy and Its Geo-Strategic Imperatives*, New York, 1997.

20 Brzezinski, op. cit., p. 61.

21 See: Stephen Haseler, *Super-State: The European Challenge to American Power*, chapter 5 for my argument for the emergence of 'Core Europe' built around the Eurozone.

Index

Black, Conrad 28, 142, 194-196
'Black Wednesday' (1992) 169, 181-183
Blair, Tony 1-3, 10-14, 15-40, 45, 68, 89-90, 142, 143, 158-161, 164,
    165, 168, 175, 184-186, 188-190, 191-194, 195, 204-206, 208, 209,
    211, 213, 218, 223, 228
Blue Streak 60, 79
Blue Steel 60
Body, Richard 97
Bowes-Lyon, Elizabeth 67
British Commonwealth of Nations 57, 59, 78-79, 120, 121
Brittan, Leon 184
Brown, George 96, 97, 152, 153
Brown, Gordon 27-28, 34-35
Bruges Group 140
Brzezinski, Zbigniew 225-226
Buchanan, Pat 148
Buckley, William F 143, 148
Buffet, Warren 160
Bullock, Alan 156, 74
Burnet, Alistair 134
Bush, George W 2, 3, 5, 11-14, 16-24, 32, 34, 148, 160, 198, 206
Bush, George H.W 135, 179, 180, 201
Butler, Rab 55, 71, 73, 74
Byrnes, James 59, 60

Callaghan, James 5, 104, 107-109, 110, 111, 131, 136, 165, 174
Cameron, David 27, 28, 185, 186, 210
Carlton, David VIII, 73, 110-112, 147
Carter, President Jimmy 2, 150, 153
Cecil, Hugh 65, 66
Chamberlain, Joseph 44, 78
Chamberlain, Neville 45, 81, 82
Charlton, Michael 134
Charmley, John 47, 48
Cheney, Dick 16
Chesterton, G.K 66
Chirac, Jacques 33, 189, 198
Churchill, Winston VI, 5, 7, 8, 21, 42, 46-54, 55-69, 69-74, 79, 90,
    93, 104, 164, 172, 173, 200, 228

Printed in the United Kingdom
by Lightning Source UK Ltd.
120106UK00001B/94-315